RECORDS OF EARLY ENGLISH DRAMA

Records of Early English Drama

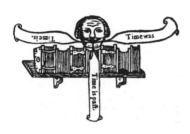

NEWCASTLE UPON TYNE

EDITED BY J. J. ANDERSON

UNIVERSITY OF TORONTO PRESS

TORONTO BUFFALO

MANCHESTER UNIVERSITY PRESS

© University of Toronto Press 1982
Toronto Buffalo London
Printed in Canada
ISBN 0-8020-5610-5

Published in Great Britain by Manchester University Press
ISBN 0-7190-0892-1

Canadian Cataloguing in Publication Data

Main entry under title:

Newcastle upon Tyne

(Records of early English drama)
Bibliography: p xlviii
Includes index.
ISBN 0-8020-5610-5 1000752529 T
1. Performing arts – England – Newcastle upon Tyne (Northumberland)
– History – Sources. 2. Theater – England – Newcastle upon Tyne (North-
umberland) – History – Sources. I. Anderson, J.J. (John Julian), 1938–
II. Series

PN2596.N48N48   790.2'0942876   C82–094614–1

The research and typesetting costs of Records of Early English Drama
have been underwritten by the Social Sciences and Humanities Research
Council of Canada.

Contents

Records of Early English Drama

The aim of Records of Early English Drama (REED) is to find, transcribe, and publish external evidence of dramatic, ceremonial, and minstrel activity in Great Britain before 1642. The general editor would be grateful for comments on and corrections to the present volume and for having any relevant additional material drawn to her attention.

ALEXANDRA F. JOHNSTON University of Toronto GENERAL EDITOR
SALLY-BETH MACLEAN University of Toronto ASSOCIATE EDITOR

Preface

Almost all of the records used in this volume are civic and guild records. Most are now in the Archives Department of Tyne and Wear County Council, West Blandford Street, Newcastle upon Tyne, but some are in the Northumberland Record Office, Melton Park, North Gosforth, Newcastle upon Tyne. The following repositories yielded one item each: the Library of the Society of Antiquaries of Newcastle upon Tyne, The Black Gate, Newcastle upon Tyne; Newcastle Central Library, Newcastle upon Tyne; Trinity House, Trinity Chare, Newcastle upon Tyne; Department of Palaeography and Diplomatic, University of Durham, South Road, Durham; The College of Arms, Queen Victoria Street, London. No Newcastle ecclesiastical records with relevant material have survived.

I wish to thank those responsible for the collections I have used, for assisting me in my search and for giving me permission to publish from their records: The Director of Administration of the Newcastle City Council and Dr W.A.L. Seaman, the Archivist for Tyne and Wear County Council; Mr R.M. Gard, the Archivist for Northumberland County Council; Mr Arthur Wallace, City Librarian, and Mr D. Bond, Deputy Local History Librarian, Newcastle Central Library; the Secretary, Dr Constance M. Fraser, and the Council of the Society of Antiquaries of Newcastle upon Tyne, who have permitted me to use not only the one relevant document at the Black Gate but also items from the Society's collection deposited in the Northumberland Record Office; the Secretary, Captain A.H. Kent, and the Corporation of The Newcastle upon Tyne Trinity House; Mr M.G. Snape and Miss Margaret McCollum, of the University of Durham, and Mr W.K. Wills, Durham Diocesan Registrar; Mr F.S. Andrus, Lancaster Herald of Arms, and the Chapter of the College of Arms. His Grace the Duke of Northumberland has kindly allowed me to read Hugh Hornby's manuscript history of Newcastle in the library of Alnwick Castle.

Most of my time in Newcastle was spent in the search room of the Tyne and Wear Archives Office, where I made considerable demands on the knowledge and patience of Mr Andrew Champley and Mrs Susan Craig, amongst others. I owe a great deal to the entire staff of the Office, most of whom seem to have been involved in my researches in one way or another. Mr Champley undertook document description on my behalf, and the descriptions in the Introduction of the guild documents, in particular, are based on his work. Mr Gard has also helped me with document description.

The editorial team in the Toronto office of Records of Early English Drama have checked my transcriptions against microfilms of the originals, and have prepared my manuscript for publication. The indexing of names and places has been done in Toronto by Mr Willard McCarty. I have also profited from the special expertise of Dr Mary Blackstone, Dr Ian Lancashire, Dr Cameron Louis, Ms Anne Quick, and Dr Theodore DeWelles. As volume editor, Dr Sally-Beth MacLean has attended to numerous matters of detail, bringing sense and sensitivity to bear on sometimes tricky problems, and the final shape of the book owes much to her work. Dr Alexandra Johnston, the General Editor of REED, has always given me both encouragement and practical help; in particular, she has checked on the spot in Newcastle my transcriptions of material which did not microfilm well. Others in the Toronto office whom I wish to thank are Mrs Sheena Levitt, Mr Andrew Rossman, Mrs Arlene Gold, Mrs Nancy Rovers-Goheen, Mrs Darlene Money, and Miss Patricia Tolmie. Miss Prudence Tracy, of the University of Toronto Press, has treated me with unfailing courtesy as she has guided the book towards publication. My typist in Manchester, Miss Penny Evans, has done an excellent job with a difficult manuscript.

Many other people have helped me in the course of my searching and editing, and I am particularly grateful to Professor A.C. Cawley, who first suggested to me that research in Newcastle might prove rewarding, Mr J.K. Bishop, Dr R.W. Ingram, Dr C.E. McGee, and Mr Gordon Tams. I wish too to acknowledge here the invaluable advice given me by Dr Fraser concerning the dating system used in the Newcastle Chamberlains' Accounts.

I began work in Newcastle in 1968, when I was the holder of an Eleanor Sophia Wood Travelling Fellowship from the University of Sydney. Since then some of the cost of my research has been defrayed by the University of Manchester, and some by the Social Sciences and Humanities Research Council of Canada, which has also supported the publication costs of this volume. A generous grant from the British Academy has covered my typing expenses.

JJA
University of Manchester, 1982

Newcastle and its Early Drama

In the later middle ages and in Tudor and Stuart times, the period with which this volume is concerned, Newcastle upon Tyne was one of the most substantial towns in the kingdom, with a population rising from an estimated four thousand in 1400 to ten thousand in 1560 and eighteen thousand by 1700.[1] Its position not far from the Scottish border gave it military significance, and this together with the fact that it was well sited on an easily navigable river led to its becoming an important manufacturing and trading town. Already by 1400 coal was important in Newcastle's economy, and in the sixteenth and earlier seventeenth centuries, when Tyneside coal production increased rapidly, trade in coal made Newcastle into a busy port and a city of some wealth, though the wealth for the most part was concentrated in the hands of a ruling class of merchants.

CIVIC OFFICERS

Like other English towns of importance, Newcastle had considerable rights of self-government granted by the crown.[2] The corporation of Newcastle, and an elected mayor, are first heard of in the thirteenth century. In articles confirmed by Edward III in 1342, it is ordered that the mayor is to be elected annually by twenty-four electors who are themselves to be chosen, through a complicated procedure, by twenty-four representatives of the twelve mysteries or principal guilds of the town. The new mayor and the twenty-four electors are then to elect the bailiffs and 'all other officers.' The mayor and bailiffs are to be assisted by chamberlains in computing and recording in a roll the accounts of the town every week, and auditors (elected by the mayor and chamberlains) are to make yearly account, in the fifteen days before Michaelmas (29 September), of all receipts and payments. In 1345, new articles fix the date of the mayoral election as the first Monday after Michaelmas.

By 1400, with the granting of a new charter by Henry IV in that year, Newcastle was 'a county of itself,' with a sheriff and six aldermen replacing the bailiffs. The aldermen, with the mayor, were to act as justices of the peace. In 1516, a decree of the Star Chamber states that the officers to be elected each year on the first Monday after Michaelmas are the mayor, six aldermen, the recorder, the sheriff, eight chamberlains, two coroners, the sword-bearer, the common clerk (of the chamber), and eight sergeants at mace. Twenty-four auditors are to be chosen by the twelve mysteries. Charters of Philip and Mary in 1557 and of Elizabeth in 1600 give the same list of officers to be elected as in 1516, except that in 1557 the number of aldermen is increased from six to ten, and from 1600 they are to hold office for life ('during good behaviour'). Also in 1557, the electoral college of twenty-four representatives of the guilds is constituted a common council, with the duty of assisting the mayor and aldermen for the year.[3]

THE GUILDS

In 1215, the burgesses of Newcastle were granted a guild merchant by King John. It is likely that this body, probably made up, at least originally, of all the burgesses, was the ancestor of the incorporated companies, or traders' and craftsmen's guilds, which emerged in the fourteenth, fifteenth, and sixteenth centuries.[4] In 1342, the articles of Edward III were ratified 'in full guild,' and in the fifteenth and earlier sixteenth centuries 'the common guild,' which has been explained as 'the mayor and burgesses at large,'[5] is found in the records as the ultimate authority of civic government. The trade and craft guilds were enfranchised, usually by the municipal authorities, to regulate the conduct of a trade or craft for the benefit of the members of the guild and of the town. The document of enfranchisement, in which the duties and privileges of the guildsmen are set forth, is called an 'ordinary.' The guilds also had social, religious, and ceremonial functions, the most important expression of which, in the fifteenth and earlier sixteenth centuries, was the requirement, usually announced at the beginning of the ordinary, that the members of the guild should participate annually in the Corpus Christi procession and play.

Newcastle had many trade and craft guilds. The most important of these, all formed before 1342, were the twelve mysteries. They were the Drapers (or merchants of woollen cloth); Mercers (or merchants of silk and small wares); Boothmen (or merchants of corn); Skinners; Tailors; Saddlers; Bakers and Brewers; Tanners (and Barkers); Cordwainers; Butchers; Smiths; and Fullers and Dyers (walkers). There were also fifteen 'by-trades,' listed by Brand as follows: Masters and Mariners (Trinity House); Weavers; Barber Surgeons and Chandlers; Cutlers; Shipwrights; Coopers; Housecarpenters; Masons; Glovers, Joiners; Millers; Curriers, Feltmakers, and Armourers; Colliers, Paviors, and Carriage-men; Slaters; and Glaziers, Plumbers, Pewterers, and Painters. Brand also lists companies not of the fifteen by-trades: Goldsmiths; Waits; Scriveners; Bricklayers; Rope-makers; Upholsterers, Tin-plate Workers, and Stationers; Sailmakers; Mettors ('measurers' of capacities of keels and boats); and Porters. His last list is of companies extinct by the later eighteenth century: Cooks; Spicers; Furbishers; Sword-slippers; Bowyers; Fletchers; Spurriers; Girdlers; Vintners; Watermen (never properly constituted); and Keelmen. Newcastle crafts not in Brand's lists, but mentioned in the 1516 Star Chamber decree and the 1557 charter of Philip and Mary, are the Daubers, Tilers, Chalon Weavers (ie, blanket weavers), and Wallers.[6]

Standing outside the structure of mysteries and by-trades were two other companies of great importance, the Merchant Adventurers and the Hostmen. The first of these grew out of an association of the guilds of Drapers, Mercers, and Boothmen, made up of wealthy wholesale merchants who from the fourteenth century on largely controlled Newcastle's trading activities. Some time before 1480 they formed themselves into the Merchant Adventurers' company, which continued to play a leading part in the town's affairs in the sixteenth and seventeenth centuries. The Hostmen gave lodging to visiting merchants and conducted their business, each visitor being assigned a particular hostman who levied a duty in return for his services. They are first mentioned as a company in 1517, in the Merchant Adventurers' records, but their rise to power as a group appears to belong to the later sixteenth century, when they attempted to monopolise the Newcastle coal trade. Between them, the Merchant Adventurers and the Hostmen comprised the ruling oligarchy of Newcastle. Both companies were formally incorporated by royal charter, the Merchant Adventurers in 1547, the Hostmen in 1600.[7]

Associations of guilds were often far from stable. The Goldsmiths were incorporated with the Glaziers, Plumbers, Pewterers, and Painters in 1536, but separated from them in 1717; the Joiners were incorporated with the Housecarpenters in 1579 but were reconstituted a separate company in 1589; and the Slaters were on their own at least in 1452 and 1568, but were associated with the Bricklayers in 1579, and, according to Brand, with the Coopers in the eighteenth century. The Bricklayers were joined with the Plasterers in 1454. In 1442, the Barbers were a company on their own, but later they were associated with the Chandlers.

In the Chamberlains' Accounts for 1508–10, there are three payments to 'the prestes (off corpus christi gild) ffor ther wyn.' Nothing else is known of a Corpus Christi guild in Newcastle, but in some other towns (eg, York, Beverley) the Corpus Christi guild was a religious guild, with priests and laymen as members, and it was chiefly responsible for the management of the procession on Corpus Christi Day.

THE CORPUS CHRISTI PLAY AND PROCESSION

The records show that there was considerable dramatic and semi-dramatic activity in Newcastle in the fifteenth, sixteenth, and seventeenth centuries. Pride of place must go to the annual Corpus Christi play, first referred to, as an ancient custom, in an ordinary of the Coopers' company dated 1427, and last referred to in the Masons' Ordinary of 1581, in which masons are enjoined to participate 'whensoeuer the generall plaies of this towne of newcastle antientlie called the Corpus Christi plaies shall be plaied.' In the Joiners' Ordinary of 1589, the phrase is 'any generall playe or Marshall exercise,' with no reference to Corpus Christi.[8] There is a list of players' apparel, dated 1599, in a book belonging to the Goldsmiths, Plumbers, Glaziers, Pewterers, and Painters' company. Most ordinaries up to and including that of the

Curriers, Feltmakers, and Armourers in 1545 make it clear that the day of performance of the play was Corpus Christi Day, though the Tailors' Ordinary of 1537 has at one point: 'yt is ordand that all the Tayllorz ... shall euery yere at the lost [for fest] of corpus christi day Amyably go to gider in procession in Aliueray and play ther play,' and at another point: 'it ys Ordand that euere brother of the seid felliship com in his lyueray when he shalbe warned by ther beddell that ys to sey to the procession vppon corpus christi day Saynt Iohn day in may the day that the plays shall be played And vppon the day of ther generall diner....' Elsewhere in the ordinary, the tailors are required to make payments to the play 'euery yere when yt shalbe played.' No reference later than 1545 ties the plays to Corpus Christi Day, apart from the doubtfully dated order of the Tailors (between 1560 and 1587); the next ordinary with a reference to the play is the Cooks' of 1575, which states that the Cooks must 'sett forth ther play among the rest of the Corpus Christi playes ... whensoeuer the whole playes of the sayd Towne shall proceed.'

The text of only one of the plays survives, in a bad eighteenth-century copy—the Shipwrights' play of the building of Noah's ark.[9] The names of several other plays and the guilds responsible for them, at least at a particular date, are known from ordinaries as follows:

Barbers (1442)	'The Baptising of Christ'
Bricklayers and Plasterers (1454)	'The Creation of Adam'
	'The Flying of Our Lady into Egypt'
Weavers (1525)	'The Bearing of the Cross'
Goldsmiths, etc (1536)	'The Three Kings of Cologne'
Millers (1578)	'The Deliverance of the Children of Israel out of the Thraldom Bondage and Servitude of King Pharaoh'
Housecarpenters and Joiners (1579)	'The Burial of Christ'
Slaters and Bricklayers (1579)	'The Offering of Isaac by Abraham'
Masons (1581)	'The Burial of Our Lady St Mary the Virgin'

The Goldsmiths' list of items of costume in 1599, and the Slaters' Accounts for 1568, confirm the subjects of their plays.

The Fullers and Dyers' Accounts for 1561 show that their play must have been 'The Last Supper.' It appears, from the list of names at the beginning of the account, to have been farmed out to four men, whose job may have been to oversee the production. From the entry in the Chamberlains' Accounts for 4 week July 1568,[10] the Hostmen performed a play involving fire and gunpowder, possibly a harrowing of hell or doomsday play. In a side-note on page 21 of his *History of Newcastle*,

Bourne writes: 'This Company [ie, the Saddlers] has belonging to it, an ancient Manuscript, beautifully wrote, in Old English Rhime; it relates to our Saviour's Sufferings.'

Companies known from their ordinaries to have performed plays, though the title of the play is not given, are the Cooks; Coopers (1427); Curriers, Feltmakers, and Armourers; Glovers; Joiners; Skinners; Smiths; Tailors; and Tanners.[11] The Walkers' Ordinary refers to a financial levy for the procession and play, though it does not state specifically that the Walkers were to perform a play of their own. According to their accounts for 1552, the Merchant Adventurers were responsible for mounting five plays, including the Hostmen's play, for which the town was to pay four pounds; as has been seen, the town also paid for the Hostmen's play in 1568. The other four were probably the plays of the three constituent companies of the Merchant Adventurers (Drapers, Mercers, and Boothmen), and the play of the Vintners, who paid the Merchant Adventurers 39s 10d 'for ye play' in 1552. Again, in 1561, the Merchant Adventurers paid 'ffor the settinge ffowrthe of the Corpuschristye plays.' The Bricklayers and Plasterers' Ordinary of 1454 contains the names of two plays performed by the company, and other ordinaries refer to 'plays' or 'pageants' in the plural, namely those of the Tanners (1532) and Saddlers (1533), and the undated Order of the Tailors (1560–87).[12] Companies which certainly or probably existed in the sixteenth century or earlier, but which have no surviving ordinary from that period and no other record which makes mention of the Corpus Christi procession or play, are the Bakers and Brewers, Bowyers, Butchers, Chalon Weavers, Cutlers, Daubers, Fletchers, Furbishers, Girdlers, Keelmen, Masters and Mariners (Trinity House), Rope-makers, Spicers, Spurriers, Sword-slippers, Tilers, Waits, and Wallers.

The Corpus Christi plays appear to have been played at several places in the town in the course of a single day's performance. In their ordinary of 1578, the Millers are required 'to attend upon their said plaie in decent manner in euerie plaice of the said towne where antientlie the same among other plaies usalie hath bene plaicd.' In their ordinary of 1536, the Goldsmiths, Plumbers, Glaziers, Pewterers, and Painters are required to 'mayteygne ther play of the thre kynges of coleyn as the plays shall goo forth in cours.' The only places named in the records in connection with performance of the plays are the Sandhill (see pp 38, 55) and the Head of the Side (see p 55). The Fullers and Dyers' Accounts for 1561, the Slaters' Accounts for 1568, and the Chamberlains' Accounts for 4 week July 1568 (charges for the Hostmen's play) refer to 'bearers of the car' or 'bearing the car'; the cars on which the plays were performed were evidently carried about the town by porters. The word 'carres' is also used in the reference to the plays in the Chamberlains' Accounts for 1 week August 1568: 'Item paid to rudderfurthe for leddinge of sand to the hed of the syde for stainge the carres when the playes was played.' The word seems to have the sense 'pageant vehicle,' not 'wheeled vehicle.' No other word for the pageant vehicle is used in the records;[13] several company ordinaries refer to the 'pageant,' but with the sense 'pageant' or 'play' rather than 'pageant vehicle.' The steepness of some of

Newcastle's streets, such as the Side, may have helped determine the method of moving the cars from one part of the town to another.[14] The sand brought to the Head of the Side was presumably spread over the sloping and uneven surface of the street in order to give stability to the wheel-less pageant vehicles when they were set down.

The banns of the Corpus Christi play are referred to in entries in the Chamberlains' Accounts for 18 May 1510, 24 May 1510, 13 June 1511, and 1 week September 1568; this last detailed entry indicates that the crying of the banns was itself a considerable performance, involving many people and much show and expense.

In the company ordinaries, the Corpus Christi play is associated with the Corpus Christi procession. The formula 'To the worship of God and sustentation of the procession and Corpus Christi play' begins the ordinaries of the Coopers (1427), Glovers (1437), Smiths (1437), Skinners (1438), Barbers (1442), Saddlers (1460 and 1533), Walkers (1477), Tanners (1532), Goldsmiths, Glaziers, Plumbers, Pewterers, and Painters (1536), and Tailors (1537). The ordinary of the Tanners and the 1533 ordinary of the Saddlers, which are closely similar in wording, state clearly that the guildsmen shall meet at the appointed hour in the customary place or places, go out with the procession and return with the procession to the same place or places, and then immediately set forth and play their pageants. Most of the fifteenth-century ordinaries use the formula (here quoted from the ordinary of the Coopers): 'go to gedder in procession As other Craftes Doyes And play ther play at ther costes.' The Barbers' Ordinary uses this formula, and adds: 'And that euery man of the said craft shall be att the procession when his hour is assigned att the Newgate on paine of a pound of wax. And alsoe the said Craft shall goe with their pageants when it is played in a Liuery of [for on] paine of a pound of wax.' Evidently the procession and play were separate and the pageant cars went only with the play; there is no evidence that they were ever carried in the procession. The Merchant Adventurers' Order of 23 March 1480 relates to the Corpus Christi procession only. Members of the company are to assemble in the beer (ie, barley) market ('meal market' is deleted),[15] and wait until mass is over ('by seven o'clock in the morning' is deleted). The rest of the order has to do with the regulation of the order of the marchers. The 'lattast Mayd burges' are to go first, except that should any of the company be mayor, sheriff, or aldermen, they together with their officers and servants are to attend upon the Host (which in other towns, eg, York, Beverley, Norwich, was carried at the head of the Corpus Christi procession), and past mayors, sheriffs, and aldermen are to go 'princypall,' ie, presumably, ahead of the 'lattast Mayd burges.'

The Barbers' Ordinary and the Merchant Adventurers' Order refer to specific places in Newcastle. The Tailors' Ordinary of 1537 also mentions the Newgate: 'euery man ... shall come to the procession at the tyme Assigned and yf he com nott to the felliship before the procession passe the newyat to pay A li of wax and if he com not afor the procession be endid to pay twoli of wax.' Possibly the procession regularly began from St Nicholas church, after morning mass, with the Host attended by ecclesiastics, including the members of the guild of Corpus Christi, as in York and Beverley. The mayor and other officers of the city may have attended mass and set out with the procession from the church. The procession evidently went north-wards, through the meal market and beer market, where it was joined by the members of the Merchant Adventurers' company, and then along a well-defined route to Newgate, the main gate in the northernmost part of the city wall, with groups of marchers and individuals joining it on the way. The procession then re-turned to its starting point; there are no more place-names, but the only obvious route, unless the marchers simply retraced their steps, was eastwards along High Friar Chare, following the wall to Pilgrim Street, then down Pilgrim Street and back to the central area by Upper Dean Bridge or Nether Dean Bridge (though it is possible the marchers worked their way right down to the Quay before returning).[16] The plays would then be taken down the Side to the Sandhill and the lower part of the town. However, the evidence is not sufficient to enable one to venture a reconstruc-tion of the pattern of events on Corpus Christi Day with any confidence, and in any case the pattern may have varied over the years.

FESTIVALS OTHER THAN CORPUS CHRISTI

There are traces in the records of other popular festivals besides that of Corpus Christi Day. The Chamberlains' Accounts for 18 and 19 April 1510 and 10 May 1511 refer to 'the Dragon,' evidently a construction of timber and canvas, which probably belonged to a St George's Day (23 April) celebration.[17] The Chamberlains' Accounts for the latter half of the sixteenth century regularly have an entry of expenses at the end of the financial year 'for keeping of Hogmagog this year,' or sometimes for keeping Hogmagog's coat; the entry for 2 week October 1594 has: 'paide for keepinge hogmago*es* koate and him self in licknes.' The reference must be to the effigy of a giant. London pageantry had a famous giant named Gogmagog,[18] and giants were a feature of Midsummer and other shows all over Britain. In the earliest book of orders of the Merchant Adventurers' company, two entries for 1554 and 1558 record substantial payments 'ffor the charges in ande a boute hoggmaygowyk' and 'for the charges of hogmagoge as apers by perteculars.' Both entries come im-mediately before entries for the charges of Corpus Christi Day, and their wording suggests that the giant may have given his name to a Newcastle festival of unknown date.

St John's Eve (23 June) and St Peter's Eve (28 June) were regularly marked by festivities. In the Chamberlains' Accounts for 28 June and 2 September 1510, there are payments 'to the Schippmen ffor Dansyng affor the mair vppon Saintt Iohns Ewyn' and 'to the Schipmen vppon Sannt Pett*er* Ewyn.'[19] The accounts of Trinity House record payments for minstrels on St John's Eve and St Peter's Eve in 1553 and for feasts, with music, on St Peter's Eve in 1623 and 1624.

MUSICIANS, PLAYERS, AND OTHER ENTERTAINERS

Payments to waits, musicians, and minstrels are frequent in the account books of the city and of the guilds. In Newcastle as elsewhere, the terms 'wait' and 'musician' are more or less interchangeable. The phrase 'waits and musicioners' is used constantly in the Waits' Ordinary of 1677.[20] Minstrels too are usually and primarily musicians, though the term may have a wider meaning. In the 1560s and 1570s, the Chamberlains' Accounts record several annual payments of £5 to the mayor to cover his expenses for 'Iestars & mynstrilles' for the year. 'Waits' is the preferred term in the accounts for musicians who were in the employment of the city. In the 1508–11 section of the Chamberlains' Accounts, there are regular payments, beginning 31 July 1508, to 'thomas Carr mynstrall' and 'William Carr mynstrall,'[21] each of whom appears to be paid 3s 4d per quarter. In the entry for 8 November 1508 there is a reference to 'the thre watt*es*,' and the waits are paid 10s on 26 July 1509. There is no further reference to Thomas Carr and William Carr after the entries recording payment of their wages on 28 September 1509 and 17 November 1509, but there are now regular entries, from December 1509 until July 1511, for the payment of the waits' quarterly wages of 13s 4d; presumably the number of waits went up from three to four from the first quarter of the financial year 1509–10. From February 1562 to August 1563 only one wait, Henry Carr, receives regular quarterly payments of 6s 8d, but from November 1563 to May 1568 he is joined by three others who are paid at the same rate, though Henry Carr retains his separate entry in the accounts. In 1580–1 there are again four waits, and the rate is unchanged, and again in 1590–8. With the entry for 3 week February 1599 the number goes up to five. In the 1607–8 section there are six waits, paid a total of £2 per quarter, until the entry for 3 week March 1608, when the number is increased to eight, though the total quarterly payment remains at £2. In the 1615–17 section the number of waits is not given; the half-yearly payments begin at £4, but later there are payments of £3 and £3 6s 8d for the half-year. In 1631–5 there are six waits, paid at the rate of 10s each per quarter. The Waits' Ordinary of 1677 gives the names of five waits who apparently make up the whole company. Waits continued to be employed by the city in the eighteenth century.

Liveries for the waits (gowns of broad cloth, 'new-coloured' in 1594, 1601, black in 1595), as for other employees of the city, are a regular item of expenditure. No doubt the civic waits had the duty of playing music at official functions, such as the annual banquets for the auditors, though there is little trace of their activities in the records as they were not paid by the performance, and where there is a reference to 'the waits' one cannot be certain that only the official waits are meant. In the Chamberlains' Accounts for 4 week February 1565, there is a reference which indicates that the waits accompanied the mayor when he rode the fair the preceding Lammas. In 1638, Trinity House paid 10s to 'the Towens Mizsitions' for playing at a dinner. The Waits' Ordinary gives the members of the guild something of a monopoly for playing at weddings.[22]

The Chamberlains' Accounts record several payments by the city for the maintenance of the organs in St Nicholas' church, and, up to 1568, for singers in the church.
In 3 week November 1634, 'the waites' received £5 from the city for a year's service
at the church.[23] St Nicholas, the largest church in Newcastle, was also the parish
church, and the city had always given it strong financial support.

There are occasional references to performances of music by children. In 1503,
Princess Margaret is welcomed to Newcastle by children at the bridge end singing
hymns, and in 1597 'mr Anthoniyes children' play music on the coronation day
anniversary.

The drum, flute, and fife are mentioned in the Chamberlains' Accounts in the
context of military or semi-military occasions out of doors. In 1592–4, there are
three references to the playing of the flute and fife by Robert Askew, one of the
official waits.

The city made frequent payments to visiting musicians, for example, 'to Sir
henry persy mynstrilles,' 'to the wayttes of ledes' (p 30), 'to the Kinge of skotes
his musicioners playeinge before mr maiore his Bretheren' (p 129).

In 2 week December 1596 there is a payment 'to a skottes poyett.' There are
many payments to bearwards, in 1 week September 1580 a payment of 10s 'to hym
that had the lyon,' and in 1 week September 1607 a payment to players with
baboons. There are two references to men with hobby-horses. In 2 week November
1590, there is a payment 'to my Lord of essexs tvmbleres,' and in 1 week October 1600
'to a ffrenchman a fune ambule or rope walker playing before mr maior the
aldermen with others....' In 2 week June 1562, there is a payment 'to lockye the
quenes mayiesties Iester.'

The accounts bear witness to the fact that many professional companies of actors
included Newcastle in their itineraries. In September 1593, the mayor gave the earl
of Sussex's players £3 for putting on a free play, and there are other references to
free or public plays in Newcastle. Sometimes visiting players are known simply by
the name of a town: 'the players of Durham,' 'the players of Hull.' In 1600 and 1601,
plays were performed in front of the mayor and his brethren by the boys of the
grammar school. In 5 week October 1600, the mayor paid compensation for the loss
of some items of clothing which were stolen from the merchants' court during a
performance of a comedy by Terence. The merchants' court is frequently named as
the venue for plays in the 1560s; no other place is ever so named, apart from the
mayor's house (once in 1566, possibly also in 1608).

FOOLS

From 1561 to 1635, the Chamberlains' Accounts record many payments to or for
fools. Particularly prominent in the accounts are long and detailed entries relating to

clothes for the fools, which were a significant item in the city's expenditure. The articles of clothing most frequently mentioned are caps, hats, shirts (sometimes with ruffs and bands), waistcoats, coats, petticoats, jerkins, doublets, slops, breeches, hose, short hose, stockings, garters, gloves, shoes, and points (sometimes specified as belonging to coats). Coats and other garments were regularly lined and trimmed. Fabrics were usually coarse: broad cloth, canvas, cotton, frieze, harden, kersey, linen, rug, russet, sheep skins (for breeches), silk russet, stammel, and straiken. Bright colours and patterns were common: yellow and blue for the fools' coats and caps, with white lining to the coats, in 1561; 'skie culler carsey' for stockings and 'checker cullerd clothe' for a coat in 1596; 'oringe cullerred Carsey' for a petticoat and 'brode popenioye green' for trimming to a coat in 1599; motley for one of the fools in 1607. Clothing was frequently renewed; thus in the financial year 1562–3, John Watson, the only fool mentioned in the accounts for that year, received one cap, three shirts with ruffs (one of these also with bands), one shirt apparently without ruffs, two coats (one for Christmas and another for Easter), one petticoat, one pair of hose, three pairs of short hose, one pair of gloves, and five pairs of shoes, plus two pairs of shoes mended, at a total cost to the corporation of £3 11s 10d (including making). This frequency and level of expenditure for a fool's clothes appears to have been maintained fairly consistently over a long period. Until 1580, there are regular annual payments to the barber for shaving the fools' heads.

Undoubtedly the fools who were treated in this way had a ceremonial function, though the records tell us very little about what they did. Probably at least one fool at any given time was regarded as the personal fool of the mayor, but only once, in 1596 (p 114), is a fool referred to as 'mr maiores foole,' though John Lawson, the fool so named, is in the records from 1590 until at least 1607.[24] The only reference to something done by a fool is in the Chamberlains' Accounts entry for 3 week October 1576, in which we are told that John Watson the fool rode the fair with the mayor. The fools must have been in attendance on the mayor and probably other civic officials on other kinds of occasion, but there is no information.[25]

One of the fools whose name occurs frequently, Thomas Dodds, is sometimes called 'a natural fool,' indicating natural simple-mindedness, but he goes with the other two fools of the time in the accounts and is given the same kinds of special costume that they are given. The term 'natural' is not used for any of the other fools, but at least some of the others may have been more or less simple-minded too.[26] What is clear is that there is an element of charity in the maintenance of some if not all of the fools. From 1590 to 1600 there are regular weekly payments 'to Dame Clark for keeping Allon the fool,' 'for keeping Allon the fool,' and 'for keeping Allon the fool in relief.' In the same decade, there are payments for keeping John Lawson, and in the latter part of the decade several payments to a woman for looking after Lawson's bedding and washing his clothes. Both Allon and Lawson, and members of their families, were given money by the city when they were sick. Clothing for the fools is frequently associated in the accounts with clothing for the poor, eg, in 4 week May 1591: '7 yardes of hardne to be shartes to allon the foole and to ij poore childer.' In the seventeenth-century accounts, items headed 'paid for the poor folks' gowns' or 'paid for shoes for the poor folks,' etc, usually include the fools in the list of beneficiaries. Most of the fools whose names recur regularly in the accounts, whether they are associated with the poor or not, receive 'ceremonial' clothing from time to time, of a kind which the other beneficiaries do not. There is however one fool, Henry Atkinson, who regularly receives payments 'in relief' in 1599–1600, but never 'ceremonial' clothing. A few named fools occur only once or twice, in contexts which give little indication of their standing. It seems that the term 'fool' was used both for simple-minded unfortunates who, like other unfortunates, received regular or occasional charitable payments or gifts, and for others who were given a kind of official position and were expected to perform in return for the considerable sums of money spent on them.[27]

In 1561–2 there seem to be two official fools, one of whom is John Watson, the other unnamed. In 1562–8 there is only John Watson. From October 1576 to 1579 there are two fools, John Watson and Edward Errington, and from 1580 to 1581 there are three, Watson, Errington, and 'Allayne the fovll.'[28] From 1590 to October 1593 there are two fools, 'Allon' and John Lawson, and from October 1593 to 1601 there are three, these two and Thomas Dodds. In July 1601, 'Allon,' Lawson, and Dodds are joined by 'marshall the foole.' In the 1606–8 section of accounts, Lawson, Dodds, and Marshall are evidently the three official fools, but the last mention of Lawson in this section is in 2 week October 1607. In the 1615–17 section, the fools mentioned are Robert Marshall and Errington; a John Lawson is also mentioned, though he is not called a fool. In the 1631–2 section there is evidently only one fool, William Errington. In the 1634–5 section there is one mention of 'the fooles coate,' but the fool is not named.

ROYAL VISITS

Many English and foreign monarchs, and other exalted personages, visited Newcastle, but the records are not informative. Brief accounts of visits by James I in 1603 and Charles I in 1639 state that the king was very well entertained, but they do not give details, concentrating instead on the exchange of official courtesies.[29] John Young's description of the visit of Princess Margaret in 1503 is the fullest account, and it mentions feasting, sports, and music, but, compared with the receptions mounted by other large towns on her route, York and particularly Edinburgh, as reported by Young, Newcastle's effort seems modest; Young notes 'they maid non sound of artyllery & ordonnaunce' (f 89). There is no evidence that pageants were ever built or deployed for a reception in Newcastle.

The Documents

Civic Records

CHAMBERLAINS' ACCOUNT BOOKS

Most of this edition of Newcastle dramatic records is made up of extracts from the Chamberlains' Account Books, which are kept by the Tyne and Wear Archives Department. They are a series of one hundred and seventy-seven large volumes, with entries beginning in 1508 and ending in 1835 (TW: 543/14–189, and 543/212; they continue to 1870 as Treasurers' Account Books). They contain the only municipal accounts to 1642 which survive; indeed, very few other civic records of any kind are extant from the pre-1642 period. The earlier volumes are of reasonably uniform size, their leaves (paper) measuring approximately 415mm x 280mm. There is wide variation in the number of pages in each volume. Some volumes have been foliated, in full or in part, at various dates, the volumes used in the edition were foliated or refoliated by the Tyne and Wear Archives Department in 1979–80. The volumes to 543/172 (1817–18) were uniformly bound in brown leather, probably in 1818 or 1819, and it is likely that the disrupted chronological sequence in some of the early volumes originated with this binding. The year titles on the spines of the early volumes do not always indicate the contents accurately.

The accounts for the years 1508–11 are entered on a daily basis (under headings such as 'The xxij day of Maye'), though not every day, and blocks of receipts and payments items alternate within the daily entries. The later accounts follow a different system, with weekly entries under headings such as 'The furste weke of November,' 'The 2 weke,' 'The 3 weke,' etc. Receipts and payments are usually kept separate; receipts for a sequence of years normally come first in the volume, and the payments for the same years follow, though there are several examples of variation from this pattern, for example, 543/17 is receipts only for 1590–6 and 543/18 is expenditure only for 1590–6, and 543/19 is expenditure for 1596–1600, followed by receipts for April–October 1601.

The receipts entries to 1642 are mainly concerned with shipping dues. Typically, they record — in Latin to 1600, in English thereafter — the names of ships using the port of Newcastle, their ports of origin, their captains' names, their hostmen's names, and the dues paid. From 1561 on, income from other sources is also recorded regularly, in English, at the end of each year (with occasional items at the end of a month), particularly income from rents, quarries, freemen's dues, quarter sessions, and the sheriff's court. The contents of the payments sections, in English throughout, are very miscellaneous, and the weekly entries vary considerably in length; occasionally, although there is a heading, there are no payments at all. As well as payments to players, fools, minstrels, waits, etc, there are payments to poor people, for equipment for mining and quarrying operations and for roadworks, to workmen, to those who have travelled on the town's business, for presents to men of importance, for repairs to the church of St Nicholas, for rents, for clothes for civic officials, for expenses connected with the working of the town chamber (paper, counters, etc), for civic occasions of various kinds, and for many other purposes.

In most years, there are regular weekly payments, with the first items for each week (in some years as many as forty or so items) showing little variation from one week to the next.[30] There are also regular quarterly payments at Candlemas (2 February), St Ellenmas (3 May),[31] Lammas (1 August), and All Saints' Day (1 November), for example, to the town's waits and other civic officials, and regular annual payments at Michaelmas (29 September), such as the fees for the mayor, sheriff, and recorder, which make for longer weekly entries at these times. Some half-yearly payments occur, especially in the seventeenth century.

The accounting year runs from Michaelmas to Michaelmas, in arrears of the calendar year. In the early sixteenth-century accounts, the first entries for the financial year have an early October date, the last entries a late September date. In the later weekly accounts, however, the first entries for the year come under a heading for the first week of October, and the last under a heading for the fourth, sometimes the fifth, week of October. There are thus two sets of October headings for each year's accounts. The explanation is that the accounts were made up on a seven-day basis and entered under weekly headings which followed in mechanical sequence, four headings to a month. As there are more than twenty-eight days in each month, except in February, this means that the headings get further and further ahead of the actual date as the year goes on, so that, for instance, in the years after 1561 the All Saints' Day quarterly payment to the waits is regularly entered under 1 week November, but the payments for Candlemas, St Ellenmas, and Lammas are regularly entered under 2 week February, 3 week May, and 4 week August, respectively. After the sequence of forty-eight headings from the first week of October to the fourth week of September, four more headings are required for weeks forty-nine to fifty-two of the financial year. Hence the second set of October headings, which actually relate to September and not October. Over the years there is still some slippage, however, as there are 365 days in a year, not 364 (=7x52), and there are 366 days in a leap year. Thus the actual dates corresponding to a heading vary from one year to the next, and in some years a fifty-third week is needed, headed 'the fifth week of October.' [32]

Conversions of headings to actual dates are written in regularly in the margins of the receipts sections from 543/20 on, beginning with the heading for 2 week September 1599, which is converted to 13 August. The only payments sections, at least in the pre-1642 period, which have conversions written in are those in 543/21 and 543/22. From 543/22 on, the receipts sections may show two or three dates in the margin, under the one heading, as the week's entries proceed; thus under the heading 1 week October 1616 in 543/22, at the beginning of the financial year 1616–17, appears the one date 1 October, but under the next heading, 2 week October, the dates 7, 9, and 12 October appear down the margin. The payments sections never have more than the one date per heading, which is always some days after the first receipts date entered for that week (thus 4 October, 11 October under the headings 1 week October and 2 week October 1616, in the payments section). The conversions gave the clerks trouble; they often cross out, alter, make an obvious error, or omit the conversion altogether. [33]

The early sixteenth-century accounts have only a simple two-line heading at the beginning of each financial year, in the following style: 'The buke off the Cham*er* the iij Day off octobre the first 3er off the Reyn off kyng henriy the viij^th John brandlyng mair Eduerd baxtter scheroff,' followed by the first accounts entries. The accounts from 1561 on regularly have a title page at the beginning of each year's receipts section, followed by lists of those made free of the city during the year, and the names of civic officers, usually including the mayor, sheriff, the twenty-four auditors, and the twenty-four common councillors. The payments sections from 1561–1600 regularly begin with another title page, in the following typical style:

Anno / 1567 /

Incipt liber istius Anno primo die octobris Anno regni regine nostri Elizabethe Nonno / de omnibus huius Anni Integri Solucionib*us* Mr Robert Anderson maior / and [henrye Brandlinge] Iohn watson sheiriffe of this towne of Newcastell vpon tyne chamberlayns of the same towne william Iennyson myghell Mylburne cuthbert Hunter & marke shafto marchauntes Robart Bewicke & george symson taylyer*es* william dowe tannar & george carr Sadler /1567/

Anno / 1567

Clarke of the chamber George
Dent Marchaunte

From 1606 on, there is no separate title page, only the year date ('An*n*o Dom*i*ni 1616,' etc), followed by the first payments entries.

The accounts regularly give weekly (from 1561 on), monthly, and annual totals for both receipts and payments, though occasionally a total is omitted. Roman numerals are standard, though very occasionally an arabic numeral is used in the payments column, and arabic figures are not unusual within entries (eg, 'Paid for 5

yardes of brode clothe iij s'). In the payments sections, weekly and monthly totals in
small arabic numerals are regularly written in the margins, alongside the formal
entries in larger roman numerals (the formal entry is sometimes missing). Running
totals in small arabic numerals are also found in the margins in both receipts and
payments sections.

The scribes make no use of illumination (though letters and figures in headings
may be modestly flourished) or of coloured inks. There are no catchwords. Nine
hands may be distinguished in the payments sections of the accounts from 1508–1635
(normally, the hand in the receipts section is the same as that in the payments section
for the same period). Hand A is found throughout 543/212. It makes much use of
abbreviation and contraction, and there are frequent superfluous flourishes and
marks of various kinds. Hand B is found throughout 543/14 and also throughout the
year 1565–6 in 543/15. This hand makes less use of abbreviation than A; 'n' and 'm'
often end in a meaningless flourish, and the macron mark is sometimes without significance. The distinction between small 'l' and capital 'l' is particularly difficult in
this hand. Hand C is found in the remainder of 543/15, in 543/16, and again in 543/18,
ff 165v–184 (1 week October 1590 – 3 week April 1591). It is characterised by very
broad and heavily-inked strokes which may show through the page, obscuring writing on the other side. It has very few superfluous marks. Hand D is found throughout
543/18, apart from ff 165v–184, and throughout 543/19, apart from the last section
(4 week April 1601 – 4 week October 1601). This hand is clear, and the shapes of
the letters are consistent, but it is sometimes very compressed, at other times spread
out, and the writer has used both broad and fine pen-points. The hand has almost no
superfluous flourishes or marks. Hand E is found only in the last section of 543/19
and is a regular hand with few superfluous flourishes. Hand F is found only in 543/21
to f 207v (1 week November 1607); it is less tidy than previous hands, and there are
a few superfluous marks. Hand G is found in the remainder of 543/21. This is a
sharper hand than F; there are virtually no superfluous flourishes or marks and not
much abbreviation or contraction. Hand H is used throughout 543/22, and Hand I,
which has occasional superfluous flourishes, for final 'n', for example, is used throughout 543/24 and 543/26.

There follow further details of the volumes from which excerpts have been taken.

543/212
'Chamberlains' accounts, 1508–11'; i + 109 + i; ff 1–21v receipts and payments 25 May 1508 – 30
September 1508, f 22 blank, f 22v heading for year 1508, ff 23–56v receipts and payments 2
October 1508 – 28 September 1509, ff 57–86v receipts and payments 2 October 1509 – 28
September 1510, ff 87–109v receipts and payments 4 October 1510 – 9 August 1511; condition
good after major restoration; all margins have extensive water marks, but text usually legible, f 77
lost except for fragment of inner margin, some rodent damage and erosion of top outer corner,
ff 79–109, affecting relevant items (figures lost) on ff 84, 98, 104, 109; rebound 1980 in quarter
brown calf, brown buckram sides, blind tooled on sides and spine, label on spine.[34]

543/14

'Chamberlains' account book, 1561', actual 1561-5; ii + 188 + ii; ff 1–109v receipts, ff 110–13v
blank, ff 114–36v payments 1 week October 1561 – 4 week October 1562, ff 137–7v blank,
ff 138–57v payments 1 week October 1562 – 4 week October 1563, ff 158–8v blank, ff 159–75
payments 1 week October 1563 – 4 week October 1564, f 176 heading for year 1564, ff 176–7v
blank, ff 178–87v payments 1 week October 1564 – 4 week June 1565 (4 week January – 2 week
February missing), ff 188–8v blank; condition fair, considerable damp staining and some tearing,
with occasional illegibility and loss of text at margins affecting relevant items on ff 135, 161v, 178,
181, 181v, small holes in paper affect relevant items on f 180v; pages repaired and cut away in
thumb index form; half bound in brown leather with grey cloth boards on raised bands (modern),
with title in gold near top of spine.[35]

543/15

'Chamberlains' accounts, 1566–1569', actual 1565-8; iii + 302 + iii; ff 1–218v receipts, ff 219–32v
blank, ff 233–53v payments 1 week October 1565 – 4 week October 1566, ff 254–4v blank,
ff 255–81 payments 1 week October 1566 – 5 week October 1567, ff 281v–3v blank, f 284 heading
for year 1567, ff 284v–5v blank, ff 286–302v payments 1 week October 1567 – 4 week October
1568; condition good, though ink considerably faded, with purple tinge, on f 289 and occasionally
in margins elsewhere, the result of an attempted modern restoration with silk; extensively repaired;
bound in green and brown morocco (modern), with red title panel and title in gold near top of spine.

543/16

'Chamberlains' accounts, 1576–81'; i + 168 + i; ff 1–104v receipts, ff 105–8 payments 1 week October
1576 – 4 week October 1576, ff 108v–9 blank, ff 109v–18v payments 1 week October 1576 – 4
week January 1577, ff 119–43 payments 2 week December 1579 – 4 week October 1580, ff 143v–52
blank, ff 153–68v payments 1 week October 1580 – 1 week May 1581; condition good, some damp
staining and tearing, but only headings significantly affected; at present (1981) being rebound.[36]

543/18

'Chamberlains' accounts payments only, 1590–1596'; ii + 318 + ii; ff 1–55 1 week October 1594 –
5 week October 1595, ff 55v–7 blank, ff 57v–110v 1 week October 1593 – 4 week October 1594,
f 111 blank, ff 111v–59 1 week October 1592 – 4 week October 1593, ff 159v–165 blank, ff 165v–
208 1 week October 1590 – 4 week October 1591, ff 208v–12 blank, ff 212v–64v 1 week October
1591 – 4 week October 1592, f 265 blank, ff 265v–318 1 week October 1595 – 4 week October
1596 (year and other headings often in error); condition good, some fading, damp staining, ink
showing through page, and tearing, particularly at beginning and end of volume, but very little
loss of text, apart from the last page (f 318) which has a large piece missing, small tear affects
relevant item on f 147v; repaired and bound as 543/15.

543/19

'Chamberlains' accounts, 1596–1601'; ii + 297 + ii; f 1 blank, ff 1v–57v payments 1 week October
1596 (MS heading 1597 in error) – 4 week October 1597, f 58 blank, ff 58v–113 payments 1 week
October 1597 – 4 week October 1598, ff 113v–14 blank, ff 114v–63 payments 1 week October
1598 – 4 week October 1599, ff 163v–4 blank, ff 164v–205 payments 1 week October 1599 –
5 week October 1600, ff 205v–14 blank, ff 214v–76 receipts, ff 277–91v payments 4 week April

1601 – 4 week October 1601, ff 292–7 presentments and lists of councillors 1597–9, f 297v blank; condition good, minor damp staining in right-hand margins sometimes makes figures difficult to make out; repaired and bound as 543/15.

543/21
'1607–1608', actual 1606–8; i + 251 + i; ff 1–161v receipts, ff 162–77v blank, 178–203 payments 1 week October 1606 – 4 week October 1607, f 203v blank, ff 204–51v payments 1 week October 1607 – 1 week October 1608; condition fair, considerable damp staining affects text in upper part of pages, progressively worsening tears damage inner margin at top and bottom, affecting text from f 244 on; bound in brown leather with raised bands (early nineteenth century), with dark blue title panel and title in gold near top of spine.

543/22
'Chamberlains' accounts, 1615–1617'; ii + 310; ff 1–263v receipts, ff 264–4v blank, ff 265–94 payments 1 week October 1615 – 4 week October 1616, ff 294v–7v blank, ff 298–310v payments 1 week October 1616 – 2 week July 1617; condition good, some damp staining at margins, some loss of corners and margins by tearing from f 300 on, but text little affected; repaired and bound as 543/15.

543/24
'1629–1632'; 296 leaves; ff 1–263v receipts, ff 264–83v blank, ff 284–96v payments 4 week October 1631 – 4 week August 1632; condition reasonably good, slight damp staining, inner top corners affected by progressively worsening tears from f 261 on resulting in some loss of text; bound as 543/21, but binding broken.

543/26
'Chamberlains' accounts, 1635–1636', actual 1634–6; 265 leaves; ff 1–125 receipts, ff 125v–7 blank, ff 127v–143v payments 1 week October 1634 – 4 week October 1635, ff 144–265 receipts; condition good, slight water damage, some erosion of margins but text little affected; repaired and bound as 543/15.

543/212 See above, p xxiii.

CIVIC ENROLMENT BOOKS

There is a run of thirty-one civic enrolment books which are kept by the Tyne and Wear Archives Department (TW: 544/1–25 and 544/71–5). Enrolments begin in 1637 with volume 1 and end in 1834 with volume 31. The books are used mainly for the enrolment of contemporary deeds (leases, indentures, etc), but there are some other items, including company ordinaries in volumes 3, 4, and 5. In these three volumes the documents are copied with their original dates and often the dates of enrolment are given as well. Most of the originals are lost.

544/72
'Enrolment Book 3', 1659–69; title on flyleaf 'The Book of Enrolment'; English; parchment, except flyleaves (paper); iii + 102 + ii; 435mm x 280mm; early foliation, ff 1–65 from front of volume

and ff 1–35 from back; some modest elaboration of initial letters; good condition; bound in original brown leather, '3, 1662' on front cover, red title panel with gold letters, binding broken.

544/73
'Enrolment Book 4', 1661–75; English; parchment, except flyleaves (paper); i + 120 + i; 455mm x 300mm; early foliation, ff 1–51 from front of volume and ff i–lxix from back; some modest elaboration of initial letters; good condition; bound in original brown leather with Newcastle arms and motto on front cover, red title panel with gold letters, binding broken and front cover detached.

544/74
'Enrolment Book 5',1675–81; English; parchment, except flyleaves (paper); i + 124 + i; 460mm x 325mm; early foliation, ff 1–68 from front of volume and ff 1–54 from back; some modest elaboration of initial letters; good condition; binding as for 544/73.

Records of the Incorporated Companies

Most of the documents formerly in the possession of the various companies are now in the Tyne and Wear Archives Office. The substantial collection of the Society of Antiquaries of Newcastle upon Tyne, which contains many guild items, is now divided between the Society's own library in the Black Gate and the Northumberland Record Office. The only document used in this edition which is still in the hands of one of the guilds is a book of accounts belonging to Trinity House.

Five originals and one early copy of company ordinaries which make reference to the Corpus Christi procession and play have survived. They are those of the Coopers (1497 copy of 1427 original); Saddlers (1459 and 1533); Goldsmiths, Plumbers, Pewterers, Glaziers, and Painters (1536); Tailors (1537); and Curriers, Feltmakers, and Armourers (1545). The substantial Merchant Adventurers' Order Books contain orders (including two versions of one for the procession on Corpus Christi Day, and others concerned with the unruly behaviour of apprentices), accounts, and other material. The other original guild documents made use of in this edition are essentially small account books, though they may contain other matter besides accounts, and they tend to be poorly written and erratically kept: an account book of the Bakers and Brewers, a minute book of the Barber Surgeons and Chandlers, a meeting book of the Butchers, a company book of the Goldsmiths, etc, a meeting book of the Housecarpenters, a minute book of the Saddlers, and two Trinity House Account Books. The Goldsmiths' book has a short list of items of costume for their Corpus Christi play, but usually the only relevant items in these books are occasional payments for music at a dinner. For late copies of guild records, other than the ordinaries in the enrolment books, see under 'Antiquarian Material' (pp xxx–xxxi)

Bakers and Brewers' Company
Newcastle upon Tyne, Northumberland Record Office, ZAN M17/51, Bakers and Brewers' Account Book, 1637–96; English; paper; i + 369; 293mm x 193mm (265mm x 155mm); ff 63–5, 94–334,

361, 363–4, 367–9 blank, ff 335–60 written from back of volume; unfoliated; no decoration; good condition; bound in brown leather with raised bands, no title, binding broken and front cover loose.

Barber Surgeons and Chandlers' Company
Newcastle upon Tyne, Tyne and Wear County Council Archives Department, 786/1, Barber Surgeons and Chandlers' Minute Book, 1616–86; English; paper; i + 374 + ii; 300mm x 190mm (variable); collation irregular, some sections written from back of volume; extensively repaired, good condition; modern binding in cream vellum, title 'Minute Book of the Company of Barber Surgeons & Chandlers of Newcastle upon Tyne, Vol. I, 1616-1686' on spine in gold letters.

Butchers' Company
Newcastle upon Tyne, Tyne and Wear County Council Archives Department, 859/1, Butchers' Meeting Book, 1634–1782; English; paper; 349 leaves; 285mm x 185mm; unfoliated; no decoration; slight staining, otherwise good condition; bound in soft dark brown leather with no markings.

Coopers' Company
Newcastle upon Tyne, Tyne and Wear County Council Archives Department, 432/1, copy (dated 3 November 1497) of Coopers' Ordinary (original date given as 20 January 1427); English; parchment; one leaf, 275mm x 380mm, folded; signatures at foot, 13 seal tags with no seals; some fading, especially in folds.

Curriers, Feltmakers, and Armourers' Company
Newcastle upon Tyne, Tyne and Wear County Council Archives Department, 151/1, Curriers, Feltmakers, and Armourers' Ordinary, 1 October 1545; English; parchment; one leaf, 575mm x 405mm; signatures at foot, 11 seal tags with no seals; good condition; note of enrolment in city enrolment books (on 10 September 1669), new order (1579) relating to armourers, and title of ordinary, inscribed on dorse.

Goldsmiths, Plumbers, Pewterers, Glaziers, and Painters' Company
Newcastle upon Tyne, Tyne and Wear County Council Archives Department, 940/1. Goldsmiths, Plumbers, Pewterers, Glaziers, and Painters' Ordinary, 1 September 1536; English; parchment; one leaf; 648mm x 680mm with left hand margin of 50mm; signatures at foot; 15 seal tags with 2 seals; extensively repaired, one hole.

Newcastle upon Tyne, Tyne and Wear County Council Archives Department, 861/1, copy (17th century) of 940/1; English; parchment; one leaf of irregular shape, indented at foot; 675mm x 602mm (approximate); lower half in ruled columns listing names of members of company; no seals or tags; faded at foot and in folds, two small holes, otherwise fair condition.

Newcastle upon Tyne, Tyne and Wear County Council Archives Department, 940/3, Goldsmiths, Plumbers, Pewterers, Glaziers, and Painters' Company Book, 1598–1671; English; paper; i + 133 + i; 290mm x 190mm; early foliation in ink (ff 1–10 only), later foliation in pencil (incomplete); little decoration; many pages in poor condition; bound in original brown leather, title 'Plumbers, Glaziers, Pewterers' on spine in gold, binding broken and front cover loose.

Housecarpenters' Company
Newcastle upon Tyne, Tyne and Wear County Council Archives Department, 903/1, Housecarpenters' Meeting Book, 1590–1661; English; paper; 211 leaves, 407mm x 150mm; unfoliated; no
decoration; several pages fragmentary; bound in dark brown leather, labelled '1590–1624', binding
badly decayed and broken.

Masters and Mariners' Company (Trinity House)
Newcastle upon Tyne, Trinity House, No 60 (old catalogue), Account Book, 1530–1650; English;
paper; iii + 199 + iii; 405mm x 140mm; paginated; no decoration, some larger initial letters; ff 1–23
cut to form thumb index, mostly blank; fair condition; bound in brown leather with raised bands,
tooling, and decoration, label on spine and gold lettering on front cover 'Trinity House, Newcastle,'
spine partly broken.

Newcastle upon Tyne, Tyne and Wear County Council Archives Department, 659/446, Account
Book, 1622–45; English; paper; ii + 177; 310mm x 200mm; ff 151–77 blank; unfoliated; accounts
in ruled columns; no illumination, occasional flourishes; fair condition, some damp stained pages;
half bound in brown leather with paper covered boards and raised bands, date in centre of spine in
gold letters.

Merchant Adventurers' Company
Newcastle upon Tyne, Tyne and Wear County Council Archives Department, 988/1, Merchant
Adventurers' Book of Orders, 1480–1568; English; paper; i + 217; 385mm x 280mm; ff 175–9
and 211–16 blank; early and irregular foliation; no decoration; some repair, good condition; fully
rebound with raised bands, original brown leather panels mounted front and back, title on spine.

Newcastle upon Tyne, Tyne and Wear County Council Archives Department, 988/2, Merchant
Adventurers' Book of Orders, 1554–1627; English; paper; 163 leaves; 360mm x 265mm; ff 70–155
and 158–63 blank; early foliation; no decoration; some repair, good condition; bound as 988/1.

Saddlers' Company
Newcastle upon Tyne, Northumberland Record Office, ZAN M13/A3b(1), Saddlers' Ordinary,
6 March 1460; English; parchment; one leaf, approximately 325mm x 245mm (305mm x 220mm);
signatures at foot, 16 seal tags with 12 seals or fragments; fair condition; title inscribed on dorse.

Newcastle upon Tyne, Northumberland Record Office, ZAN M13/A3b(2), Saddlers' Ordinary,
4 February 1533; English; parchment; one leaf, approximately 545mm x 480mm (500mm x 440mm);
signatures at foot, 14 seal tags with 22 seals or fragments; fair condition.

The two items above are wrapped in paper inscribed '3 old ordinaries of the Society
of Sadlers, Directions respecting Corpus Christi Plays etc. Dates March 6th 1450,
February 4th 1532.'

Newcastle upon Tyne, Northumberland Record Office, ZAN M13/A3, Saddlers' Minutes Book
1594–1707; English; paper; iii + 183; 405mm x 150mm (360mm x 140mm) variable; ff 71–162
and 177–81 blank; unfoliated; no decoration; unrepaired, fair condition; bound in dark brown
leather, no title, binding broken.

Tailors' Company
Newcastle upon Tyne, Tyne and Wear County Council Archives Department, 98/1/3, Tailors'
Ordinary, 31 January 1537; English; parchment; 2 leaves joined at bottom, 585mm x 585mm;
initial words in larger hand; signatures at foot, 26 seal tags with some seals and fragments, one silk
cord with seal; condition only fair, some parts badly faded, very severe stains on first membrane,
lesser staining on second; note of enrolment in civic enrolment books (on 8 September 1669)
inscribed on dorse.

Miscellaneous

Three of the items included under this heading are concerned with royal visits to
Newcastle. The first is a manuscript in the College of Arms which is a collection of
descriptions of four royal occasions; the last of these descriptions is one by John
Young, Somerset Herald (d. 1516), of the progress of Princess Margaret, daughter of
Henry VII, from London to Edinburgh for her marriage to James IV of Scotland,
including her reception at Newcastle. This piece was printed, in a not very accurate,
but complete transcription in the 1774 edition of John Leland's *Collectanea*, vol 4,
pp 258–300. Now about ten folios (which have nothing to do with Newcastle) are
missing at the beginning of the manuscript. The account of the visit of James I is
from *The True Narration*, which was published as a small printed book in 1603; part
of a later version by John Stow and Edmond Howes is included in an endnote. The
visit by Charles I in 1639 is briefly described by John Nalson in *An Impartial
Collection* (1682).

The last miscellaneous item is a Durham Consistory Court Act Book, a manuscript
record mainly of criminal cases, probates, and administrations. A transcript of litigation in 1568 concerning a disputed will of Sir Robert Brandling of Newcastle
supplies an incidental reference to the Newcastle Corpus Christi plays. Extracts from
the Act Book are edited by James Raine in *Depositions and Other Ecclesiastical
Proceedings from the Courts of Durham*, Surtees Society 21 (London, 1845).

The Progress of Princess Margaret, 1503
London, College of Arms, M13; early 16th century; English; paper; 117 leaves; 290mm x 215mm;
modern foliation; some moderately decorated initials; condition good, occasional staining and torn
corners, some restoration; bound in with M16, which follows; bound in brown leather, 18th–19th
century.

Visit of James I, 1603
The |True Narration of | the Entertainment of his | Royall Maiestie, from the time of his depar- | ture
from *Edenbrough*; till his receiuing at | London: with all or the most spec- | ciall Occurrences. |
Together with the names of those Gentle- | men whom his Maiestie honoured | with Knighthood. |
AT LONDON | Printed by Thomas Creede, for Thomas | Millington. 1603. | 4⁰, 24 leaves unnum-
bered. STC 17153.

Visit of Charles I, 1639
AN | Impartial Collection | OF THE | Great Affairs of State, | From the Beginning of the | SCOTCH REBELLION | In the Year MDCXXXIX. | To the Murther | OF | King CHARLES I. | WHEREIN | The first Occasions, and the whole Series of the late Troubles | IN | England, Scotland, & Ireland, | Are faithfully Represented. | Taken from Authentick Records, and Methodically Digested, | By *JOHN NALSON*, LL.D. | VOL. I. | Published by His Majesties Special Command. | *LONDON*, | Printed for *S. Mearne*, *T. Dring*, *B. Tooke*, *T. Sawbridge*, and *C. Mearne*, MDCLXXXII. | folio, lxxix + 844 pages (817 numbered, 27 unnumbered). STC N 106.

Litigation concerning Sir Robert Brandling's will, 1568
Durham, University of Durham, Department of Palaeography and Diplomatic, D.R. III. 2 (new classification pending), Consistory Court Act Book November 1567 – August 1572; English; paper; 305mm x 200mm; i + 436 + i; early foliation, ff 6–370, 73 leaves at end unfoliated; first section to f 53 has leaves bound in erratic order, some leaves missing, ff 6, 45, 50 and an unnumbered fragment not bound in; no decoration; condition generally good, but some leaves fragmentary or torn, and text lost through progressively worsening erosion across top outer corner near end of volume; only unbound leaves repaired; bound in dark brown quarter calf with card boards, probably early 19th century, title 'Acts 1567 to 1572' on spine.

Antiquarian Material

The work of Newcastle antiquarians is not very significant for this edition, as most of the source material on drama and minstrelsy which they used is still extant. Brand has a few relevant items the originals of which are not now to be found, the most important being his extracts from the Fullers and Dyers' Accounts for 1561 and the Slaters' Accounts for 1568. Brand's extensive collections for the *History*, most of which are in Newcastle Central Library, are used in this edition in preference to the published *History of Newcastle* itself; transcriptions in the collections are not tidied up to the same extent as in the *History*, and are therefore likely to reflect the originals more accurately. An eighteenth-century transcript of a Glovers' Order Book and a nineteenth-century collection of Tailors' Records are also included here; one item from each is used in the edition.

The Bricklayers and Plasterers' Ordinary of 1454 cannot be traced back beyond the summary in Walker and Richardson's *Armorial Bearings* (see Select Bibliography).

Brand MSS
AC Newcastle upon Tyne, Newcastle Central Library, L942.82 N536 B, Brand MSS collections of material relating to Newcastle, 18 vols; English; paper; unfoliated; 300mm x 200mm (average); loose miscellaneous papers, 18th century, some printed, mounted on pages; modern bindings, maroon morocco with black title panel and gold lettering.

AC Newcastle upon Tyne, Northumberland Record Office, ZAN M13/B13, Brand MSS among the collection of the Society of Antiquaries of Newcastle upon Tyne; English; paper; 219 leaves; foliated; 210mm x 170mm; loose miscellaneous papers, 18th century, mounted on guards and bound, or bound independently; 19th-century binding, half vellum with marbled paper covers, ink title on spine: '6 Newcastle upon Tyne.'

Glovers' Order Book
Newcastle upon Tyne, Northumberland Record Office, ZAN M13/A3a, 'Book of Orders belonging to the Company of Glovers in Newcastle upon Tyne, transcribed in the year 1734, John Potts, Clerk' (on flyleaf); English; paper; ii + 85; ff 1–8, paginated 1–15, contain transcripts of originals, rest mostly blank; bound in brown leather with raised bands and no title.

Tailors' Records
Newcastle upon Tyne, Society of Antiquaries of Newcastle upon Tyne, Black Gate Library, M13/D10, Tailors' Company Orders etc; English; paper; 99 leaves (20 blank) + 2 printed notices inserted; unfoliated; 345mm x 215mm; decorated binding with leather spine, card boards, title on spine in gold letters on red; probably 19th-century binding of artificial collection.

Editorial Procedures

Principles of Selection

It has been the intention of the editor to give full transcriptions of every documentary reference to dramatic, musical, and ceremonial activity in Newcastle before 1642, of the kinds discussed in the first section of the Introduction. In accounts, an entry is usually given in full if most of the items in it are relevant to the interests of this volume. In extracts from documents written as continuous prose, such as guild ordinaries, full quotation is preferred to a series of short passages linked by dots indicating ellipsis; dots are used only where there is a substantial amount of irrelevant material between relevant passages.

One exception to the principle of comprehensiveness is the many references in the Chamberlains' Accounts between 1590 and 1600 to the keeping of Allon the fool; these are omitted from the edition. From 1 week October 1590 to 2 week May 1595 there is a weekly entry (with some variation of spelling, and occasional minor variation of wording): 'paid to Dame Clark for keeping Allon the fool xij d.' From 3 week May 1595 to 2 week September 1596 the sum paid goes up to 18d. From 3 week September 1596 to 1 week October 1600 the entry is 'paid for keeping Allon the fool xviij d,' and it occurs monthly in the payments for the first week of each month, apart from September 1596 (where it is made in the third and fourth weeks), August 1597 (first and fourth weeks), and September 1597 (fourth week). In 1 week March 1596 the entry is 'paide to dame younge for keeping allon clarke foole xviij d.'[37]

Also omitted from the edition are the sixteen entries recording regular payments to Henry Atkinson between 1 week August 1599 and 1 week October 1600: 'paid to Henry Atkinson (a) fool in relief vj d,' and the one reference to 'henry Atkinson the foole' in a list of recipients of clothing (Atkinson received a pair of stockings) in 4 week July 1607. It is unlikely that Atkinson was an official fool (see above, p xix). All other references to fools are included; even incidental references may help clarify the town's attitude towards them, in particular the extent to which the town was prepared to support them. Incidental references to waits and others are included for the same reason.

The following have not been included in the edition as being irrelevant:

— references to church music and ceremonial activities (except for those to church music paid for by the city, which are included).
— references to bellringing by the four churches (St Nicholas, St John's, St Andrew's, All Saints) on the coronation anniversary, the fifth of November, and for royal visits, unless the bellringing is accompanied by other music or ceremony. The Chamberlains' Accounts record expenses for bellringing on twenty-one separate occasions in all.
— references to bonfires on Midsummer Eve and the coronation anniversary, unless accompanied by musical activity.
— references to dinners, breakfasts, etc, unless the occasions are accompanied by music or other entertainment.
— references to fairs, though the few references to fair riding in the Chamberlains' Accounts are included. Newcastle had three annual fairs, established by royal grant, beginning on Lammas Day (1 August), St Luke's Day (18 October), and Martinmas Day (11 November).
— occasional references in accounts to preparations (street dressing, provision of food, etc) for the visits of royal personages and other notables.
— references to guns, gunners, and the town armour, of which there are many in the Chamberlains' Accounts. There is no evidence that the armour was ever used in a show.
— references in the Chamberlains' Accounts to delivery charges for the liveries of waits and others.
— references to expenses for lights and torches in the accounts of the Masters and Mariners' company (Trinity House) and the Merchant Adventurers' company. Every year from 1555 to 1559 Richard Thompson the barber is paid five shillings for looking after the lights for the Merchant Adventurers. In 1558 there is also a separate item in the Merchant Adventurers' Accounts 'ffor the charges of the torges' which comes immediately before the expenses for Hogmagog and Corpus Christi Day, but there is no more definite association of torches with festival occasions.
— references to civic regalia.

Edited Text

The material in the edition is arranged chronologically from year to year, but within the year the arrangement is document by document. The order of documents within the year follows a regular sequence determined by the type of document: first, civic records; second, guild records; third, any other material. The editorial headings give dates, in as much detail as possible, document identification, and folio or page numbers where these exist.

An attempt has been made to give some idea by the format of the edited text of the general layout of the manuscript originals. As far as possible, headings, marginalia, and account totals are printed in the position in which they appear in the manuscripts. Original paragraphing has been preserved, but not original lineation.

As far as possible, the texts in the edition are given as they stand in the originals, with a minimum of editorial interference. In the few cases where two copies of a document survive, a base text has been chosen, with reasons for the choice given in an endnote, and significant variants are collated at the foot of the page. Mere spelling differences and differences in capitalisation, form of abbreviation, word-division, and punctuation are ignored. Footnotes are also used to give simple explanation and clarification of the text (for example, to draw attention to scribal dittography), but no attempt is made to note every error. Some textual problems are discussed in the endnotes. The texts themselves are not emended in any way. Original spelling, capitalisation, and punctuation have been preserved, though diacritics, braces, and line-fillers have been ignored. 'I' and 'J' have been uniformly transcribed as 'I'.

Abbreviations

Most scribal abbreviations have been expanded, with italics to indicate letters supplied. Few offer any difficulty. The sign 'γ' has been expanded consistently to 'es' even when it follows 'e'. The abbreviation 'x' has been expanded to 'ch*rist*' and 'xp' to 'ch*rist*'. Signs for 'and' have been transcribed uniformly as '&'. Other abbreviations which have been retained are 'li', 's', 'd' (for 'denarius' and 'dimidium'), 'ob'('obolus,' half-penny), 'mr', 'st', 'viz', and '&c'. If a form has some sign of abbreviation in the manuscript but is not expanded in the edited text, a stop is used to indicate the presence of an abbreviation mark. In accounts, 's' for 'solidus' and 'd' for 'denarius' often end in a flourish; the 's' has two distinct kinds of flourish, one a curved upstroke, the other a loop and downstroke. Unless there is some more definite sign of abbreviation, however, such forms are transcribed simply as 's' and 'd', without stops. Shortened forms of personal first names have been expanded to the usual full forms. All superior letters have been silently lowered to the line, except when they are used with numerals, for example, 'xxiiij^tie'.

Dating

Regnal years, and, where possible, financial years are converted in the edition to calendar years. When the financial year is not known, as is usual in the guild accounts, the year headings found in the documents are used.

The weekly headings in the Chamberlains' Accounts become more and more out of step with the actual dates as the financial year, from Michaelmas to Michaelmas, goes on (see above, pp xxi–xxii), but no attempt is made to convert the manuscript headings to actual dates. Most such conversions would be problematical. A table of conversions for the financial year 1607–8, based on converted dates written in beside the weekly headings in the accounts book, is given below, pp xl–xli. Superscript numerals are used to differentiate the first set of October headings in the calendar year ('October[1]') from the second ('October[2]').

The modern calendar year begins 1 January, but the calendar year in use in England in the fifteenth, sixteenth, and seventeenth centuries did not begin until 25 March. Documentary dates between 1 January and 24 March are therefore converted; thus original 12 March 1451 becomes 12 March 1452 in the edition.

No attempt is made to date individual accounts entries apart from the headings. It is of course usual for payment to be made and/or recorded after the event, sometimes long after, occasionally before. Thus the payment to the shipmen for dancing on St John's Eve is given in the edition under the heading 28 June 1510, which is the heading in the Chamberlains' Accounts, not under 23 June, the date of St John's Eve.

Where the edition makes use of an enrolment or other copy of a document, the date under which it appears is that of the original document as recorded by the copier.

Notes

1 These estimates are taken from the table of population figures in Sydney Middle-brook, *Newcastle upon Tyne: its Growth and Achievement* (Newcastle, 1950), p 321.

2 There is a clear if not entirely comprehensive survey of the charters and other documents important to the development of the civic government of Newcastle in E. Mackenzie, *A Descriptive and Historical Account of Newcastle upon Tyne*, vol 2, pp 601–11.

3 The enrolment of the 1557 Privy Council Ordinance (Public Record Office C 78/9, no 81) states that the electors shall be 'taken as of the Comen Counseill,' ie, taken as comprising the common council, not, as Brand states (vol 2, p 181), 'taken of the common council.' At the beginning of many of the receipts sections of the Chamberlains' Accounts volumes from 1561 on, there are lists of the names of the twenty-four common councillors and twenty-four auditors for the year. In both lists the names are in pairs, each pair attached to the name of one of the twelve mysteries. The common council is often referred to in the records as 'the 24tie.' The phrase 'the mayor's brethren,' also of frequent occurrence in the records, has been taken as another name for the common council (eg by Middlebrook, p 30). But references in the records to the mayor, his brethren, and the 24tie (see below, pp 128–9) count against this view. The brethren are more likely the aldermen; compare the phrase 'mr maior the aldermen with others' with 'mr maior his bretheren & others,' below, pp 136–7.

4 Most published work on the Newcastle companies goes back to John Brand, *History and Antiquities of Newcastle upon Tyne*, vol 2, pp 311–61. There is no comprehensive modern study. F.W. Dendy has edited the records of the Merchant Adventurers' company (2 vols, Surtees Society 93, 101 [London, 1895, 1899]) and the Hostmen's company (Surtees Society 105 [London, 1901]); both volumes have solid introductions.

5 Mackenzie, 2, p 636.

6 See I.S. Leadam, *Select Cases before the King's Council in the Star Chamber*, vol 2, 1509–44, Selden Society Publications 25 (London, 1911), p 112. In the record of the litigation leading up to the decree (Leadam, p 96) there is mention of 'Robert

Thewe ... Bootlere' (bottler, a maker or seller of glass bottles?), and 'Thomas
dennand Cardmaker' (Leadam, p 99), but there is no evidence that these occupations were constituted as guilds.

7 The Masters and Mariners' company (Trinity House) was the only other Newcastle
company to have its franchise directly from the crown. It too was a prestigious
company with a commercial involvement, though it did not have the civic power
of the Merchant Adventurers and the Hostmen.

8 There is no reference to the Corpus Christi play or procession, or any kind of
dramatic activity, in the ordinaries of the Drapers (1512), Porters (1528),
Cordwainers (1566), and Coopers (1575).

9 Henry Bourne's transcript is printed in his *History of Newcastle upon Tyne*,
pp 139–41. Brand, 2, pp 373–9, also prints the play, following Bourne. A facsimile
of Bourne's text is available in J.J. Anderson and A.C. Cawley, 'The Newcastle
Play of *Noah's Ark*,' *Records of Early English Drama Newsletter*, 1977: 1, 11–17.
The play is edited by Norman Davis in his *Non-Cycle Plays and Fragments*, Early
English Text Society, Supplementary Text no 1 (London, 1970).

10 The chamberlains' methods of dating their accounts are explained on p xx.

Most scholars' lists of plays in the Newcastle cycle assign 'The Descent into Hell'
to the Tailors. The first to make the attribution were apparently J. Walker and
M.A. Richardson, *The Armorial Bearings of the Several Incorporated Companies
of Newcastle upon Tyne* (Newcastle, 1824), p 59; they also assign 'The Purification'
to the Smiths. The present editor can find no warrant for either attribution.
Walker and Richardson evidently misunderstood a footnote in Brand, 2, p 370:
'Mr Warton [Thomas Warton, *The History of English Poetry*, vol 1 (London, 1775),
p 243], who smiles at the idea of their having anciently committed to the black-
smiths the handling of the "Purification" [in the Chester cycle], an old play so
called, would have had still greater reason, could he have assigned with truth to
the company of taylors "the Descent into Hell".'

In the ordinary of the Barbers (1442), the plural form 'pageants' evidently has
singular sense.

'Karre' is also used, once, for a pageant vehicle in Beverley, according to an agree-
ment dated 1391 and recorded in the Great Guild Book (f 13). Whether the
Beverley 'karre' had wheels or not is uncertain. A Beverley Town Chartulary entry
for April 1448 refers to 'seruientes [of the Tilers] ... ducent & ponant pagendam
suam in festo corporis christi.' See Diana Wyatt, 'The Pageant Waggon: Beverley,'
Medieval English Theatre, 1 (1979), 55–60.

Wheel-less pageants which were carried were common in England in the later
middle ages and the sixteenth century, notably in London. The Lincoln
Cordwainers' pageant of Bethlehem, which was carried, makes a suggestive com-
parison with Newcastle, for in Lincoln too a steep street had to be negotiated by
the marchers, from the High Bridge up to the Cathedral. See transcript of records
and discussion in Hardin Craig, 'The Lincoln Cordwainers' Pageant,' PMLA, 32

(1917), 605–15, and Stanley Kahrl's edition of the Lincolnshire dramatic records, *Collections Volume VIII*, Malone Society (London, 1974 [for 1969]).

15 The meal market, also called oatmeal market and later groat market, was on the west side of Middle Street, just above St Nicholas church. The beer market, more usually 'bigg market,' was in the next stretch of road further up towards Newgate. Bourne refers to the beer market twice (pp 13,15), drawing on an old account of the wards of the town.

16 The Chamberlains' Accounts for 8 May 1510 have a reference to breaking down 'ij gappys off the guddy Deyn ffor procescion,' and those for 11 May 1510 refer to the 'making upp' of the same 'gayppis,' but what this procession was is uncertain. Corpus Christi Day in 1510 fell on 30 May, and the first reference in the accounts to the Corpus Christi play in that year is a payment for the banns of the play on 17 May. The present editor has been unable to locate 'the guddy deyn,' though the name occurs regularly in lists of rentals in the receipts section of the Chamberlains' Accounts in the 1560s. Brand (1, p 418) notes a seventeenth-century sheriff's rental: 'Item the Forth and the Gooden-Deane letten to Thomas Cook.' This need not mean that 'the guddy deyn' was near the Forth, but it is worth noting that, according to Bourne (p 146), the Forth was traditionally 'a Place of Pleasure and Recreation,' and it was the custom for the mayor, aldermen, and others to go in procession to the Forth at Easter and Whitsun.

17 Compare with the spars and canvas the items relating to the rebuilding of the Norwich St George's Day dragon in the Norwich St George's Guild Surveyors' Account Rolls for 1533–5 (Norwich Record Office, case 8, shelf f): 'And payed to the man that made the dragon ij s vj d And payed ffor Canwas for the dragon vj d...And payed for vj ffadom of lyne & for nayles ffor the dragon iiij d' (1533–4); 'And payed for the makyng of the dragon to Roose Steyner v s And payed ffor canvas ⌈6 d⌉ for his nekke & for anew staffe ⌈ij d⌉ ...' (1534–5).

18 On the London Gogmagog and his origins in legend and biblical lore, see Robert Withington, *English Pageantry*, 2 vols (Cambridge, Mass., 1918,1920), especially vol 1, pp 58–64.

19 Cf the entry for 1 week May 1562: 'paid to the fellyshyp of a shype albroughe ffor dansyng in the fyrthe.'

20 See Appendix II, pp 164–8.

21 A few names of individuals designated 'minstrel' occur in Newcastle parish registers, and Professor Ian Lancashire has picked up a reference to 'my tenement in Pilgrime-strete in the teanor of Edwarde Davynson, mynstrell' in the will of Robert Shadforth dated 7 August 1545 (J.C. Hodgson, ed, *Wills and Inventories from the Registry at Durham*, part 3, Surtees Society 112 (London, 1906), p.3).

22 Two post-1642 entries in the Common Council Books of Newcastle corporation give some further scraps of information about the waits. In the Common Council Book for 1645–50 (TW: 589/4), f 72, is the following minute from a meeting of the council held on 4 November 1646: 'Moved that the Waites of the town should

be allowed to proceed as on former occasions and to go morning and evening according to the ancient custom & usage of the Corporation. They were to be warned not to go into taverns & if they did so they were to be punished.' In the Common Council Book for 1650–9 (TW: 589/5), f 554, there is a reference, dated 20 August 1655, to '...the sagbott which Iohn Allanby, late one of the waites of this town did play his part upon...'

Information on the kind of 'service' is lacking. Dr Sally-Beth MacLean has pointed out to the editor that in Norwich, individual waits were employed as singing men in church.

In the register of burials of St John's church for August 1589 is found the designation 'town's fool': 'Edward erington the townes fooll the 23 of August died in the peste.'

Occasionally fools were used for the purpose of running errands (see, eg, p 121).

On the distinction between natural and artificial fools see Enid Welsford, *The Fool: His Social and Literary History* (London, 1935), p 119.

For 'half-witted town-fools' in later medieval France, see Welsford, p 121.

'Allayne the fovll' is always so referred to and his name is always so spelt, in 1580. From 1 week October 1590 to 2 week April 1591 the spelling is 'Allan,' and from then on, with change of hand, 'allon' is usual, occasionally 'allen.' The name in its various forms occurs some four hundred and fifty times, almost always without surname, but there are four references to 'allon clarke foole' in 1596 and six to 'Allon younge (foole)' in 1597–1600. Probably there is only one 'allon the foole.' He may be called 'allon clarke' after 'Dame Clarke,' the woman who regularly looks after him until 2 week September 1596, when she disappears from the accounts. 'Dame Clarke' may have been succeeded as Allon's keeper by 'Dame Young,' whose name the fool then took (there is one reference to a Dame Young, in 1 week March 1596: 'paide to dame younge for keeping allon clarke foole'). Of course, it is also possible that either Clarke or Young was the fool's true surname.

Charles I was also in Newcastle in 1633 (see Brand, 2, p 455), 1639, and 1641. Dr Theodore DeWelles has drawn the editor's attention to references to these visits in the *Calendar of State Papers, Domestic Series, Charles I*, vols 6 (for 1633–4), p 92; 14 (for 1639), pp 136, 144–6; 18 (for 1641–3), pp 101, 105; and Addenda 1625–49, pp 606–7.

In 543/18, the scribe may omit the amounts paid for whole blocks of regular weekly entries, leaving the column on the right-hand side of the page blank; he does this on (1594–5) ff 4v, 8v, 10v, 11–11v, 12v, 13v, 14–14v, 15, 15v–16, 16v, 17v, 18–18v, 23, 24, 25–5v, 30v, 31v–2, 34–4v, 35–5v, 36v, 38v, 39v, 41v–2, 42v–3, 43v–4, 45, 46v–7, 49, 50–0v, 51v, 53–3v; (1593–4) ff 91v–2, 92v–3, 93v, 94–4v, 95–5v, 96–6v, 98v, 100, 101, 102, 103, 104, 105, 106v, 107v; (1595–6) ff 273v, 274v–5, 275v–6, 278, 280v, 286v, 290, 290v–1, 291v, 293, 294, 295, 295v, 296v, 297v, 299, 300, 300v–1, 301v. In blocks of regular entries for the four weeks of March 1595 the scribe leaves out not only the amounts but the main part of the entries as well, so that on part of folio 19v there are only the words 'paide to' written twenty-six times down the left-hand side of the page; similarly ff 20–0v, 21–1v, 22–2v.

31 St Ellenmas (also Saintelmas, St Tellenmas, etc) must be the feast of the Invention of the Cross, 3 May in the calendar in the Book of Common Prayer. In legend, St Helena the mother of Constantine was the finder of Christ's cross, buried near Calvary.

32 The editor is grateful to Dr Constance M. Fraser, who first saw, and pointed out to him, that the chamberlains worked according to a lunar month system, and who drew his attention to the conversions in some of the volumes of accounts. A weekly and lunar monthly system is found also in the accounts of the Cellarer of Durham Abbey, 1307–1535 (J.T. Fowler, (ed), *Extracts from the Account Rolls of the Abbey of Durham*, vol 1, Surtees Society 99 (London, 1898), pp 1–112), but in this system the months are simply numbered 1–13, and the weeks, often attached to a feast day, 1–4.

33 The following table is compiled from dates written in the margins of the accounts for the financial year 1607–8 (in 543/21).

Heading	Receipts conversion	Payments conversion
1 week October	6 October	10 October
2 week October	no conversion	17 October
3 week October	21 October	24 October
4 week October	28 October	31 October
1 week November	1 November	7 November
2 week November	7 November	14 November
3 week November	14 November	21 November
4 week November	21 November	28 November
1 week December	not legible	5 December
2 week December	9 December	12 December
3 week December	17 December	19 December
4 week December	19 December	26 December
1 week January	26 December	2 January
2 week January	2 January	9 January
3 week January	9 January	16 January
4 week January	not legible	23 January
1 week February	23 January	30 January
2 week February	31 January	6 February
3 week February	6 February	13 February
4 week February	13 February	19 February
1 week March	20 February	26 February
2 week March	27 February	4 March
3 week March	5 March	11 March
4 week March	12 March	18 March

1 week April	19 March	26 March
2 week April	30 March	2 April
3 week April	7 April	9 April
4 week April	no conversion	16 April
1 week May	no conversion	23 April
2 week May	26 April	30 April
3 week May	2 May	7 May
4 week May	not legible	14 May
1 week June	17 May	21 May
2 week June	23 May	28 May
3 week June	30 May	4 June
4 week June	6 June	11 June
1 week July	13 June	18 June
2 week July	not legible	25 June
3 week July	27 June	2 July
4 week July	4 July	9 July
1 week August	11 July	not legible
2 week August	18 July	23 July
3 week August	no conversion	20 (*error for* 30) July
4 week August	1 August	6 August
1 week September	8 August	13 August
2 week September	no conversion	20 August
3 week September	22 August	27 August
4 week September	29 August	3 September
1 week October	no conversion	not legible
2 week October	11 September	not legible
3 week October	no conversion	not legible
4 week October	25 September	not legible

This 1508–11 section of accounts was brought to light only in 1978 by Mr Gordon Tams. It was formerly bound together in one volume (543/16) with the 1576–81 section, which it followed.

In this volume the payments accounts run continuously, with weekly headings in regular order, from 1 week October 1561 to 1 week November 1563 (f 161). The next weekly headings, on f 161v, are 'The 2 weke' and 'The 3 weke,' but the next heading, on f 162, is 'The 4 weke off dessember.' The headings then continue in regular order until 4 week October 1564. Then follows the year heading for the next fiscal year, '1564' (f 176); the next three pages are blank, and the accounts begin again on f 178 at 3 week February 1565 and continue regularly till 4 week June 1565 (f 182v). The next headings are: f 183, 'The 4 weke off november,' 'The ffurste weke off december'; f 183v, 'The 2 weke,' 'The 3 weke'; f 184, 'The ffurste weke off november'; f 184v, 'The 2 weke,' 'The 3 weke.' Much of the next sheet (ff 185–5v) has been lost through a tear, but f 185 evidently contained two sets of accounts headed 'The 1 weke' and 'The 2 weke,' and f 185v two sets of accounts headed 'The 3 weke' and 'The 4 weke off october.' On each side, the first heading is lost, part of the first set of accounts remains, including the weekly total at the end, and the second heading remains. There follow f 186, 'The 4 weke of november,' 'The ffyrste weke of dessember'; f 186v, 'The 2 weke,' 'The 3 weke'; f 187, 'The ffurste weke of Januarye,' 'The 2 weke,' 'The 3 weke'; f 187v, 'The 4 weke of december' (the last set of accounts in the volume).

F 186 is out of place; it should come after f 161, where it fills the apparent gap in the sequence of accounts between 3 week November 1563 and 4 week December 1563. Ff 183–5 and f 187 are out of place and out of order; the correct order is: f 185, 1–4 week October 1564 (beginning of financial year); f 184, 1–3 week November 1564; f 183, 4 week November, 1–3 week December 1564; f 187, 4 week December 1564, 1–3 week January 1565; this last sheet has been bound wrong way round. The weekly totals add up correctly to the monthly totals in the re-arrangement. The list of regular items beginning each week's accounts on f 186 conforms to the pattern for the year 1563 rather than for 1564 or later.

36 In this volume the payments accounts run continuously, with weekly headings in regular order, from 1 week October 1576 (end of financial year) to 4 week January, but the next heading, after 4 week January, is 2 week December. There is then a regular sequence from 2 week December to 4 week October. At the end of the entries for 4 week October there is a note of the sum of the payments for 'this holl yeare begynnynge at myghelmas last past in anno / 1579 / and endinge at myghelmas last past in / anno / 1580 / .' The next heading is 'Anno 1580,' and the weekly headings are then in regular sequence until the end of the volume. It seems that the point of disjunction in the sequence of accounts, when the heading 4 week January is followed by 2 week December, marks a jump from the fiscal year 1576–7 to the fiscal year 1579–80. As one would expect if this were the case, one set of regular entries occurs at the beginning of each week's accounts up to the point of disjunction, and another set, different though not entirely dissimilar, appears from then on.

37 Exceptionally, a sum other than 12d or 18d is recorded, as follows: 1,4 week December 1594 4d each week; 4 week September 1597 2s. The figures column is blank in 1, 2, 3, 4 week July 1594; 1, 2, 4 week August 1594; 3, 4 week September 1594; 1, 2, 3 week October 1594; 3 week December 1594; 1, 2, 3, 4 week January 1595; 1, 2, 3, 4 week February 1595; 4 week March 1595; 1, 2, 3 week April 1595; 2, 4 week June 1595; 2, 3 week July 1595; 2, 4 week August 1595; 1, 2, 3 week September 1595; 1, 3, 4, 5 week October 1595; 2, 3 week November 1595; 1, 4 week December 1595. There is no entry at all for keeping Allon the fool in 3, 4 week April 1591; 2, 3, 4 week May 1591; 1 week June 1591; 1 week December 1593; 2, 3 week March 1595; 4 week April 1595; 3 week June 1595; 1, 4 week July 1595; 3 week August 1595; 4 week September 1595; 2, 3 week December 1595; the period 1 week January 1596 to 4 week July 1596 (with the exception of the 1 week March payment to Dame Young quoted in note 28, above); 1, 2, 3, 4 week October 1597 (end of financial year); 1, 2, 3, 4 week July 1599.

Select Bibliography

With one or two exceptions, only books and articles with first-hand transcriptions of documents relating to dramatic, ceremonial, and musical activity in Newcastle before 1642 are included in this list.

General Histories of Newcastle

Bourne, Henry. *The History of Newcastle upon Tyne: or, the Ancient and Present State of that Town* (Newcastle, 1736).

Brand, John. *The History and Antiquities of the Town and County of the Town of Newcastle upon Tyne*. 2 vols (London, 1789).

Grey, W. *Chorographia, or a Survey of Newcastle upon Tyne* (Newcastle, 1649).

Hornby, Hugh. *An Attempt towards Some Account of the Ancient and Present State of the Town of Newcastle upon Tyne* (MS). 4 vols. Library of the Duke of Northumberland, Alnwick Castle, Alnwick, Northumberland, MS 187A 200–3 (nd, but compiled between 1774 and 1798).

Mackenzie, E. *A Descriptive and Historical Account of the Town and County of Newcastle upon Tyne including the Borough of Gateshead*. 2 vols (Newcastle, 1827).

Sykes, John. *Local Records; or, Historical Register of Remarkable Events, which have occurred in Northumberland and Durham, Newcastle-upon-Tyne, and Berwick-upon-Tweed*. New edition. Vol. 1 (Newcastle, 1866).

Welford, Richard. *History of Newcastle and Gateshead*. 3 vols (London, 1884, 1885, 1887).

Studies and Editions

Anderson, John J. 'The Newcastle Pageant "Care",' *Medieval English Theatre*, 1 (1979), 60–1.

Boyle, J.R. 'The Goldsmiths of Newcastle,' *Archaeologia Æliana*, ns 16 (1894), 397–440.

Dendy, F.W. *Extracts from the Records of the Merchant Adventurers of Newcastle-upon-Tyne*. 2 vols. Surtees Society, vols 93, 101 (London, 1895, 1899).

Dodds, Madeleine Hope. 'The Northern Stage,' *Archaeologia Æliana*, 3rd series, 11 (1914), 31–64.

— 'Northern Minstrels and Folk Drama,' *Archaeologia Æliana*, 4th series, 1 (1925), 121–46.

Embleton, Dennis. 'The Incorporated Company of Barber-Surgeons and Wax and Tallow Chandlers of Newcastle-upon-Tyne,' *Archaeologia Æliana*, ns, 15 (1892), 228–69.

Gleason, John MacArthur. 'The Corpus Christi Pageants at Newcastle in the Middle Ages,' MA thesis (Yale, 1928).

Halcrow, Elizabeth. 'Mr Treasurer — Newcastle upon Tyne before 1835,' *Local Government Finance* (July and September, 1953), 1–6.

Hodgson, J.C. 'The Company of Saddlers of Newcastle,' *Archaeologia Æliana*, 3rd series, 19 (1922), 1–34.

Leland, John. *Antiquarii De Rebus Britannicis Collectanea, Cum Thomae Hearnii Praefatione Notis et Indice ad Editionem Primam, Editio Altera*. 6 vols (London, 1774).

Nelson, Alan H. *The Medieval English Stage: Corpus Christi Pageants and Plays* (Chicago, 1974).

Raine, James. *Depositions and Other Ecclesiastical Proceedings from the Courts of Durham, extending from 1311 to the Reign of Elizabeth*. Surtees Society, vol 21 (London, 1845).

Richardson, G.B. *Extracts from the Municipal Accounts of Newcastle upon Tyne* (Newcastle, 1848). Reprinted in *Reprints of Rare Tracts & Imprints of Antient Manuscripts, etc., Chiefly Illustrative of the History of the Northern Counties; and Printed at the Press of M.A. Richardson*, Historical Vol 3 (Newcastle, 1849), section 1.

Thompson, A. Hamilton. 'On the Books of the Companies of Glovers and Skinners of Newcastle upon Tyne,' *Archaeologia Æliana*, 3rd series, 18 (1921), 121–202.

Walker, James, and M.A. Richardson. *The Armorial Bearings of the Several Incorporated Companies of Newcastle upon Tyne* (Newcastle, 1824).

Welford, Richard. 'Players and Minstrels at Newcastle upon Tyne,' *Notes and Queries*, 10th series, 12 (1909), 222–3.

Key for map on facing page

Places mentioned in the records

A Newgate (Corpus Christi procession); **C** The Manner(s), earlier Austin Friars (rope walker); **D** Beer Market (Corpus Christi procession); **F** Carliol Croft; **H** Meal Market (Corpus Christi procession); **I** St Nicholas Church; **K** Head of the Side (Corpus Christi plays); **L** Forth *or* Firth (dancing); **P** Mayor's House (so Bourne; travelling players); **Q** Sandhill (Corpus Christi plays); **S** Merchant's Court (travelling players); **T** Bridge End (reception for Princess Margaret); **U** ?New Quay

Other places

B St Andrew's Church; **E** Upper Dean Bridge; **G** St John's Church; **J** Nether Dean Bridge; **M** All Saints' Church; **N** Trinity House; **O** The Side; **R** Guildhall

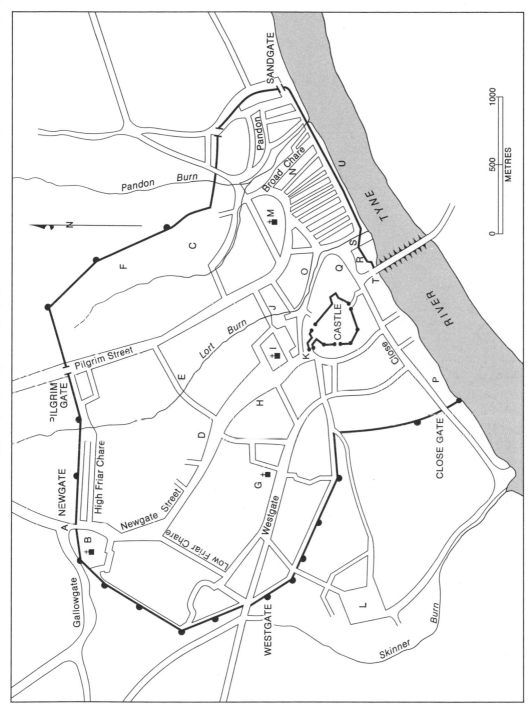

Map of medieval Newcastle upon Tyne, adapted from Leslie W. Hepple, *A History of North-umberland and Newcastle Upon Tyne* (Chichester, 1976), by kind permission of Phillimore and Co Ltd

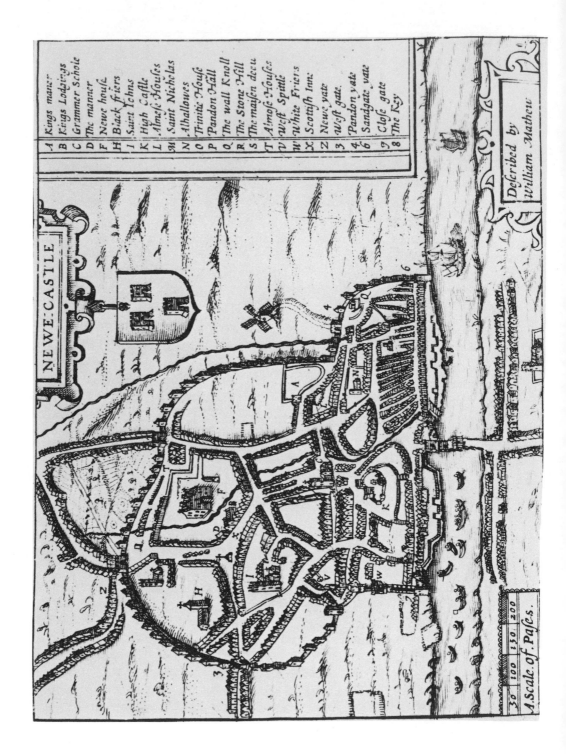

Map of Newcastle upon Tyne from John Speed, *The Theatre of the Empire of Great Britaine* (1611 edition), by kind permission of Georgetown University Library

RECORDS OF EARLY ENGLISH DRAMA

Symbols

AC   Antiquarian collection of material from diverse sources
BG   Black Gate
CA   College of Arms
NCL   Newcastle Central Library
N ZAN   Northumberland Record Office, Collection of the Society of
            Antiquaries of Newcastle upon Tyne
TH   Trinity House
TW   Tyne and Wear County Council, Archives Department
UD   University of Durham
nf, np   not foliated, not paginated
*   (after folio, page, or membrane number) see endnote
⟨...⟩   lost or illegible letters in the original
[ ]   cancellation in the original
(blank)   a blank in the original where writing would be expected
° °   matter in the original added in another hand
⌐ ¬   matter in the original written above the line
∟ ⌐   matter in the original written below the line
∧   caret mark in the original
...   ellipsis of original matter
| change of folio or membrane in passages of continuous prose

Note: In excerpts from the Newcastle Chamberlains' Accounts, superscript
            numerals are used to differentiate the first set of October headings in
            the calendar year ('October^1') from the second ('October^2'). For
            explanation of the chamberlains' use of headings, see pages
            xxi–xxii.

The Records

1427
Coopers' Ordinary (1497 copy) TW: 432/1
single leaf *(20 January)*

To the Worshippe of godde And sustentacion of the procession   5
And Corpus chr*ist*i play in the towne of the Neucastell vppon
Tyne Aftur the laudable And the amycient Custome of the seide
towne And in eschewyng of discencion And discorde that has
benne emong diuerse Craft*es*. of the seid towne is ordinet And
Assentid by the mare sherif Aldermen Iustice of peas by Auctorite   10
of the co*m*myn Gilde of the seide towne the xxᵗⁱ Day of Ianuary
in the yere of our lorde godde ⌈m¹⌉CCCCxxvj That the coupers
Now dwellyng or in tyme to co*mme* reparyng to dwell in the
seide towne shall amyabilly yerly atte the fest of Corpus chr*ist*i
go to gedder in procession As other Craftes Doyes And play ther   15
play at ther cost*es* of the seid coupers Aftur the ordinance of
ther Wardeyns yerly of them by ther co*m*myn Assent to be
chossyn And that eu*ery* man of ye seid craft shalbe Atte the
procession Whanne his oure is assignede by the seyd wardens o
payn to pay Aponde of wax to the seide wardennes & craft...   20

1437
Smiths' Ordinary (1669 copy): Enrolment Books
TW: 544/73
ff 6–6v *(14 January)*   25
...
                    The Smiths Ordinary
To the Worship of God And in sustentac*i*on of the procession
and Corpus Chirsti play in the Towne of Newcastle upon Tine

7 / amycient *presumably for* auncient   29 / Chirsti *for* Christi

after the laudable and old Custome of the said towne And in
Eschewing of all dissention and disorder that hath been amongst
[D] Diverse Craftes of the said Towne It is defyned and fully
Assented by Richard Hall Mayour Thomas Wardell Sheriffe
Roger Thorneton Robert Whelpington Lowrence Acton Simon   5
Welldone and William Ellerbie Aldermen and Iustices of peace
by the authority of the Common Guild of the said Towne
Assembled the ffourteenth day of Ianuary in the yeare of our
Lord God One thousand ffoure hundred Thirtie and Six That all

Procession

Smiths now dwelling or in time to come repaireing to dwell in   10
the said Towne shall Amiably att the ffeast of Corpus Christi goe
together in procession in their place and order to them by the
said Cominalty Assigned And play their play att their owne
Costs after the Ordinance of their Wardens yearly of them by
their Common Assent to be chosen and that every of them shall   15
be att the Procession when his houre is Assigned by the said
Wardens upon paine to pay to the said Crafte One pounde of
Waxe And that every Brother I of the said Crafte be att St Nicholas
kirke att the setting forth of the procession on St Loy Day upon
paine of one pound of Waxe And it is Agreed by the whole   20
ffellowship of the Smiths that noe man shall come to agree
with their bodie of Corpus Christi even then and there to lay
downe All there Agreements without any thing oweing to the
said Crafte and all to be paid in Lawfull money and noe pledge./...

25

Glovers' Ordinary (1669 copy): Enrolment Books
TW: 544/72
f 64v* *(20 January)*

Glouers ordinarie. ⌜1440⌝

To the worshipp of God & Sustentacion of the procession &   30
Corpus christi play in Newcastle vpon Tine of the laudible & the
ancient Craft of the said Towne It is now ordained & assented by
Richard Hall Maior Thomas Wardele Sheriffe Roger Thorneton
Robert Welpington Lawrence Acton Simon Welden William
Ellerby Aldermen Iustices of peace by the Authoritie of the   35
Common Guild of the aforesaid Towne the xx^th day of Ianuary
in the yeare of our Lord One Thousand ffoure Hundred Thirty
& Six That all Glouers now dwelling in this Towne or repaireing

Corpus christi

to dwell in the said Towne shall amiably yearly att the ffeast of

Collation with N: ZAN M13/A3a, f 1:   29 & *(1st)*] and the   30 the *(2nd)*]
omitted   34 of peace] of the peace, and   36–7 One ... Six] 1436

Corpus christi goe in procession & Liuery & play together their
play att the Costs & charges of the Masters Glouers after the
ordinance of their wardens & each of them by their Common
assent to be chosen & that euery man of the aforesaid Craft
se⟨..⟩e att the procession when his hour is assigned by the aforesaid   5
wardens paine 1 li. of wax to the said wardens & craft....

1438

AC *Skinners' Ordinary: Brand MS* N: ZAN M13/B13
    f 180* *(20 January)*   10

Copy of
A Book of Orders belonging to the Company of Skinners in
Newcastle upon Tyne transcribed in the Yeare of our Lord one
Thousand Seven Hundred and thirty five. By Iohn Potts Clerk.   15
(1) To the Worsshipp of God and the Sustentation of the
procession and Corpus Christi play in NewCastle upon Tyne of
the Laudable & antient Craft of the said Towne....

1442   20
Barbers' Ordinary (1669 copy): Enrolment Books
TW: 544/72
ff 64v–5 *(10 October)*
...

                    Barbours Ordinarie 1442   25
To the Worshipp of God & in Sustentacion of the procession &
Corpus christi play in the Towne of the Newcastle vpon Tine
after the laudible & the ancient Custome of the said Towne &
in eschewing of dissencion & discord that now late hath been
among diuerse crafts of the aforesaid Towne. It is now ordained   30
& assented By the Maior Sheriffe Aldermen Iustices of the peace
by Authority of the Common guild the x[th.] day of October In
the yeare of our Lord m[l].cccc[mo]xlij[o]. And in the yeare of the
Reigne of King Henry the Sixth after the conquest xxij[o]. That all
manner Barbours now dwelling & in time to come repaireing to   35

Collation continued: 1 goe] together 1 & Liuery] in *(blank)* 2 Costs]
Cost 2 Masters] Master 3 their] your 3 them ... Common] you be there,
giueing 4 aforesaid] foresaid 5 se⟨..⟩e] shall be 5 the *(1st)*] *omitted* 5 his
hour] he 5 aforesaid] foresaid 6 paine 1 li.] upon payne of one pound

5 / se⟨..⟩e: *possibly* serue

dwell in the said Towne shall amiably yearly att the ffeast of
Corpus christi goe together in procession in a Liuery & play their
play the baptizeing of Christ att their allers Costage after the
ordinance of their two wardens yearly to their Common assent to
be Chosen And that euery man of the said craft shall be att the   5
procession when his hour is assigned att the Newgate on paine of
a pound of wax. And alsoe the said Craft shall goe with their
pageants when it is | played in a Liuery of paine of a pound of
wax....

    10

1452
AC *Slaters' Ordinary (summary): Brand MS 18*
NCL: L942.82 N536 B
nf *(12 March)*

    15

They are to go together in a Livery and play the play at their
Cost at the Feast of Corpus Christi yearly — Each to be at the
procession when his Hour is assigned on pain of a pound of Wax.

1454   20
AC *Bricklayers and Plasterers' Ordinary (summary)*
Walker and Richardson: *Armorial Bearings*
p 58 *(12 November)*

An ancient record of this society, which is still in their possession,   25
dated 12 Nov. 1454, enjoined them to meet yearly at the Feast
of Corpus Christi, to go together in procession as other crafts did,
and play, at their own charge, two plays, viz. 'The Creation of
Adam' and 'The Flying of our Lady into Egype'. After the plays,
the wardens were to be chosen by the common assent of the   30
fellowship; each man of the said craft to be at the procession
when his hour was assigned him.

1460
Saddlers' Ordinary N: ZAN M13/A3b(1)   35
single leaf *(6 March)*

To the Worship of god & in Sustentacion of the procession &
corpus christi play In the town of the New Castell on Tyne eftir

8 / of *(1st) for* on
25 / this society: *of Bricklayers and Plasterers*

the lawdabyll & the Auncient Custom of the sayd town & in
eschewyng of discenc*i*on & discord. that now late has bene
ymong diuers Craftis of the forsayd town. It is now ordaynet &
assentyd be the Mair Aldermen Iustic*es* of pese be auctorite of
the Comon Gyld of the forsaid town. the sext day of Marce In   5
the 3er of our lord M^l.CCCC^{mo}lix. And in the 3er of ye Regn of
kyng henri the sext eftir the conquest of Ingland xxxviij. That all
the Sadlers now duellyng or in tyme to come repayryng for to
duell in the sayd town. Sall amyabli 3erly at the fest of Corpus
chr*i*sti go to gedir in p*ro*cession in a lyu*er*ay. And play to gedir   10
thair play at thair allers costagez eftir the ordenaunce of thair
wardeyns 3erly of thaym be thair comon assent to be Chosen.
And at eu*er*yman of the forsayd Craft sall be at the p*ro*cession
when his our is assignet be ye forsayd wardeyns opayn to pay
xl d to ye said wardeyns & Craft....   15

1477
Walkers' Ordinary (1669 copy): Enrolment Books
TW: 544/72
f 50 *(6 May)*   20
          Walkers' or ffull*er*s and Diers Ordinarie.
To the worshipp and pleasure of God And in Sustentation of the
procession and Corpus chr*i*sti play in the Towne of Newcastle
vpon Tine after the old Custome and for the auoydeing and
suppressing as well of dissention & discord in the ffellowshipp of   25
the Craft of Walkers of the said Towne as of deceipt in workeing
in the same Craft...

f 50v

                                                                                30

...Alsoe it is ordeyned that none of the said ffellowshipp vpon
Procession on
Corpus chr*i*sti
day</div>Corpus chr*i*sti day faile to be setting forth of the procession
yearly att the hour assigned by the said Wardens vpon paine of
two pound of wax to be paid to the susteyning of the said
Charges without they haue reasonable cause founden & allowed   35
by the said wardens And that each one of the said ffellowshipp
shall pay vj d. to the procession & play yearly....

f 51v*

                                                                                40

...Also it is ordeyned that euery man of the ffellowshipp shall
meet with dew warning *(blank)* att six of the Clock vpon paine of

a pound of wax. Alsoe it is ordeined that euery man of the same
ffellowshipp shall meet without warning on chr*ist*ie euen att
morne att Six of the Clock in the Carlolcroft vpon paine of a
pound of wax.

Memorand*um* that it was agreed vpon by the ffellowshipp vj⁰.   5
May 1596 that euery one that came not by Six of the Clock
this day should pay xij d.

...

1480   10
Merchant Adventurers' Book of Orders TW: 988/1
f 3* (23 March)

...

the ackit of the pr*o*sescicio*n* of corp*us* chr*ist*e day
[Also it is asentit acordit and agreit by the Said felleship*p* in   15
prosescio*n* Affermyng of Gwd rewll to to be Maid and had the whilk hath
lang tym beyn Abused Emank*es* thaym That wppon Corpus
chr*ist*i day yerly in hono*ur*yng and wirhippyng of the Solemp*ne*
pr*o*cession Eu*er*y Man of the Said felleship*p* beyng w*ith*in the
franches of yis Town the Said day as it shall fall Shalle apper in   20
the ⌈beer⌉ [Meel] m*er*cath ⌈abyd contynentt af*ter* to mes be
donne⌉ [by vij of clok in the morning] but he haff laytyng by
infyrmyte other Ell*es* he af speciall licanse by the Said Maist*er* of
the said felleship*p* wppon payn of A fin*e* by the defauters to be
paid for Eu*er*y Syke defaute j pond wax to the felleship*p*. Also   25
that thair be A Rowll Mayd of all the names of the same felleship*p*
for the Said pr*o*cession and acordyng to that Rowll Callyd by the
Clark the lattast Mayd burges to go formest in pr*o*cession
w*ith*utyn Any contraryyng wppon of forfet*ur* wnto the felleship*p*
for Eu*er*y sik defawte xl d pr*o*vyded always that all Those of the   30

Collation with TW: 988/1, f 4 (at back of book): 14 the *(2nd)*] goyng in
14 of *(2nd)*] vpon 15 prosescio*n (margin)*] *omitted* 15 Also] *omitted*
15 Said] holl 19 Eu*er*y] That euery 19 of the Said] beyng free of this
21 abyd] even 21 to] the hye 22 but] but yf 23 speciall] a speciall
23 by] of 24 said] *omitted* 24 by the defauters] *omitted* 25 j pond] A
pounde of 26 same] saide 28 Clark] steward*es* 28 lattast] last 29 of] a
30 xl d] iij s iiij d

16 / to to MS *dittography*
21–2 / abyd ... donne *apparently squeezed in above deletion, but difficult to read*
29 / wppon of *for* wppon payn of

Said felleshipp that shalbe Mair Shereff and Aldermen *with* thair
Officers and *ser*uandes than beyng Attend wppon The holy
Sacramente. P*ro*vydet also that all those of the Said felleshipp
that as beyn Maires Shereff*es* and ald*er*men in yerys by Passyt
Shall Go p*r*incypall in the Sayd Solemp p*ro*cession Acordyng as   5
thay war Chossen into the Sayd Officese]

      [of] the akit [⟨.⟩ of] thoyis y*at* be vnfre not *with* the Sayd
      felyshyp be not amyt to go i*n* p*ro*ssescioon
Also it is asentit &c. That no man be admyt fre nw beyng wnfre   10
To Go in p*ro*cession nor To gyff leccion *with* the Saym felleshipp
from this day in Tym Comyng but he that shalbe p*r*enttas at the
Ocupacion of the Said felleshipp vij yer at the leest Exept A
Speciall Agrement Mayd *with* the holl felleship for the Saym
lib*er*te to be had ᵒor elles that he be afrema*n*s sonᵒ   15
…

1503
Progress of Princess Margaret from London to Edinburgh
CA: M13   20
ff 89–90

The xxiiij day of thesaid monneth dep*ar*ted the said qwene from
the said durham aco*m*payned of hyr nᵘble ⌐company as she had
bene In⌐ [trayn and of y*at* sam happen of] the days past. In fayr*e* 25
man*er*e & ₍⌐goode⌐ ordre for to com to the town of the new
castell*es*
At thre mylle ⌐[f⟨..⟩] thens came to her⌐ [of thesaid place cam
befor*e* hyr*e* my lord] the p*r*ior of tynemouth well apoynted &
in ⌐his⌐ company [of xxv to] xxx horsys hys folk*es* in ⌐his⌐   30
lyu*er*ay
And y*er* was in lyke wys Syr*e* Rawff harbotell knyght Rychly
appoynted well ⌐horsed⌐ [monted] and hys folk*es* in ⌐his⌐
lyu*er*ay [of] to the nombre of xl. horsys
And at the intrynge of thesaid town of new Castell the qwen   35
apoynted hyr*e* / and intred in noble astat Ich lord / & oy*er*s
tuke[d] newes horsys Rychly appoynted. in specyall [the Conte]
⌐therle.⌐ of northu*m*berlaund / as in the man*er*e of the entryng

Collation continued: 2 than beyng] *omitted* 4 as] hathe 6 Officese] office

23 / thesaid monneth: *July*

of york and hys folk*es* in lyke wys / & y*er* entred well desyred of
the people for to be sen / & knowen
And apon the bryge cam in processyon Rychly Revested the
College of thesaid town *with* them the freres carmelist*es* / and
Iacoppyns *with* the crossys the wich was gyffen to thesaid qwen | 5
to kysse as befor*e* by the ∧ ⌐arch⌐ byschop
After them was the mayr*e* of thesaid town aco*m*payned of ye
Scheryff*es* & aldermen well apoynted ⌐on⌐ [at] fowt / the wich
Receyved honorably thesaid qwene. and aft*er* the ⌐receyuynge⌐
[recepcyon] monted thesaid maire ∧ ⌐on⌐ horsbak beryng hys   10
mass*e* before hyr*e*
At the bryge ende apon the yatt war many chyldren Revested of
surpeliz syngynge mellodyously / hympnes. & oy*er*s instrume*n*t*es*
of many sortez
And *with*in thesaid town by ordre the borges [mananns] &   15
habitanns war honnestly apoynted. the streytt*es* hanged / [& in
thes] / & at ye wyndowes loupp*es* / topp*es* & schypp*es* so full of
people. gentylmen & gentylwomen in so grett nombre / y*at* it
was a plaisur for to se bot they maid non sound of artyllery &
ordonnaunce. [I belyve it was for fawte of powdre/.]   20
In such a stat & fayr*e* aray was thesaid qwene brought & co*n*veyd
to the freres austyns wher*e* she was lodged. and honestly Receyved
by thos Revested *with* the crosse / in the man*er*e as it is Rehersed
before and ⌐she broght⌐ [hyr*e*] to hyr*e* lodgyng eu*er*y men hym
[owt] drew to hys awn | 25
The next day after ∧ ⌐the⌐ xxv day of thesaid monneth / [day of]
on Sannt Iamys ∧ ⌐Day⌐ she abode⟨.⟩ all the day in thesaid town
and was ∧ ⌐at the church⌐ at [the] masse [to the church] varey
nobly aco*m*payned
That sam day at even [ther lord Conte] ⌐therle⌐ of northu*m*berlaund   30
maide ∧ ⌐to⌐ [at] many lord*es* knyght*es* / & oy*er*s A ∧ ⌐goodely⌐
bannkett [fayr*e* & honest] & lasted to myd[*es*] nyght. for cause
of the games / dauncers sport*es*. & song*es* *with* foice of ypocras.
succres. and oy*er*s mett*es* of many delicyousez man*er*es
To thesaid new castell cam ⌐the lord Dacre.⌐ [my lord of acres]   35
of ye north acompaneyd [Of] ⌐of⌐ many gentylmen honestly
apoynted / & his folk*es* [vested &] arayd ∧ ⌐in his⌐ [of] lyveray
The xxvj. day of thesaid monneth Dep*ar*ted thesaid qwene of
thesaid place. ∧ ⌐after the⌐ [to the] custome[s] [&] *p*recedent[*es*]
[man*er*es] varey Rychly. and in fayre aray. and thesaid mayre   40

36 / [Of] O *written over original* De

conveyd hyr*e* owt of thesaid town. and after tuke lyve of hyr*e*

...

1508
Chamberlains' Account Books TW: 543/212   5
f 10 *(18 July)*

...

Item paid to the kyng*es* berward in reward   xiij s iiij d

...
                                                                            10

f 12 *(28 July)*

...

Item paid to my lord off northombreland Berward in
Reward   vj s viij d

...   15

f 12v *(31 July)*

...

Item paid to thom*a*s Carr mynstrall ffor his ffee   iij s iiij d

...   20

f 14 *(8 August)*

...

Item paid to Weddells Son ffor playng off the orgons ress*eived*
be Dawy man   vj s viij d   25
Item paid to the mynstrall that playitt Affor the mair vppon
lam*m*es Day   xij d

...

f 19v *(23 September)*   30

...

Item paid to thom*a*s Carr mynstrall the ffull off hys ffee iij s iiij d

...

Item paid to Will*i*am Carr mynstrall the last paymentt off his
ffee   x s   35

...

f 20v *(30 September)*

...

Item paid to the prest*es* ffor ther wyn   iiij s   40

...

f 21

...

Item paid to the Syngger of Santt nycolles kyrk   xxvj s viij d

...

f 25v* *(8 November)*

...

Item paid to Robert herrison *sergeant* ffor the thre watt*es*
gow*n*nys   xxxiiij s iiij d

...

f 26v *(18 November)*

...

Item paid to Will*i*am Carr mynstrall ffor makyng his Coller
thatt was granttyd be the Com*m*on Gyld in weght xvj ownc*ces*
be tayll   iiij li. vj s

...

f 28 *(22 December)*

...

Item paid to thom*a*s Carr mynstrall in p*ar*ty payment off his
ffee   iij s iiij d

...

1509
Chamberlains' Account Books TW: 543/212
f 35 *(6 April)*

...

Item paid to thom*a*s Carr mynstrall in p*ar*ty paymentt off his
ffee   iij s iiij d

...

f 50 *(26 July)*

...

Item paid to the watt*es* in p*ar*ty paymentt off ther ffee   x s

...

f 54v *(16 September)*

...

Item paid to the prest*es* off corp*us* chr*ist*i ffor ther wyn   iiij s

...

f 56 *(28 September)*

...

Item paid to thom*a*s Carr mynstrall ffor his q*uarter*
wag*es*   iij s iiij d

f 58v *(17 November)*

...

Item paid to Willi*a*m Carr mynstrall off his last ʒer
wag*es*   vj s viij d

...

f 59v *(25 December)*

...

Item paid to the watt*es* ther ffirst q*uarter* wag*es*   xiij s iiij d

...

1510
Chamberlains' Account Books TW: 543/212
f 61v *(16 February)*

...

Item paid to my lord off northombreland berrwerd in
reward   vj s viij d

...

f 65v *(30 March)*

...

It*e*m paid to the watt*es* ffor ther q*uar*tter wag*es*   xiij s iiij d

...

f 68 *(18 April)*

...

Item paid to Gorg howghell ffor xij ʒerd*es* Canwes to the
Dragon   iij s
Item paid to Iohn Dod*es* ffor nallis to the Dragon   iij d

...

f 68v *(19 April)*

...

Item paid to Rogg*er* Sewior ffor goyng with the
Dragon   iij s vj d
Item paid to Rogg*er* Sewior ffor beldyng the Dragon   viij d
Item paid to Iohn Swynnow ffor paynttyng the Dragon   ij s viij d

...

Item paid to Eduerd baxster ffor iij Sparris to the Dragon   iiij d
Item paid ffor ij gyrtthis to the Dragon   viij d
Item paid ffor Saylltwyn & Canddyll to the Dragon   vj d
Item paid to Rogger Seveor and his ffellowis in reward   iiij d   5
...

f 70v *(8 May)*

...

Item paid ffor brekyng down ij gappys off the guddy Deyn ffor   10
procescion   ij d
...

(11 May)

                                                                                15
Item paid ffor makyng vpp ij gayppis in the guddy Deyn   ij d
...

f 71* *(18 May)*
...   20
Item paid to thomas Skelltton ffor vncostes paynttyng &
writtyng the bayn off the play   xxj d

f 72 *(24 May)*
...   25
Item paid to thomas Skellton ffor bryngyng fforth the bayn off
the playe   x s
Item paid to ther mynstrall ffor goyng with the players   viij d
...

                                                                                30
f 72v *(25 May)*

...

Item paid to the mair resseived be Russell ffor the kynges
berrward in reward   xiiij s iiij d
...   35

f 74 *(8 June)*

...

Item paid to Iohn Cukk for v skowchons makyng to the playis   x d
...   40

1 / Eduerd: rd *run together*

f 75v *(28 June)*

...

| Item paid to lord Darccy berwerd in reward | vj s viij d |
| Item gyffyn the berward & his Son in reward | iiij s ij d |

...   5

f 76

Item paid to the Schippmen ffor Dansyng affor the mair vppon
Saintt Iohns Ewyn   ij s   10

...

f 81v *(17 August)*

...

Item paid to the wattes ffor ther quarter wages at   15
lammes   xiij s iiij d

...

f 84* *(2 September)*

                                                                            20
Item paid to the Schipmen vppon Santt Petter Ewyn   〈...〉

...

f 85v *(28 September)*

...   25
Item paid to the wattes ffor ther ffee   xiij s iiij d

...

f 86

...   30
Item paid to the prestes off corpus christi gild ffor ther
wyn   iiij s

...

f 90 *(24 December)*   35

...
Item paid to the wattes ther quartter wages   xiij s iiij d

...

1511
Chamberlains' Account Books TW: 543/212
f 91 *(8 February)*
...

Item paid to weddell Son ffor keppyng the orgons *in* Santt   5
nycolles   vj s viij d
...

f 92v *(4 March)*

...   10
Item paid to the lordd off northombreland berwardd in
reward   x s
...

f 94v *(8 April)*   15
...
Item paid to weddells Son ffor his q*ua*rtt*er* wagg*es* ffor keppyng
the orgons   vj s viij d
...
Item paid ffor s*er*gand*es* leuerayis & the watt*es* at   20
Cristynmes   vij li xiiij s
Item paid ffor Caryag toull Canwes & thred off them   v s iiij d
...

f 95v *(17 April)*   25
...
Item paid to the watt*es* ffor ther q*ua*rtter wag*es*   xiij s iiij d
...

f 97v *(10 May)*   30
...
Item paid to Rogg*er* brown ffor the attendans off the Dragon   iiij d
...

f 98 *(17 May)*   35

Item paid to Weddells Son ffor keppyng the orgons *in* Santt
nycolles kirk iij q*ua*rt*er*   ⟨...⟩
...

f 100 *(13 June)*

...

Item paid to thomas Skelltton ffor the bayn off the playe   xvj s

...

f 104 *(4 July)*

...

Item paid to Iohn Cuke ffor v Skoutt3ons makyng to the
playis   〈...〉

...

f 109 *(31 July)*

...

Item paid to the watt*es* ffor ther q*uarter* wag*es*   〈...〉

...

1519
Merchant Adventurers' Book of Orders TW: 988/1
f 8v

...

The copye of Andrew bewyk*es* byll is xiij s iiij d paid hym by
Robert Millot in mone whiche was Ressaved of the money to pay
for the playes xij s iiij d Rest clere to hym xij d Althyng clere
Rekened wit*h* hym *th*e xxv day of Sep*tem*ber A*nn*o nono and he
is clere & payd

...

1525
AC *Weavers' Ordinary (summary): Brand* MS 10
NCL: L942.82 N536 B
nf *(31 August)*

...at the Feste of Corpus Christi — to play their Play & Pagente
of the beringe of the Crosse.

1532
Tanners' Ordinary (1669 copy): Enrolment Books
TW: 544/72
f 58v *(8 November)*

Tanners Ordinarie.
Vnto the honour worshipp lawde and p*rai*sing of Almighty God

5

10

15

20

25

30

35

40

& sustentac*i*on & maintenance of the procession of Corpus
chr*ist*i & the play of the same with in the Towne of Newcastle
vpon Tine according to the laudible vse & ancient custome of the
same Towne of Newcastle & in eschewing of diuerse great
dissenc*i*ons debates Striues & discords that heretofore hath been   5
moued & depending amongst diuerse Crafts of the said Towne of
Newcastle for lack of good order att such time to haue been
made had & executed Master Maior that now is Councelling
himself together with Mr Sheriffe Aldermen & Iustices of the
peace of the same Towne with good discreet Aduisament & good   10
discrec*i*on alway tendering com*m*on wealth of this Towne &
in auoydeing of such Inquietnesses debates Strifes & discordes
& that good vnitye peace Loue & charity from henceforth may
daily encrease & continue among the said Crafts to the pleusure
of god & their com*m*on wealth. It is therfor condescended   15
ordeined & established by the said Mr Maior Sheriffe ∧⌜Aldermen⌝
& Iustices of peace & by the grant & assent of com*m*on guild of
the said Towne of Newcastle. That all the Company associac*i*on
or ffellowshipp of the Craft of Tanners otherwise called Barkers
now dwelling in the said Towne of Newcastle & repaireing to the   20
same or hereafter shall repaire to come & dwell in the same
Towne of Newcastle & then being free of the said Crafte or
brother of the same shall from this day forward amiably &
Loueingly ∧⌜yearly⌝ att the day of the ffeast of Corpus chr*ist*i

Corpus chr*ist*i
play

shall come to the place & places of old Custome att the hour of   25
the same day to them appointed and assigned by their wardens
& from thence goe together honestly in good & due order after
the best manner like as other honest Crafts-men doe vse in the
said p*r*ocession to the time of the setting forth of the same
procession vnto the Comeing again of the same to the place or   30
places accustomed as is afore rehearsed & then imediately after
the said procession done. Their pagions accustomed to them and
belonging to be sett forth in due order & to be played together
att all their Costs & charges after their ordinance & sessing of
their wardens for the time being without any contradic*i*on or any   35
delay. Which wardens shall yearly be elected & chosen by the
com*m*on assent of the whole body of the said ffellowshipp of the

Wardens elected

said Craft or by the most part of them. And that euery man of
the said Craft shall be in his Array & apparrell att the said
p*r*ocession & soe to passe forth with the same p*r*ocession att   40
such houre as then shall be appointed & assigned by the said
wardens vpon paine of euery default ffor his or their non

appearance & attendance vpon the said procession & play to pay
to the said wardens of the said craft for the time being a pound
of wax to be taken & leuied to the vse & behoofe of the said
crafte...

5

1533
Saddlers' Ordinary N: ZAN M13/A3b(2)
single leaf* *(4 February)*

Vnto the lawde honor & preyse of Alemyghty godde And to the   10
Sustentacion and Mayntenance of the procession of Corpus
christi And the Pley of the same Within this worsshipfull towne
of Neucastell Appon tyne After the laudable Vse And Auncient
Custome Vsed within the same towne And for Asmoche As ther
hath byn dyuers greate discencions debates Stryves & discordes   15
that here to fore hath byn Moved & dependyng Emonges dyuers
Craftes of this seyd towne of Neucastell And specially emongest
the Company or ffelowshippe of this Crafte of Sadlers ffor lacke
of goode Order At Suche tyme to have byn made & Executyd
Master Mair that nowe ys Incounceyllyng hym selfe to gedder   20
with Master Shireffe And Masters the Aldermen and Iustices of
the kynges peace within the same towne of Neucastell with
goode discreate Aduisement & good discression All wey tenderyng
the Comen welth of this towne And In Adwydyng of Suche
Ingreetnesses debates & discordes And goode vnitie concorde   25
love & charytie ffrome hensforth may daily increase & contynue
Amonge the said craftes & occupacions & namely emonge the
felawshyppe & Crafte of Sadlers Affore ⌐seid⌐ to the pleasure of
all myghtty godd & their Comen Welth Yt ys therfor condiscendid
ordeyned & establesshedd by the sayd Mr Meir Mr Shireffe   30
Masters the Aldermen & by the graunte & Assent of the Comin
gilde of the seyde towne of Newcastell Thatt all the Company
Association or ffelisshype of the Crafte of Sadlers nowe dwellyng
in the seyd towne of Naccastell or in Any tyme hereafter
Repayryng to the same or shall Repayre come & dwell in the   35
same towne of Neucastell & then beyng ffree of the seyd Crafte
or broder of the same shall ffrome hensforth Amyably & lovyngly
yerely atthe day of the ffest of Corpus christi Shall in their best
Apparell or Array come to the place or places of olde Custome
vsed Atthe ower of the same to them Appoyntid & Assigned by   40
their wardens And ffrome thence so ⟨.⟩o gydder honestly in good
& dewe order After the best Maner lyke as other honest Craftes

Men doo vse to goo in the seyd procession ffrome the tyme of
the Settyng fforthe of the same procession vnto the Comyng
Agayne of the same procession to the seyd place or places
Accustomed And then Inmediatly After the seyd procession
doone Then their pagions to them Accustomed & be longyng to   5
be Sette fforth indew order And to bee pleyd to gydder Att all
their Costes & charges After the ordynaunces & Sessyng of their
wardens ffor tyme beyng withoute Any contradiction or Any
deley Which wardeyns shalbe yerly ellecte & chosen by the
Comen Assent of the hole body & felowshyppe of the seyd   10
Crafte or by the moste parte of them And that euery Man of the
seyd Crafte of Sadlers shall mete to gydder in hys & their best
Arraye & Apparell Atthe procession And soo to passe ff⟨..⟩th
with the same procession Att Suche ower As then shalbe
Appoynted & Assigned by the seyd wardens Appon payn of euery   15
Suche defaute ffor hys or their non Apparence & Attendaunce
Appon the seyd processione or pleye to pay a pounde of wax to
be takyn & lyvyed to thuse & behofe of the said Crafte.... Allsoo
Any man that shalbe Resceyued into the seyd or he goo with the
seyd felowshippe in procession As ys A boue wrytten shall pay   20
iij s iiij d sterling to thuse of the seyd ffellysshyppe.
...

1536
Goldsmiths, Plumbers, Pewterers, Glaziers, and   25
Painters' Ordinary TW: 940/1
single leaf* *(1 September)*

Vnto the honour And worsshippe of Almyghti godd And In the
Sustentacon of the precession of Corpus christi play within this   30
town of Neucastell Appon tyne After the Laudable Antik And
Ancient Costome of the seyd town And to Avoyd & Eschew the
High Discencions ⟨....⟩tes And Stryffes that hath byn in tymes
past in & Amongest Dyuers craftes and Occupacions of the seid
town And ffor the good Reformacion therof And for the good   35
contynuance of Vnite peace concord love And charite to be All
ways hadd and Daly to be contynued Amo⟨...⟩ In councillyng
hym self to geddes with Thomas Bewyk Shiref Thomas Horsseley
Iames Lawson Henry Annderson peter Chater Andrew Bewyk

30 / precession *for* procession   33 / ⟨....⟩tes: Debaytes (TW: 861/1)
37 / Amo⟨...⟩ amongst us We Thomas Baxter Maior (*ibid*)

And Iohn Sanderson Aldermen And Iustices of pece to our
most doubtyd Soueraigne lord Kyng ⟨...⟩ haue by good disc⟨..⟩scon
advise of councell lerned and by comyn Assent and concent of
the hole cominalltie of this seid town hath Estabillyd made And
ordeyned That all goldsmythes plumers Glaciers puderers And   5
paynters dwellyng within this seid town ⟨...⟩ that nowe ys Aggred
with the seid occupacions or in tyme to come shall Aggre with
the seid occupacions or Any of them shall yerly frome hensforth
Amyably in the ffest and Day of corpus Cristi louyngly goo to
gedders in procession All in A leuerey After Dew order and ⟨...⟩   10
they shall seem good And mayteygne ther play of the thre
kynges of coleyn as the plays shall goo forth in cours Appon
all ther costes & charges to gethers After the ordynance &
Appoyntment of the ffowre Wardens of the seid Craftes ... And
that euery hiredman of any of the seyd ffyve craftes shall pay   15
half as his master pays to the pagiant...

1537
Tailors' Ordinary TW: 98/1/3
mb 1-2* (31 January)   20

To the Worshepp off god And in Sustentacion off the procession
of Corpus christi plays in the towne off Neucastell Apon tyne
After the laudabell and Aunciant coustome of the same towne
And in Avoydyng off Dissencion And Discord that hath bene   25
Amonges the Craftes off the seyd town As off man Slawghter &
morder And other myscheves in tyme comyng the Whiche hath
bene laitly Attempted Amonges the ffeloship of the seyd craftes
off the tayllorz of the same town And to induce loue charite
pease And Ryght to be had Amonges the seyd ffellishipp ffrome   30
hensforth The eight Day of October in the yere of our lorde god
Mˡᵛᶜxxxvj yt ys Assentyd Agreed ffully concludid And Accordid
by all the holle ffeloship of the seyd Craft of Tayllorz then beyng
And that in tyme to come shalbe Abyd And Dewell in the seyd
town of neucastell Robert Brandlyng then mayre Iohn Vrde   35
Sheryff Thomas horseley Iames lawson Gilbert Middilton henry
Annderson peter Chater And Andrew Bewyk Aldermen And sir
Thomas Tempest knyght Recorder of the seyd town that ys to sey
ffyrst yt ys Agreed And ordaned that euery mane that haue been

2 / ⟨...⟩ Henry the Eight (TW: 861/1)   2 / disc⟨..⟩scon Discretion (ibid)
10 / ⟨...⟩ manner as (ibid)

Aprintice in the seyd town And haue ffully Sarveed his yerez of
Appṙynticeshipe by the purporte of the tayllorz register And
record of his master shalbe admitted to Sett vp Shope of Tayllorz
craft and Work it payng at his begynyng after ye olde vse &
custome ⌈to ye⌉ fellyship of the same craft and a pott with aill   5
to the same fellishipe and yerly to the Stewerdes of the seyd
fellishipe xiij d to our lady lyght whiles he shalbe of powre and
dwellyng in the same town or within xij mylles of it And viij d
to the play euery yere when yt shalbe played And that euery
sewer pay vj d And euery hierman workyng by the weyke iiij d in   10
the yere And euery hierman by the holl yere or by the half yere
iij d to the play euery yere when yt shalbe played
Also it is ordoned that Euery man of the same Craft beyng off
the kynges legeaunce borne and ffre with the seyd town of
Neucastell that was neuer pryntice in the seyd town shalbe   15
admitted to Sett vp Shope of tayllour Craft within the same
town for ffourty poundes and to pay one li. of waxe to the
fellishipe of the same craft and A pott of aill at his furst admittance
paying Also xiij d to our lady light and viij d to the play as it ys
aforseid...   20
...
Also it is Ordand that euery man of the seid fellishipe yerely
vppon corpus christi day shall come to the procession at the
tyme Assigned and yf he com nott to the felliship before the
procession passe the newyat to pay A li of wax and if he com not   25
afor the procession be endid to pay twoli of wax Also that he
come in his leueray yf he be warned soo to doo vppon payn of a
li. of wax And also that non of the seid craft shall have liuerey
nor goo in procession with the seid felliship Afor he haue holden
shope in the seid town by A holl yere to thentent that his gud   30
condicions and demenor shalbe knowen
...
Also yt is ordand that all the Tayllorz now being And that in
tyme comyng shalbe dwellyng as fellowes in the seid town shall
euery yere at the lost of corpus christi day Amyably go to gider   35
in procession in Aliueray and play ther play at ther alleres costage
after ther ordinance of ther Stewardes
...
Also it ys Ordand that euere brother of the seid felliship com
in his lyueray when he shalbe warned by ther beddell that ys to   40

35 / lost *for* fest

sey to the procession vppon corpus christi day Saynt Iohn day
in may the day that the plays shall be played And vppon the day
of of ther generall diner and that the fellishipe disposes them to
haue A messe and dirge for the brether of the seid fellishipe
and other metynges to be assigned...   5

1545
Curriers, Feltmakers, and Armourers' Ordinary
TW: 151/1/1
single leaf *(1 October)*   10

...Therfore it is ordeyned Decreed and constituted by Robert
Lewen Mayor ... ffyrst that the said Occupacions and Companies
of Armorers Coriors and Hatters nowe being and in tyme coming
repayring hither to Dwell shalbe oone ffelowship combyned and   15
knyt vnder this Ordynance as to the bering of charge of the same
to be equally susteyned by theym according to their nombre And
shall yerelie amyablie associat theym self in the ffeast of Corpus
christi / And goo to gither in procession as other Misteries
Doethe and sustein the charges of the Lightes pagiant and plaie   20
on the same ffeast according to olde auncyent Customes and the
ordinance therin to be Devised by the wardeins of the same for
the tyme being. / And that every oone shalbe redie attendant
vpon the same whan the Hower is assigned vpon payne to Lose
and forfaict oone pownde of wax to be applied to the vse of the   25
hole ffeloweship of the said occupacions/...

1552
Merchant Adventurers' Book of Orders TW: 988/1
f 34*   30
...
Resauid for the Entraunce of apprentices and fremen for this
yere as aperes   xl s
Receyved for the monthe pence of this yere   iiij li. xj s.
Receyved for Shipe mony with the imposecions of this hole   35
yere   xiij li
Receyved for Sesmony and absence mony this yere   vj li. iiij s. ij d
Receyved for Craftesmony yat ys to saye for drapers mercers
and Bouthemen   xl s

3 / of of MS *dittography*

Receyved that was gathered of the Ventyners for ye
play   xxxix s x d
    Sum*m*a Totalis of all
    the hole receiptes of this   xxix li. xv s
    hole yere ys   5
...

Item paide of this Revenus abouesaid for the fyve
playes whereof the towne must paye for the
ostmen playe iiij li. and so theis playes paid for   xxxj li. j s xj d
with the fees and ordynarie char*ges* as aperes   10
by perticulers wrytten in the steward*es* booke
of this yere ys

    And so more paid nor Receyved
    of this hole yeres receiptes and   15
    paymen*tes* by the said steward*es*   xxvj s xj d
    w*hi*ch ys awen ⌈to⌉ Andrewe
    sureteys and Cuthbert hunt*er*
...
                                                                            20

1553
Masters and Mariners' Account Book (Trinity House)
TH: No. 60
p 44
...   25
Ite*m* p*ai*d to the menstrell*es* on saint Iohn & saint peter
ewen   xiiij d
...

1554   30
Merchant Adventurers' Book of Orders TW: 988/1
f 27* *(November)*
  An Act for the Apperell of Appryntyses mayd in november in
A*n*no D*om*i*n*i 1554 Mr Cuthbert Ellyson then beyng gou*er*noure
                                                                            35
Whereas in the Educacion and bringing vp of apprentices no litle
regarde and studye hathe Remaned in oure elders, That like as
the dewtie of the apprentize wae enstructed him to god, So was
the same not forgotten what reverence ought to be doone to the
maister and mystres: what obedyence to there Superiours, what   40

17 / xxvj s *converted from* xxxj s

honest loove vnto there equall*es* / What temperaunce in meate
dryncke and apparell Insomoche that theis vertuous m*aste*rs with
good enstruccions, had no les good Servaunt*es* obedyent vnto the
same, Than likewise the Servaunt*es* throughe the vertuous
asign*m*ent*es* and lessons of there good m*aste*rs haue heretofore   5
Comme forward in the worlde, not to be doubted bothe to the
glorye of god and to the Comforte of those whiche brought
theim vp / But whan as nowe lewde libertye in stede of the former
vertuous life haithe of late taken place in apprentizes and chiefelye
of those as ar servyng in this worshipefull fellyshipe of marchant*es*   10
whether the occasion thereof ys imputable vnto vs m*aste*rs that
by oure good lifes and wordes do not enstructe oure apprentizes
of there Dewtie. orels to be ascribed vnto the negligent or
stubberne servaunt that regardeth litle the good Lessons of vs
there m*aste*rs. ffor neuer amonge apprentizes and Chiefelye of   15
this said feoloshipe, hathe bene more abused and inconvenyent
behauour than ys of theim at this daye frequented. for what
dyseng. cardeng. and mummyng. what typlinge: daunseng and
brasenge of harlot*es*. what garded cotes. Iagged hose. lyned with
Silke. and cutt shoes. What vse of gitterns by nyght. what wearynge   20
of berd*es* / what daggers ys by theim worn crosse ouerthwarte
theire back*es* / that theis theire dooing*es* are more cumlye and
decent for rageng ruffians than seemlye for honest apprentizes /
So that yf vnto theis enormyties Spedye remedyes be not
provyded. let not in this feoloshipe be looked fromhensfoorth   25
theim to be honest and vertuous m*aste*ris to Succede vs in this
worshipefull feoloshipe for the mayntenau*n*c⟨.⟩ of the feate of
marchaundize whiche so vngodlye haue bene brought vp being
apprentizes / ffor Reformacion whereof be it therefore enacted
by Cuthberte Ellisone gouernor of this feoloshipe. the assistant*es*   30
and brethren assembled at this courte and by the authorytie of
th⟨.⟩ Same also establyshed that no m*aste*r in this feoloshipe of
marchant*es* aforesaid havinge any apprentize permytt or Suffre
his suche apprentize duringe the tyme of his apprentishood to
daunse. dyse. Carde. or mvm. or vse any gytterns. or Suffer him   35
to weare any cuthose. cut shoes or pounced Ierkens. nor to weare
any berd*es*. But that the same apprentizes maye be well and
godlye brought vp / in the feare and love of god, his duettye
toward*es* his m*aste*r and mystres To make reverence vnto his
Superyors. and that theye weare none other hoses than slopped   40
of course clothe. whereof the yarde not to excede [xij d] ⌜ij s⌝
[theire shooes and] theire cotes to be Like of course clothe of

•nota
or such lyke
[ap*er*p*er*ell] [as]
decent apperrell
as by the feoliship
shall be thought
con venyent•

houswifes making. And that thei shall weare no straite hoose but
Suche as be playne without cuff*es*. pounseng. or gard*es*. and the
same to be woorn but vpon the holye dayes or whan as they shall
ryde out of the towne or otherwise attende vpon theire m*aster*s
vpon payne the maister of euery apprentize permytting his   5
apprentize to worke or do against any parte of theffecte of this
acte to paye vnto the vse of the feoloshipe aforesaid for euery
tyme so offendinge of his apprentize. xl s. And the apprentize to
forfaict those yeres whiche the said prentice shall haue alredye
serv⟨.⟩d.....   10

f 38v *(payments)*

...

ffor the charges in ande a boute hoggmaygowyk   iiij li. ij s
ffor the charges in ande a bout the p*ro*session of corpus   15
Criste day   xxx s v d

...

1555
Merchant Adventurers' Book of Orders TW: 988/1   20
f 40

...

paid for the Charg*es* of the procession on corpus
[christi da] Daye for this yere   xl s xj d
...   25

1556
Merchant Adventurers' Book of Orders TW: 988/1
f 42v

...   30

paide for ye charg*es* of ye procession on corpus christi daye as
apereth by ye steward*es* Booke   lij s ix d ob
...

1557   35
Merchant Adventurers' Book of Orders TW: 988/1
f 43v

...

Paide for the charg*es* of corpuschristi daye as apereth
by p*er*ticulers   L s x d   40
...

1558
Merchant Adventurers' Book of Orders TW: 988/1
f 44v

...

Item paide for the charges of hogmagoge as apers by   5
perteculars   xiiij s ij d
Item paid for the charges of corpuschristie daye as
apers by p*er*teculars   iij li. xij d

...
                                                                     10

1559
Merchant Adventurers' Book of Orders TW: 988/1
f 45v

...

paid on Corpus Christye daye in char*ges* as apers by   15
perteculars   iij li. x s
...

1561
Chamberlains' Account Books TW: 543/14   20
f 115 (*1 week October²*)

...

Item paid to Mr maior that he gave to wayttes when he was
maid maior at nyght as apers by his bill   iij s
Item mor that he gave to thc wayttes on the morrowe after   xx d   25
Item mor that he gave to the [wai] new wayttes in arlles   iij s
Item paid to hym that he gave to mynstrilles the xiij daye of
october   xvj d
...
                                                                     30

f 115v (*3 week October²*)

...

Item paid to thomas pawteson ffor a payr shoes to Iohn
watson the fuell   xiiij d
Item paid mor ffor mending a nother payr of shoes to hym   iij d   35
...

f 116 (*4 week October²*)

...

Item paid for a shyrt to Iohn watson & for Rouffes to the   40
sam   iiij s ij d
...

f 116v *(1 week November)*

...

∘ᴦItem p*ai*d to henry Car the wayt for hys hallomes
qua*rteriche* grantyd to hym for his lyff   vj s viij d¹ ∘

...

It*e*m paid to Edwerd Car and Iohn payrson the
wayttes   xiij s iiij d

...

Item paid to Mr maior that he gave to two skottes mynstrilles
in Rewarde   ij s   1

...

f 118 *(1 week December)*

...

Item paide ffor vij yardes of yalowe Carsaye and vij yardes   1
of blewe Cayrsaye at ij s viij d the yarde ffor the   xxxvij s iiij d
ffulles cottes & cappes agaynste Christinmas

...

Item paid ffor xiij yard*es* of whytt lynnynge at vj d the
yard to the Sam ffulles Coottes   vj s vj d   2

...

(2 week December)

Item paid to georg brown ffor making the ij ffulles Cottes   2
[And Capes] agaynst chrystynmas   iiij s
Item mor ffor making ij Capes & ij pair of hosse to
tham   xv d

f 118v *(4 week December)*   3

...

Item paid mor to hym that he gave to two mynstrilles on
saint thomas daye   ij s

...

                                                                               3

Merchant Adventurers' Book of Orders TW: 988/1
f 49

...

paid ffor the settinge ffowrthe of the Corpuschristye

32 / hym: *the mayor*

plays as apers by the buk*es*   xiiij li. ix s xj d
...

AC   *Fullers and Dyers' Accounts: Brand MS 10*
     NCL: L942.82 N536 B   5
     nf
            1561. The Charggs of the Play this yere. A. 1561.
     The play lettine to
     S*i*r Robert Hert, Sir *Willia*m Hert —   9 sh
     George Walles, Robert Murton   10
     First for ye. Rehersall of ye play
     befor ye. Crafft   10. sh
     Item to a Mynstrell yt nyght   0 3 d
     Item for payntyng ye. Gayre   10. sh
     Item for a Salmone Trowt   15. d   15
     Item for ye. Mawndy Loves & Caks   2 sh–8 d
     Item for Wyne   3 sh–6 d.
     Item for 3 yerds & a d. lyn Cloth
     for Gods Coot   3 sh. 2 d. ob.
     Item ye. Hoysse & cot makyng   0. 6. d   20
     Item for a payr of Gloves   0. 3. d
     Item for the Care & Banner berryng   0. 20. d
     Item for ye carynge of the Trowt &
     wyn abowt ye. Towne   0–12 d
     Item for the Mynstrell   0–12 d.   25
     Item for two Spares for Stanges   0–6 d
     Item for Drynk & thayr suppers that
     watyd of the Pajent   5 sh–0
     Item for Tentor Howks   0–3 d.
     Summa totalis   50 sh. ob   30
     Item to the Clerk this yere because of the Play   2 sh–0 d.

     1562
     Chamberlains' Account Books TW: 543/14
     f 119 *(2 week January)*   35
     ...
     Item paid to mayster maior that he gave to the mynstrilles
     of this town and to other mynstrilles of the contrathe   xiij s iiij d
     in Crystynmas ⌈as apers⌉

     1 / xj d: xj d ob *Dendy Extracts; MS torn*

Item paid ffor a sherte to Iohn watsonne the full
iij yardes of lyne Clothe & ffor the Ruffes & the   iiij s
making the sam ⌈as apers⌉
Item paid ffor ij payr of shoes to the ij ffulles
agaynste [E] chrystynmas   ij s iiij d   5
Item paid to thomas kyrsope sargant ffor the Sargant*es*
And wayttes long & short leverayes as aperithe   xxx li. iiij s
by perteculars in his bill of the same the some of
...
                                                                                          10

f 120v *(2 week February)*

...
Item paid to henrye Carr the waytt ffor his lyf for his
quarteriche at candilmas   vj s viij d
...   15
Item paid to mayster maior ffor that he gave to Sir
henry persy mynstrilles in Rewarde   vj s
Item paid mor geven in Reward to the wayttes of ledes   iiij s
...
                                                                                          20

f 122 *(3 week March)*

...
Item paid by Mr maior to the wayttes of thriske geven
tham in Rewarde   iij s
...   25
Item paid mor geven in Reward to the wayttes of Carllell   iij s
Item paid mor geven in Rewarde to the wayttes of
darnton   iij s
Item paid in Reward to the skottes mynstrelles   ij s
...   30

f 122v *(1 week April)*

...
Item paid to mr maior ffor vij yard*es* of yallo carsaye
price ye yard ij s. viij d And vij yard*es* of blew   xxxvij s vj d   35
carsay price le yard ij s. viij d for the foolles cott*es*
agaynst Eastar
Item paid ffor making the sam fulles cottes
[& capes]   iiij s
...   40

5 / [E] *probably for* Easter

Item paid for making of ij payr hoses & ij Capes to the
ij fulles   xvj d

...

f 123 *(2 week April)*   5

...

Item paid ffor a payr gloves to Iohn watson ⌈and a dossen
punttes⌉   iiij d

...
                                                                             10

f 124 *(4 week April)*

...

Item paid ffor ij payr of shoun to the ⌈two⌉ fulles
agaynst ester   ij s iiij d

...   15

f 124v *(1 week May)*

...

Item paid to the fellyshyp of a shype albroughe ffor
dansyng in the fyrthe geving by Mr mayr*es* commandment   iiij s   20
and his bretheren

...

f 125v *(3 week May)*

...   25

Item paid to herre Care ye waytt ffor his q*uar*teriche
at saynt Elyngmes   vj s viij d

...

f 127 *(2 week June)*   30

...

Item paid to an yryshe mynstrell as aperithe by mr maior
byll   xij d
Item [paid] geving to the wattys of Cokeremouthe in
Rewarde   iij s.   35

...

Item geving in Reward to lockye the quen*es* mayiesti*es*
Iester at mr mayr*es* commandement   v s.

...

f 127v *(3 week June)*

...

Item paid ffor iij yard*es* & a q*uar*t*er* of lyn clothe to
watson ffor to make hy*m* a shayrt   iiij s

...   5

f 129 *(2 week July)*

...

Item gevinge in Rewarde to the quenes maiestye players
ffor playng in the m*er*chant cowrt   xxv s   10
Item paid ffor drynke to them   iiij d

...

f 130v *(3 week August)*

...   15

Item paid for a payr of shoes to Iohn watsone the
full   xiiij d

...

f 131 *(4 week August)*   20

...

Item paide to henrye Carr the waytte ffor his quarteriche
at Lammas   vj s viij d

...

Item paid mor to mayster maior that he gave to iiij   25
skott*es* mynstrilles   xvj d
Item paid mor that he gave in Rewarde to the mynstrilles
of perathe   xx d

...

°Item paid to the Dowtches of sowtfolk*es* player*es*   30
by mr Mayor*es* com*m*andement   xx s°

f 131v *(1 week September)*

...

Item paid ffor drinke in the marchant Curt to the dutchis   35
of suffolke players to Ralf Russilles wyf   xij d

f 133 v *(1 week October[1])*

...

Item paid to thomas [pott] pawtesone for a payr shoes to   40
Iohn wattson the full   xiiij d

...

f 135 *(4 week October[1])*

...

Item paide to Rychard thomson for shaving & powling
Iohn watsons head   xv⟨...⟩

...   5

f 135v

...

Item paide ffor kepinge of hoggmagogge this year to thomas
pearsonne   vj s viij d   10

...

f 136

...

Item paide to pettar ffayrbarne ffor the iiij boyes that   15
sing*es* in the Queare   xl s

...

f 136v

...   20

Item paid to thomas the singar & Iohn atcheson as
apers   iiij s

f 139 *(1 week October[2])*

...   25

Item paid in [R⟨.⟩] Reward to my lord montagles
berwarde   vj s viij d

...

t 140 *(4 week October[2])*   30

...

Item paid ffor a payr of shoes to Iohn watsonne the
fulle   xiiij d

...

Item paid ffor ij sher*tes* to Iohn watsone the full ffor   35
Ruffes & making & all som*me*   viij s
Item paid ffor on payr of hos to hym & making of
tham   xvj d
Item paid ffor ij yard*es* of playn whytt to be hym a
pettecotte [& the]   ij s iiij d   40
Item paid ffor making the same pettecotte   iiij d

...

f 140v *(1 week November)*

...

Item paid to henrye Carre the waytte for his quarteriche
at alhallowmes   vj s viij d

...   5

1563
Chamberlains' Account Books TW: 543/14
f 142v *(1 week January)*

...   10

Item paide ffor vj yard*es* of blewe at ij s. iiij d
the yarde ffor the full Iohn watsons Coott agaynste
christynmas   xiiij s
Item paid ffor a yard of whytt Cayrsaye to gard his Cott
withall   ij s iiij d   15
Item paid ffor iij q*uarte*rs of whytt clothe to be hym a
payr of short hosse   xij d
Item paid mor ffor a payr of shoes to hym & mending
a nother payre   xvj d
Item paid ffor makinge the same Cotte garding it &   20
makinge   ij s vj d
Item paid ffor blewe buttons & skean to the sam Cotte   vj d
Item paid ffor a cape to hym & making his hosse   iiij d

f 143v *(1 week February)*   25

...

Item paid ffor mending of a payr of shoes to Iohn watsone
the full   iiij d

f 144 *(2 week February)*   30

...

Item paide to henrye Carr the waytt for his quarteriche
at candilmas   vj s viij d

...

                                                                              35

f 147 *(1 week May)*

...

Item paid ffor ij yard*es* iij q*uarte*rs of brod grean to be Iohn
watsone the full a cot agaynst Easter at vj s. a yard   xvj s vj d
Item paide ffor a [q*uarte*r] yard & q*uarte*r of Reade   40
cayrsaye to gard the sam cott withe   ij s viij d
Item paid ffor silke & buttons to the sam cotte   xij d

Item paid ffor making of the saym Cott & a cape to hym   iij s.
Item paid ffor making a payr of short hose to hym & for
Clothe to the same   xvj d
Item paid mor for a payr of shoes to the sam full   xiiij d
Item paid ffor a payr of gloves to hym   iiij d   5
Item paide for iij yardes of clothe to be the sam full
a shert at x d the yarde Somme   ij s vj d
Item paid for sewing & sylke to the same   xij d
...
                                                                                10

f 147v *(2 week May)*

...

Item paid ffor a payr of shoes to Iohn. watsonne the full   xiiij d
Item paid mor for lether to his shoes at dyvers tymes   vj d
...   15
Item paide to Robart shevill draper ffor iiij yardes & a
half of brode Clothe ffor henry Carr & the paver at viij s
the yarde Somme   xxxvj s

f 148 *(3 week May)*   20

...

Item paid to henrye Car the waytt ffor his quarteriche at
Saintelmas   vj s viij d
...
                                                                                25

f 153 *(3 week August)*

...

Item paid ffor a sherte to Iohn watsone the full for iij
yardes d at x d the yarde & a quarter of fyne lyn   iij s
for Ruffes   30
Item ⟨...⟩de making of the same shart & lynnyng to the bande
& for bandes to the same   xij d
...
Item paid ffor a payr of short hosse & making tham to
Iohn watson the full   xvj d   35
Item paid ffor a payr off shoes to hyme   xiiij d
...

f 153v *(4 week August)*
...   40
Item paid to henrye Carr the waytt for his quarteriche at
lammas   vj s viij d

...

Item paid ffor [lethe] lether to Iohn watsone the full
shoes   iiij d

...

f 156v *(3 week October[1])*

...

Item paid ffor a payr of shoes to Iohn watsonne the full   xiiij d
Item paid to Rychard thompsone for dressing & powling
Iohn watsone the full this year   xvj d

...

f 157 *(4 week October[1])*

...

Item paid to thomas pearsonne ffor kepinge of hogmagogge
this year   vj s viij d

...

Item paide to thomas wegham & william Sivaime ffor
singinge in saynt nycolas churche as apers by a bill   xxx s

...

Item paide to Mr maior that he gave in Rewardes to the
Iestars & mynstrilles for this year allowide in the buk   v li.
of orders

...

f 161 *(1 week November)*

...

Item paid to henrye Carre the waytte ffor his quarteriche
at alhallomes   vj s viij d

...

Item paide to thomas stokoo ffor singing in the quear the
whiche he shulde hav haid the laste year   v s

...

Item paide to Iohn barnes Rychard sherloke and william
bennatt being wayttes ffor thar quarteriche at alhallomes   xx s

f 161v *(2 week November)*

...

Item paid to Robart smythe ffor a payr of shoes to Iohn
watson the full at Mr maior comandment   ⟨..⟩iij d

40 / ⟨..⟩iij d: xiiij d

(3 week November)

...

Item paide to thomas ⌈he⌉ the [wh] synger the which
was graunted vnto hym by the Audytt   v s ⟨.⟩ d
...   5

1564
Chamberlains' Account Books TW: 543/14
f 163v *(2 week February)*

...   10
Item paide to henrye Carre the waytt for his quarteriche
at candelmys   vj s viij d
...

Item paid to Ihon barnes william bennatt and Ihon payrsonn
beinge wattes for thar quarteriche   xx s   15
...

f 165 *(4 week March)*

...
Item paide for iij yardes of lyne clothe to be Ihon   20
watsonne the fowlle a shyrt at viij d a yarde   ij s
Itcm paide for a necke to the same shyrte   ij d
Item paide for a yarde and a half of whytt to be hyme
ijᵒ payre of howsses at xij d a yarde   xviij d
...   25

f 165v *(2 week April)*

...
Item paid ffor a payre of shoes to Iohn watsonne the ffull
agaynste Eastar   xiiij d 30
...

f 166v *(2 week May)*

...
Item paid for a payr of gloves to Iohn wattsonne the foull   ij d   35
...

f 167 *(3 week May)*

...
Item paide to henrye Carre the watt ffor his quarteriche   40
at Saynt Elingmas   vj s viij d
...

Item paide to Iohn barnes william bennat & Iohn peyrsonne
beinge wayttes for their quarteriche   xx s
...

f 168 *(2 week June)*   5
...
Item paide for a payr of shoune to Iohn wattson the
fowll   xiiij d
...
                                                                                         10

(3 week June)

Item paide ffor ij yardes and a half of brode gren to be
Iohn watsonne the fowll a cott agaynste crystenmas   xiiij s
and half a yarde of brode read to gayrde the same cott   15
...
Item paid for a payr of shorte hosses to Iohn watson of
whytt   x d
Item paid ffor makynge of Iohn watsones cott   iij s
...   20
Item paid ffor a payr of shoune to Iohn watson the fowll   xiiij d

f 168v *(1 week July)*
...
Item paide to Robart smythe ffor solinge ∧ ⌜a payr of shon⌝   25
[of] to Iohn wattsons the fowll [shonne]   vj d
...

f 169 *(2 week July)*
...   30
Item paid that was gevin in reward to my lord of
bedforthees playeres by Mr Mayores & hys brethere   xx s

(3 week July)
...   35
Item paide to vjj wryghtes ffor makinge of a skakfoll on
the sand hyll ffor the playe   [xviij d] ij s iiij d
Item paid to ix laboreres ffor beringe of hoghedes and
daylles hom and a felde to the ∧ ⌜sam⌝ skayffolde   xviij d
Item paide ffor naylles to the same   viij d   40

36 / vjj *evidently corrected from* vj

Item paid ffor a sharte to Iohn wattsonne the folle and a
[bande] necke ffor the same shart   ij s iiij d
...
Item paid in reward to my lord of Darbies berward
By Mr Mayores comandement   v s   5

f 169v *(4 week July)*

...
Item paid to henrye car ffor his laveraye goune   xxiiij s
...   10
Item paide ffor ij yardes and iij quarters of brode grean to
be Iohn watson the fowll a coott at vj s viij d a yarde   xxv s j d
and iij quarters of read to garde the same cott at ix s a yarde
Item to Robart webster ffor makyng the same cott and a
cape   iij s   15
Item paid ffor read thryde to sew the gardes of the same
cott   ij d
Item paid to hym ffor makinge ij payr of hosses to
hym   iiij d
...   20

f 170v *(3 week August)*

...
Item paid ffor a payr of shoune to Iohn watsonne the
ffowll   xiiij d   25
...

f 171 *(4 week August)*

...
Item paide to henrye Car ye watt ffor his quarteriche at   30
lamas   vj s viij d
...
Item paid to Iohn bayrnes william bennatt and Iohn peayrsonne
benge wayttes ffor their quarteriche at lamas   xx s
...   35

f 172v *(4 week September)*

...
Item paid to mr maior that he gave in Rewardes to
Iesters and mynstrelles ffor this year alowid in the boke   v li.   40
of orders
...

f 173v *(3 week October¹)*

...

Item paid to Rychard thomson barber ffor pollynge the fulles
this yeare   xvj d
Item paid to Robart smythe ffor a payr of shon to Iohn   5
watson the ffoull   xiiij d

...

f 174 *(4 week October¹)*

...   10

not p*ai*d Item paide [ffor] to thomas pearsonne ffor kepinge of
hogmogoge this yeare   vj s viij d

...

f 174v   15

...

Item paid to the iij wattes in Reward grantted by mr
maior & his bretherynge   xx s

...

Item paid to payrson waytt grantid by mr maior and   20
the awdytour*es*   iiij s viij d

...

f 175

...   25

Item paid ffor mynstrelle to the Nom*m*er of xxj at the
awdithe supper in Rewarde   xij s

...

Item paid to thomas stokoo ffor his paynes takin in
synenge in the quer this year   vj s viij d   30

...

f 184 *(1 week November)*

...

Item paide to henry carre waitt ffor his quartteriche at   35
alhallowmes   vj s viij d

...

Item paide to Iohn barnes will*ia*m bennatt and Robart Sewell
beinge wayttes ffor their quarteriche at alhallowmes   xx s

...   40

f 184v *(3 week November)*

...

Item paide ffor a payre of shoune to Iohn watsonne the
ffowll xij d
Item paid ffor ij payre of solles to hyme xij d 5

...

Item paid ffor ij payr of dobell gloves ffor gantlat*es* [off]
ffor the horse men that rod wythe Mr maior and Mr xvj d
shereff at the fayre

... 10

f 187v *(4 week December)*

...

Item paid ffor iij yardes of clothe to be a shart to Ihon
watsonne the ffowll and ffor a neck to the same ij s 15

...

1565
Chamberlains' Account Books TW: 543/14
f 178* *(3 week February)* 20

...

Item paid ffor a payr off shoune to Iohn watsome the
ffowll xij d

... 25

(4 week February)

Item paid to Robart bewicke taylor for makinge of a cott
to Iohn watson ye t⟨...⟩ ⟨...⟩
Item paid ffor a yard and a hallf of Russett to be hym a payr 30
of sloppes x⟨...⟩
mor for iij quarter*es* of whytt to be hym a payr of short
hosses xij d
Item paid ffor makinge the same slopes and and hosses to
hym ⟨...⟩ 35
Item paid ffor ij yard*es* and a half of Russett to be lynynge
to [ye] his cott ⟨...⟩
Item paid to Robart shevell for iij yard*es* of brod blew at v s
the yarde to be a coott to Iohn watson the fowll ii⟨...⟩

34 / and and *MS dittography*

more for half a yard of brod read to gard the same cott
withall   iij ⟨...⟩
Item paid ffor xj yard*es* of welche fres at xx the yard to
be cott*es* to the wattes at lammas when mr maior rod   xv d
the fayr   5
...

f 178v *(2 week March)*
...
Item gevinge in Reward to my lord stranges barwarde at mr   10
maior comandement   vij s
...

f 180v *(2 week May)*
...   15
Item paid ffor a payr of shoune to Iohn watsonne the
fowll   xij d
...
Item paide ffor v yardes and quarter of whytt to be a co⟨..⟩
to Iohn watson the ffowll at xx d the yarde Some   viij s x d   20
Item paide to thomas mylner ffor lyttinge the same
clothe Reade   iij s
Item paide for a yarde of whytt to garde the sam coott
withall   xx d
Item paide to Robart bewycke taylor ffor makinge the same   25
coott   ij s
Item paide ffor iij yardes of whyt clothe to be Hym a
paticott & a payr of short hoys ⌈at xvj d a yard⌉   iiij s
Item paid ffor makinge the same paticott and short
hoy⟨.⟩   viij d   30
Item paide for iij yard*es* of lyne clothe to be hym a shart
& for a coller to the same shart   iij s viij d
Item paide ffor a payr of gloves & a dossen pountes to
hym   iij d
...   35

19 / co⟨..⟩ *for* cott; *MS damaged*   30 / hoy⟨.⟩ *for* hoys; *MS damaged*
32 / for a *apparently, but MS torn, letters damaged*

f 181 *(3 week May)*

...

Item paid to Henrye Car the waytt ffor his quarteriche at
saynt elinmas   v⟨...⟩

...   5

Item paid to Iohn bayrnes will*ia*m bennat & Robart Sowell
beinge wattes ffor their quarteriche at Sant Elingmas   xx s

...

f 181v *(1 week June)*   10

...

Item paid ffor iij^{xx} and v yard*es* of brode clothe ffor the
sargant*es* longe and short gounes and ffor the   xxvj li. [⟨..⟩]
wattes gounes at viij s. the yarde

...   15

Item paid ffor iij yardes of brod clothe ffor a goune to
henrye Care viij s ye yard   xxiiij s

...

Chamberlains' Account Books TW: 543/15   20
f 235 *(1 week November)*

...

Item paid to henrye car the watt for his quarteriche at
halhallamas   vj s viij d

...   25

Item paid to Iohn bayrnes will*ia*m bennat and Robart
sowolde beinge wayttes ffor their quarteriche at   xx s
Hallowmas

...

                                                                                           30

f 235v *(2 week November)*

...

Item paid for a payr of shoune to Iohn watsonne the
fowll   xvj d

...   35

f 236 *(1 week December)*

...

Item paid to my lord of worssyturs plaers for plaiinge in

4 / v⟨...⟩: *possibly* vj s viij d

the marchant cowrt at the comandement of Mr maior   xx s
and his bretheringe
...

f 237 *(4 week December)*   5

...

Item paid to Robart Webster taylor ffor making a cott to
Iohn watsonne the ffowll and ffor makinge a payr of   iij s.
houses to hym

...   10

Item paid for a payr of shoune to Iohn watsonne the full   xvj d
...

AC   *Slaters' Accounts: Brand MS 18* NCL: L942.82 N536 B
     nf   15

3 d to the wates

1566
Chamberlains' Account Books TW: 543/15   20
f 238 *(4 week January)*
...
Item paid for iij yard*es* of lyn clothe to be a shert to
Iohn watson the full   ij s iiij d
...   25

f 239 *(3 week February)*

...

Item paid to Henrye Carr the wayt ffor hus quarteriche
at Candelmas   vj s viij d   30
...

Item paid to willi*a*m barnes willi*a*m bennat and Robart
sowell wattes for y*er* quarteriche   .   xx s
...

                                                                    35

f 240 *(3 week March)*

...

Item paid to henrye Car the waytt for his lyvera goune for
this year   xxiiij s
...   40

f 240v *(4 week March)*

...

Item paid for ij yard*es* ˄ ˹& a d˺ of whyt to be a payr of
slopes & a payr of short hoses to Iohn watson ˹ye foll˺   iiij s ij d

...   5

f 241 *(3 week April)*

...

Item paid to my lord of darbyes players whiche was plaid
in Mr maiore hous   xx s   10

...

f 241v *(4 week April)*

...

Item paid to my lord of hounsdons palers whiche plaid in   15
the marchant cort   xx s

...

Item paid to Robart webster taylor for makinge a cott to
Iohn watson the foull ˹a cape and a payer of housses   iiij s
& a payr off slopes˺   20
Item paid for ij yard*es* & a half of whytt to be slopes &
short housses to hym   ˄ ˹nichell d˺ [⟨...⟩j d]
Item paid for ij payr of shoune to Iohn watsonne the
foull   ij s viij d
Item paid for a payr of gloves and a dossen pountes   25
And a shart neck to hym   vj d

...

f 242v *(3 week May)*

...   30

Item paid to henrye carr the waytt for his quarteryche at
sant elingmas   vj s viij d

...

Item paid to willi*a*m barnes Iohn benat and Robart
sowell wattes for his quarteriche   xx s   35

...

f 243 *(4 week May)*

...

Item paid [fo] to ⟨.⟩ george symsone for ij yard*es* and   40

15 / palers *for* plaers

iij quarteres of brod read at v s the yard to be a cott   xiij s ix d
to Iohn wattson the fowll a gaynst crystenmas some
Item paid ffor a yard and iij quarters of whyt carsaye at
ij s the yard to gard same cott   iij s vj d
Item paid for iij yardes of fyn brod grean to be hyme a   5
cott aganst ester at 7 s yard   xxj s
Item paid for half a yarde & half a quarter of fyn brod
read to gard the same cott withall   vj s vij d
...
                                                                          10

f 244v *(3 week June)*

...

Item paid ffor a payr of shoune to Iohn watsonne the
fowll   xvj d
...   15

f 246v *(4 week July)*

...

Item paid ffor a payr of shoune to Iohn watson the fowll   xvj d
...   20

f 247 *(1 week August)*

...

Item paid ffor iij yardes of lyn clothe to be a shart to Iohn
watson the foull and for a necke and for shewinge the   ij s vj d   25
same shart
...

f 247v *(2 week August)*

...   30

Item paid ffor lvj yardes of clothe ffor the
sargantes lyverais iij yardes for vmfraye taylor
ix yardes for the wattes iij yardes for william
golyghtlye and a yard & half for william   xxix li. xix s viij d
bensone the paver wharof lix yardes at   35
viij s iiij d ye yard & xiij yardes and a half
at viij s the yard some
...

f 248 *(3 week August)*   40

...

Item paid for ij yardes of whytt to be a payr of

slopes & short houses to Iohn watsonne the foull   iij s ij d
...

f 248v *(4 week August)*

...

Item paid to Henrye car the wayt for his quarteriche at
lamas   vj s viij d

...

Item paid to *willia*m barnnes Iohn bennat & Robart
sowolde beinge wattes for their quateriche   xx s

...

Item paid for a payr of shoune to Iohn watson the full   xvj d

...

f 249v *(2 week September)*

...

Item paid for makynge a payr of slopes & short houses to
Iohn watson ye ˹full˺   viij d

...

f 251 *(1 week October¹)*

...

Item paid [ffor] to my lorde mont agle barwarde at Mr
maiore comandement   iiij s

...

f 251v *(2 week October¹)*

...

Item paid ffor ij shart nekes to Iohn watsonne the full   iiij d
Item paid ffor iiij [cott] yard*es* of Russett to be a cott
to atkenson the full   vj s
Item paid for iij yard*es* of lyn clothe to be hyme a
shart   ij s

...

f 252 *(3 week October¹)*

...

Item paid to the clarke*es* iiij boyes ffor synenge in the
churche   xxvj s viij d

...

30 / iiij *written over* a

Item paid to the wattes granted by Mr maior & his
bretherynge   xx s
...

f 252v *(4 week October[1])*   5
...

Item paid to thomas pearsome ffor kepinge of hogmogoge
ffor this yeare   vj s viij d
...

                                                               10

f 253
...

Item paid to Mr maior ffor that he gave in Rewarde to
Iesters & mynstrelles ffor this ∧ ⌐yeare⌐ as apperythe   v li.
by the bucke of orders   15
...

paid to [Robart] Rychard thomson barber ffor powlinge
the fulles   xvj d
...

Item paid to ffor a yard of read to gard atkensons cott   20
the full and for a payr of shon to hyme & a payr of   v s
shor hosses & for makinge of his cott
...

Item paid to the mynstrilles at the adytt dynnar and
at the awdyt banket   xvij s   25
...

f 253v
...

Item paid ffor a payr of shoune to Iohn watsonne the full xvj d   30
...

f 258 *(1 week November)*
...

Item paide to Henrye carr the waite for his quartryche vj s viij d   35
Item paide to william barnnes Iohn bennet & robert
sowolde beinge waites for ther quartryche   xx s
...

f 259v *(4 week November)*   40
...

Item paid to henrye carr the waite ffor his liveraye govne

this yere   xxiiij s

...

Item paid ffor A payre of shone to Iohn watson the fovll   xvj d

...

1567
Chamberlains' Account Books TW: 543/15
f 262 *(1 week January)*

...

Item paide for lvj yardes of clothe for the sargant*es*   10
lyu*er*ayes iij yardes for humfraye taylor ix yardes for
the waites iiij yardes for william golyghtlye & A yarde xxix li. ij s.
& A halffe for the paver At viij s A yarde And ij s
forther in the holl   Som*ma*

...   15

Item paide for v yardes of white to be Iohn watson the
fooll A coite At ij s iiij d A yarde Som*ma*   xj s viij d
Item paid to thomas mylner for lyttinge of the same   iij s iiij d
Item paide to Anthonye leche for j yarde & iij q*uarter*
of white [f] cayrsaye to gayrde the same coote   iij s vj d   20
Item paid for ij yardes & A halffe of white to be him A
payre of slopes & hoise   iiij s ij d
Item paide for maikinge of the saide geare   iiij s
Item paide for A sharte for Iohn watson the fooll   iij s iiij d

                                                            25

f 263v *(4 week January)*

...

Item paid for A payre of shon to Iohn watson the foll   xiiij d

...

                                                            30

f 265 *(3 week February)*

...

Item paide to henrye carr the waite for his
quartryche   vj s viij d
Item paide to *willia*m barnes Iohn bennet & robert   35
sowolde beinge waites for ther quartryche   xx s

...

Item paide to Iohn browne synger for his quartryche   xx s

...

3 / xvj d *originally* iiij d, xv *written over* iii

f 267v *(2 week April)*

...

Item paide for A [⟨.⟩] sharte to Iohn watson the foll	iij s iij d
Item paide for ij yardes & iij q*uart*eres of white to be Iohn watson the foll A paire of slopes and A paire of hoise	iiij s vij d
Item paide for makinge of the slopes & hoise	xij d
Item paid for A paire of gloves & pointes to Iohn watson the foll	iiij d
Item paid for A paire of shon to Iohn watson the foll	xiiij d

...

f 269v *(4 week May)*

...

Item paide for vj yardes of blewe carsaye to be Iohn watson the foll A coite Againste ester At ij s iiij d A yarde	xiiij s
Item paide for j yarde & A halffe of read cairsaye for to gairde the same coit w*ith* At iiij s A yairde	vj s
Item paide for makinge of the saide coote	iiij s
Item paide for threde to stiche the said coote w*ith*	xij d
Item paid for j dossen pointes to Iohn watson the foll	ij d

...

f 270 *(1 week June)*

...

Item paide to henrye carr the waite for his quartriche	vj s viij d
Item paide to w*illia*m barnes, Iohn bennet & robert sowolde beinge waites for ther quartriche	xx s

...

f 270v *(2 week June)*

...

Item paide to A player for playinge w*ith* A hobie horse in the firthe befor mr maior & his bretheren	iij s iiij d

...

f 273 *(4 week July)*

...

Item paid for A paire of A paire of shon to Iohn watson the
foll   xij d

...   5

ff 275–5v *(4 week August)*

...

Item paid to henrye carr waite for his quartriche   vj s viij d
Item paid to william barnes Iohn bennet & robart   10
sowolde beinge waites for his quartriche   xx s

...

Item paid for iij yardes of lynn clothe to be Iohn
watson the full a sharte & for a sharte neke   iij s iiij d |
Item paide for iij q*uarter* of ⌈white⌉ [russate] for a paire   15
of Hoses to Iohn watson the foll   xiiij d
Item paid for makinge of the saide hose   iiij d

...

f 280 *(4 week October*[1]*)*   20

...

Item paid to thomas pearson for kepinge of hodgmagoge
this yeare   vj s viij d

...

Item paid to m*r* maior for that he gave in rewarde to   25
Iester*es* & mynstrels for his yeare as apearithe by the   v li.
booke of order*es*

...

Item paid to the clarkes iiij boyes for singinge in the
churche   xxvj s viij d   30

...

Item paid to richard thomson for poullinge of the fooll
this yeare   xvj d

...

Item paid to the vnder clarke of sancte nicholas for   35
singinge in the churche   vj s viij d

---

3 / A paire of A paire of *MS dittography*
16 / Hoses *converted from* showes *or* shoves

f 280v

...

Item paid to the mynstrelles at the Awdite dynner   xiiij s

...

f 281 *(5 week October¹)*

...

Item paid for ij payre of showne to Iohn watson the fooll   ij s
Item paid for cowllinge of bartye Allyson the fooll this
yeare   xvj d   10

...

f 287v *(1 week November)*

...

Item paid to henrye carr waite for his quartriche   vj s viij d   15
Item paid to william barnes robart sowold & Iohn
bennet wait*es* for ther q*uartriche*   xx s

...

Item paid to Iohn browne synger for his quartriche   xx s

...   20

Item paid to *(blank)* Ascewe the waite for his sarvis
dowing to the towne betwixe myghelmes &   iij s iiij d
alhallowmes At Mr maior*es* commandemente

f 288 *(2 week November)*   25

...

Item geven in rewarde to my lord montegles barwarde   v s

...

f 288v *(1 week December)*   30

...

Item paid for iiij yardes of whit At xx d A yarde to be
Iohn watson the foll A ⌈petticote A paire of slopes & A
paire of hoise⌉ [⟨...⟩]   vj s viij d
Item paid ffor makinge of the same slopes hoies &   35
pettycote   xij d
Item paid for iij yardes & A quarter of fyne brod reede
At v s iiij d A yard to be Iohn watson the foll A coite   xvij s iiij d
Item paid for A yarde & iij q*uarter* of white cairsaye At ij s
viij d A yard to gaird the same coote   iiij s viij d   40

34 / [⟨...⟩] *possibly* [cotte]

Item paid for makinge of the Same coote   iij s
Item paid for iij yardes of lynn clothe At x d ayard to be
hym A sharte   ij s vj d
Item paid for A necke to yt   iiij d

f 289 *(2 week December)*

...

Item paid to henrye carr waite fin monaye for his
leverraye gowne   xxiiij s
Item paid for A paire of shoun to Iohn watson the ffoll   xij d
...

AC *Slaters' Accounts: Brand MS 18* NCL: L942.82 N536 B
nf

Item to the Wates   4 d.
Item to the Menstrells at Nuborne   6 d.

1568
Chamberlains' Account Books TW: 543/15
f 289v *(3 week January)*

...

Item geven in reward to the player*es* of durham At mr
mair*es* com*m*andment   iij li.
Item paid for ⌜iiij⌝ lynkes to the playe   ij s
Item paid for A quarte of wyne to the plaer*es*   iiij d
Item paid for iij laid of colles for fyer to the
player*es*   [⟨.⟩jd] xij d
...
Item paid for A paire of shone to Iohn watson the ffoll   xij d
...

f 290 *(1 week February)*

...

Item paid for lvj yardes of brod clothe for the Sargantes
leverayes iij yardes for humfraye taylyer At viij s vj d
A yard ix yardes for the waites iij yardes for   xxx li. ix s vj d
william golightlye & A yard & d for the paver
At viij s A yard Soma

...

17 / Nuborne *over erasure*

f 290v *(2 week February)*

...

Item paid to henrie carr waite for his quartriche   vj s viij d

...

Item paid to the iij waites for ther quartriche   xx s   5

...

Item paid to Iohn browne synger for his
quartriche   xx s

...

                                                                                10

f 292v *(3 week April)*

...

Item paid for iij yardes of brode blewe clothe at v s
viij d ayard to be Iohn watson the ffoll A coite   xvij s
Item paid for j yard d of read cairsaye to gaird the same   15
coite   iij s vj d
Item paid for makinge of the same coite   ij s vj d
Item paid for ij yardes d of white to be Iohn watson the
ffooll A paire of slopes & A payre of shorte hoise at
xviij d A yarde   iij s ix d   20
Item paid for makinge of the same slopes & hoise   viij d
Item paid for iij yardes of lynn clothe at x d a yarde to
be hym A sharte   ij s vj d
Item paid for A sharte coller   iiij d
Item paid for apaire of gloves and pointes to hym   iiij d   25

f 293 *(1 week May)*

...

Item paid for A paire of shone to Iohn watson the
ffoll   xij d   30

...

f 293v *(2 week May)*

...

Item paid to henrye carr waite for his q*uartriche*   vj s viij d   35

...

Item paid to the iij waites for ther quartriche   xx s

...

Item paid to robart mawe for his quartriche for singinge
in the churche   xx s   40

...

f 295 *(3 week June)*

...

Item paid for A paire of shon to Iohn watson the ffoll   xij d

...

(4 week June)

Item paid to iiij laboreres for dightinge the hill agaynst the
playes   ij s iiij d

...   10

f 295v* *(1 week July)*

...

Item paid for caryinge A keill of movke of the newe kye
⌈& for lyinge iij tydes in the playes⌉   iij s viij d   15

...

f 296v *(4 week July)*

...

Item gevyn in reward by mr maior to the players of   20
hull   iij s iiij d

...

Item the chargis of the hoistmens playe as ffolowithe
for Settinge vp of the kare xx d for vj li. of rossell
ix d for pawper mache sayltwyne & candell x d for   25
j li. q*uarter* of corn powder xv d for ca⟨.⟩ryinge of
the banner xij d for bearinge of the kare iiij s for   lvij s ij d
wynne vj ⟨.⟩ viij d to the playeres for playinge
of the playe xxx s for the playeres dynners &
the stewardes x s for payntynge of the dore of   30
the kare vj d to A man that kest fyer vj d Soma

...

f 297* *(1 week August)*

...   35

Item paid to rudderfurthe for leddinge of sand to the hed
of the syde for stainge the carres when the playes was   vj d
played

...

26 / ca⟨.⟩ryinge: *probably* cayryinge; *tail of* y(?) *visible*
28 / vj ⟨.⟩ *for* vj s; s *blotted, but characteristic tail visible*

f 297v *(3 week August)*

...

Item paid for A payre of shone to Iohn watson the ffoll   xij d

...

f 298 *(4 week August)*

...

Item paid to henry carr waite for his quartriche   vj s viij d

...

Item paid to the iij waytes for ther quartriche   xx s

...

Item paid to robart mawe for his quartrich for singing in
the church   xx s

...

f 298v *(1 week September)*

...

the chargis /
of the bone /
of the play /

Item paid to robart watson for the bone of the play
ffirst for iij^{xx} mens dinner*es* l s ffor xxxv horsse for
the player*es* at iiij d A horsse xj s viij d ffor wyne
at ther dinner*es* vj s viij d mor for A drome viij d
To the waites for playinge befor the player*es* ij s   iiij li iij s iiij d
for payntinge the S*er*gantes stavffes ij s for the
sargantes stavffes ij s mor to Iohn hardcastell for
makinge xlvj litle castelles & vj grett castelles to
the bonne of the play viij s mor for payntinge
belsyboubes clovbe iiij d So*m*ma

f 299v *(4 week September)*

...

Item paid for A yard of white to be Iohn watson the
ffooll A payre of hoise & for makinge of them   xxij d

...

f 302 *(4 week October*[1]*)*

Item paid to Robart movlde for kepinge of hogmagog this
yeare   vj s viij d

...

paid to mr maior for that he gave in reward to Iester*es*
& mynstrelles this year   [⟨...⟩] v li.

19 / l *for* 50

...

paid to the vnder clarke of sancte nycholas for singinge
in the churche   vj s viij d
paid to richard thomson barber for powllinge the ffooll
this yeare   xvj d   5

...

f 302v

...

Item paid to the mynstrelles At the Awdite dynner   10
 ∧ ⌐& bankouttes¬   xviij s

...

Item paid for A payre of shone to Iohn watson the ffoll   xij d

...
                                                                                   15

Slaters' Accounts: Brand MS 10 NCL: L942.82 N536 B
nf

1568. Item the Plaers for thear dennares   3 sh.
Item for wyne   0–8.d   20
Item for the rede clothe   2 sh
Item for the Care   20.d
Item for 4 Stoopes   6.d
Item for drea∧⌐n¬ke   6 d
Item for bearers of the Care & the Banners [⟨..⟩]   18 d   25
Item in drencke 3 d to theame that bare the Care
and a 1 d to the plaeares in drenke & 2 the Horse mete.   –6 d
Item for the Pyper   8 d
Item for Rosmare   2 d
Item for detten of the Swearde   2.d   30
Item for Charcole   2.d
Item for the detten of the Croones   2 d
Item Bertram Sadler for Plaers whan thaye came
home frome the playe in mete & drenk had   6 d.

                                                                           35

1569
Durham Consistory Court Act Book
UD: Dept of Palaeography and Diplomatic
D.R.III.2 (new classification pending)
f 123v* *(March)*   40

Ad vj^*timum* ar*ticulum* / exa*minatum* / he saithe yat about ⟨..⟩ ix
or xij dayes or therabout / about whitsonday last this exa*min*ate

spacke to yat tankerd & Mr salvayn at the said Sir Roberte
appoyntmente as he haethe said to the ⌐vth¬ [last] article and on
the fryday the same daye yat Sir Roberte dyed / this examinate
at the request of the said Sir Roberte spake to christofor chaitor
vpon the sandhill to comme to [his] Sir Roberte dynner althoughe   5
he said hym naye byfore / and vpon the same he cam to christofor
chaitor & he had promesed to Dyne other where [and Sir Roberte
said to this examinate that he wold haue had hym to haue
Drawen his will a Draught of his will] & denyed to comme
except Sir Roberte had somme speciall matter Whervpon this   10
examinate cam to hym agayn & said yat Sir Roberte wold haue
hym after Dynner to haue Drawen a Draught of his will for after
the playes he wold send for his consell and make it vp / Whervpon
the said ∧⌐x¬ chaitor said yat he must ryde yat night towardes
Darlington for markyn of horses there to be sold ∧⌐in the fair¬   15
by the conselles commandmente & promesed to comme to
hym agayn within a weke after / & further ∧⌐to this article he¬
can not depose /
...

                                                                          20

1575
Cooks' Ordinary (1668-9 copy): Enrolment Books
TW: 544/72
f 46* *(10 September)*

                                                                          25

...And alsoe the sayd fellowshipp of Cookes to be ready to sett
forth their play among the rest of the Corpus Christi playes, to

their play

be played att all such tyme & tymes hereafter at the Costs &
charge of the said fellowshipp of Cookes whensoeuer the whole
playes of the sayd Towne shall proceed vpon payne to be punished   30
at the discreccion of the Mayor & Aldermen of the sayd Towne
of NewCastle for the tyme being...

1576
Chamberlains' Account Books TW: 543/16   35
f 106 *(3 week October¹)*
...
paid for [⟨..⟩] iij yardes of lynnclothe at x d A
yarde for A sharte to Iohn watson the ffoll & for   iij s [⟨.⟩]

_____

4 / *last three letters of* Roberte *blotted*   5 / *first two letters of* comme *blotted*

A sharte collor & the maikinge

...

f 107 *(4 week October[1])*

...

paid to robart movlde for kepinge of hogmagog this
yeare   vj s viij d

...

paid to Mr maior for that he gave in rewarde to Iesteres and
mynstrelles this yeare   v li.

...

paid to raivffe russell barber for povllinge the ffoll the
yeare   xvj d

...

f 107v

...

paid for ledder to Iohn watsones shone the ffolles   viij d

...

f 108

...

paid for A paire of shone to Iohn watson the ffoll   xvj d

...

f 110v *(2 week October[2])*

...

paid for A Lether collor for baittinge the bvlles withe   iij s iiij d

...

paid for A paier of myttenes to Edwarde errington the
ffoll   iiij d

...

f 111 *(3 week October[2])*

...

paid for A horsse to Iohn watson the ffoll for the
ryddinge of the ffaire with mr maior   viij d
paid for pointes to Iohn watson the ffoll   iiij d

...

paid for iiij horsse shone yat was sett on the nage
that Iohn watson ye fovll rod ye faire on   viij d

...

f 111v *(4 week October²)*

...

paid for A paire of showes to Iohn watson the ffoole	xx d
paid for A paire for hosse to edwarde errington the ffolle	vj d

...

5

f 112v *(1 week November)*

...

paid to the iij waytes for theare quartriche	xx s

...

10

f 113

...

paid to my Lorde Darbyes player*es* geven in rewairde by mr Maior & his brether	x s.

15

...

paid for v yardes d of lynn clothe for A sharte to Iohn watson the ffooll & A sharte to henry sticknell at xj d A yardes	v s.

...

20

paid for mendinge Iohn watsones shone the ffolle	vj d

...

f 113v *(2 week November)*

...

25

paid for iiij yardes 3 q*uarters* of lynn clothe for ij shartes to edwarde errington the ffoll	iiij s. iiij d

...

f 114 *(3 week November)*

30

...

paid for ij sharte coller*es* to Iohn watson & henry stiknell	viij d

...

35

f 115v *(2 week December)*

...

geven to my Lorde staffourthes player*es* in rewarde at Mr maior*es* com*m*andment	x s

...

40

paid for A paier of showes to edwarde errinton the ffovll	xvj d

...

f 116 *(3 week December)*

...

paid for iiij yardes d of mylke & watter Clothe at 3 s. 8 d
A yarde for A cotte to Iohn watson the fovll   xvj s vj d
paid for ij yardes & A quarter of reade cairsaye to gairde   5
the saide cotte   v s iij d
paid for ij yardes of russate for A paier of britcheis to
Iohn watson   ij s viij d
paid for 3 q*uarters* of white for A paier of hosse to
hym   xviij d   10
paid for maikinge the saide clothes   v s vj d
paid for iij yardes d of mylke and water clothe at iij s viij d
A yarde for A coote to edwarde errington   xij s vj d
the ffoll
paid for A yarde d of reade cairsaye to gairde the saide   15
coote   iij s vj d
paid for viij yardes of white rvgge for lynnynge to
boithe the cottes at viij d A yarde   v s iiij d
paid for maikinge the saide cotte   v s vj d
paid for threade for sewinge the gairdes of the   20
saide cottes   xx d
paid for pointes & bvttones to theare cootcs   vij d
paid for ij sharte coller*es* to edwarde errington the
ffovll   viij d
...   25

1577
Chamberlains' Account Books TW: 543/16
f 117v *(2 week January)*
...   30
paid for A paier of showes to Iohn watson the ffoll   xx d
...

f 118v *(4 week January)*
...   35
paid for A paire of showes to edwarde errington the
ffoll   xvj d
paid for A yarde of white for ij paier of hosse to edwarde
errington   xv d
paid for maikinge the saide hosse   iiij d   40
...

AC   *Coopers' Accounts: Brand MS 10* NCL: L942.82 N536 B
     nf

     Item geiven to the Mynstrells   8 d.

     1578
     Millers' Ordinary (1669 copy): Enrolment Books
     TW: 544/72
     ff 54v–5 *(20 September)*

Corpus christi
play

...And alsoe wee the said Mayo*ur* Aldermen and Sherif of
Newcastle aforesaid doo order and decree by these presents that
the said wardens and fellowship of Millers shall whensoeuer the
generall plaies of this towne antientlie in times past called the
Co*ᵣ*pus Christi plaies shallbe | Commaunded by the Mayo*ur*
and Aldermen and their Succseso*ur*s of the said towne for the
time being to be sett forth and plaied within the said towne that
they the said wardens and felowship of Millers and their
Succseso*ur*s att their costs and charges shall cause to be plaied
the antient plaie of their said fellowship called the deliuerance
of the children of Isrell out of the thraldome bondage and
seruitude of King Pharo and also the said wardens and euery
one of the said fellowship of Millers and their Sucsessors of the
said fellowship for the time being to attend upon their said
plaie in decent manner in euerie plaice of the said towne where
antientlie the same among other plaies usalie hath bene plaied
upon paine that euerie one of the said felowship soe refusing too
attend shall paie for euerie time of his such ofence to the said
fellowship the some of twentie shillings of lawfull money of
England....

     1579
     Chamberlains' Account Books TW: 543/16
     f 119 *(2 week December)*
     ...
     paid for A payer of showes to edwarde errington the foll   xiiij d
     ...

     f 120 *(4 week December)*
     ...
     paid for ij yardes of white for A payer of britches &
     hosse to Iohn watson the ffovll   ij s ij d

paid for A payer of showes to Iohn watson the ffovll   xvj d

...

Housecarpenters and Joiners' Ordinary (1669 copy):
Enrolment Books TW: 544/72   5
ff 48–8v *(3 July)*

... And that the said felowship of House Carpenters and Ioyners
and their Succsesours of the same felowship att all times | heare
after whensoeuer the generall plaies of this towne Called anciently   10
the Corpus Christi plaies shall be played ⌄ ⌜shall⌝ [⟨...⟩] decentlie
and comlie assemble themselues together and att the charges of

Play to be
exercised

the said felowship shall in the best manner they can sett forth to
be plaied amongst other the playes of the said towne the plaie
Called the buriall of Christ partaining antientlie to the said   15
felowship...

AC   *Slaters and Bricklayers' Ordinary: Brand MS 10*
NCL: L942.82 N536 B
nf *(25 September)*   20

...And that the said fellowship of Slaiters and Bricklayers and
there Successors of the same fellowship at all tymes hereafter
foreuer whensoeuer the generall Plays of this Towne called
aunciently Corpus Christi Playes shalbe played within this said   25
Towne shall decently and cumlie assemble themselves together
and at the charges of the said fellowship shall in the best manner
they can sett forth to be plaied among other plaies of the said
Towne the play called the offering of Isaack by Abraham, And
every one of the said fellowship according to auncient Order of   30
the said fellowship there to attend and waite vpon the said Plaie
except sicknes or other lawfull cause be impediment to him vpon
paine euery one that is so absent shall pay to the use of the said
fellowship the some of Two shillings and sixpence....

                                                                      35

1580
Chamberlains' Account Books TW: 543/16
f 121 *(2 week January)*

...
paid for A payer of showes to Allayne the fovll   x d   40
...

f 122 *(4 week January)*

...

paid for A payer of showes to edwarde errington the fovll   xiiij d

...

paid for sollinge A payer of showes to Iohn watson the
fovll   vj d

...

f 123 *(2 week February)*

...

paid to the iiij waites for theare quartriche   xxvj s viij d

...

f 123v

...

paid for xix yardes of checker clothe for the 3 ffovlles cottes
at 2 s 4 d A yarde   xliiij s iiij d
paid for xviij yardes of cotton for lynynge the saide
cottes   ix s
paid to the taylyer for maikinge the saide clothes   vij s vj d

...

paid for A payer of showes to Iohn watson the fovll   xvj d
paid for canves for maikinge pokettes to the fovlles cottes   v d
paid for maikinge ⟨.⟩ payer of britches & A payer of hosse
to Iohn watson the ffovll & maikinge edward erringtones   x d
petticott

...

paid for pointes to the ffovlles cootes   vj d

...

f 124 *(3 week February)*

...

paid for v yardes of lynn clothe at x d A yarde for ij shartes
to edwarde errington the ffovll & for ij sharte coller*es*   iiij s x d

...

f 125 *(1 week March)*

...

paid for A payer of showes to edwarde errington the ffovll   xij d

...

24 / ⟨.⟩: *perhaps over-large* A *converted from some other letter*

f 125v *(2 week March)*

...

paid for iij sharte coller*es* to the ffovlles   xvj d

...

f 126v *(4 week March)*

...

paid for A payer of showes to Allayne the ffovll   x d

...

f 128 *(3 week April)*

...

paid for iij payer of showes to the iij fovlles   iij s ij d
paid for A payer of hosse to Allayne the fovll   viij d

...

paid for A payer of gloves to Iohn watson the ffovll   iij d

...

f 128v *(4 week April)*

...

paid for A payer of hosse to edwarde errington the ffovll   xij d

...

f 130 *(3 week May)*

...

paid to the iiij waites for theare *quartriche*   xxvj s viij d

...

f 130v

...

paid for x yardes of brode greane for the fovlles cottes at
5 s A yard   l s
paid for iij yardes of brode reade for gairdinge the saide
cott*es* at 5 s   xv s
paid for xj yardes of white cotton lynnynge for the saide
cottes   v s vj d
paid for canves for lynnynge the bodyes of the fovlles cottes
& maid them pockattes   xxij d
paid for threade to the ffovlles cootes   xviij d
paid for maikinge the ffovlles cootes   xiij s

...

paid for A yarde & a halfe of russate for A payer of
britches to Iohn watson   ij s j d

...

paid for A yarde & A halfe of white for A payer of hosse
to Iohn Atcheson and A payer to Iohn watson   ij s ix d   5
paid for maiking thear britches and theare hosse   xij d

...

paid for pointes to the fovlles cottes & bvttones to
Iohn atchesones cotte   viij d
paid for A payer of gloves to Iohn watson   iij d   10

...

f 131v *(1 week June)*

...

paid for iij payer of showes to the iij fovlles   iij s iiij d   15

...

f 133 *(4 week June)*

...

paid for vij yardes and A halfe of lynn clothe for ij   20
shartes to the fovlles at ix d A yarde & for maikinge them   vj s
paid for mendinge the fovlles shone   x d

...

f 133v *(1 week July)*   25

...

paid for iij sharte collor*es* for iij [of the] fovlles   xxij d

...

f 134 *(2 week July)*   30

...

paid for sollinge A payer of showes to Iohn watson the
fovll   vij d

...

                                                                         35

f 135 *(4 week July)*

...

paid to wedowe belsaye for kepinge Iohn watson the fovll
beinge vesytide withe sicknes   xvj d

...   40

paid for A payer of hosse to edwarde errington the fovll   xij d

27 / xxij d *probably converted from* xiiij d; 22 *written above* ij *in very small figures*

...

geven to the waites for playinge on mydsommer even   xij d

...

paid for sollinge A payer of showes to Iohn watson the
fovll   vj d   5

...

f 135v *(1 week August)*

...

paid to wedowe belsaye for kepinge Io*hn* watson the fovll   10
beinge sicke   xvj d

...

f 136 *(2 week August)*

...   15

paid to wedowe belsaye for kepinge Iohn watson the fovll
beinge vesitid *with* siknes   ij s

paid for A payer of showes to edwarde errington the fovll   xij d

...   20

f 136v *(3 week August)*

...

paid to wedowe belsaye for kepinge Iohn watson the foll
beinge vesytide withe sicknes this weike   ij s   25

...

paid for A payer of showes to Iohn watson the fovll &
A payer to ⌈Allayne⌉ [edwarde errington]   ij s ij d

...

   30

f 137 *(4 week August)*

...

paid to the iiij waites for theare quartriche   xxvj s viij d

...

   35

f 138 *(1 week September)*

...

geven in rewarde by Mr Maior to my Lorde of Leycester
player*es*   l s
geven in rewarde by Mr Maior to hym that had the lyon   x s   40

...

39 / 1 for 50

f 139 *(3 week September)*

...

paid for ij sharte coller*es* for ij of the fovlles   xiiij d
paid for A payer of hosse to Allayne the fovll   x d

...   5

f 140v *(2 week October[1])*

...

paid for lix yardes of brode clothe for the
sargantes leverayes & for humfraye taylyer*es*   10
leveraye at 8 s 8 d A yarde. 25. 11. 4 mor xvj   xxxj li. xvj s xj d
yardes 3 quarter*es* for the wait*es* the plumer
& ye paver at 7 s 6 d. 6. 5. 7

...
                                                                       15

f 141 *(3 week October[1])*

...

paid for iij payer of showes to the iij fovlles   iij s ij d

...
                                                                       20

f 142 *(4 week October[1])*

...

paid to robart movle taylyer for kepinge of hogmagog this
yeare   vj s viij d
                                                                       25
...

paid to bartram thomson barber for povllinge the iij
fovlles this yeare   iiij s

...

f 143   30

...

paid for A payer of hosse to Allayne the fovll   xij d

...

f 153 *(1 week October[2])*   35

...

paid for ij payer of myttenes to the fovlles   v d

...

f 155v *(1 week November)*   40

...

paid to the iiij waites for theare quartriche   xxvj s viij d

...

f 156

...

paid for iij payer of showes to the iij ffooles   iij s ij d

...
                                                                                5

f 158 *(1 week December)*

...

geven in rewarde by Mr Maior to my Lorde movntagles
player*es*   xx s
paid for ix yardes of lynn clothe for the ffolles shartes   10
at 8 d A yarde   vj s

...

f 158v *(2 week December)*

...   15

geven in rewarde by Mr Maior to the beareman   xl s
paid to gawayne Adonn & thomas bell for switching A
folle a bout the towne   viij d

...

paid for A payer of hosse to edward errington the   20
ffovll   xij d

...

f 159 *(3 week December)*

...   25

paid for sollinge the fovlles showes   xiiij d
paid for xvij yardes and A halfe of checker clothe for
the fovlles cottes at 2 s 6 d A yarde   xliiij s ix d
paid for xj yardes of white cottonn at 8 d A
yarde & viij yardes A halfe of white rvgge for   30
lyininge thear cootes & maikinge there pettecottes   xij s viij d
at 7 d A yarde
paid to the taylyer for maiking the saide clothes y*er*
cott*es* 7 s 6 d pettecotes. 8 d   viij s ij d
paid for ij payer of shorte hosse for ij of the   35
ffovlles   ij s
paid for A yarde & A halffe of graye ffreas for A payer
of britches to Iohn watson the ffovll   xxij d
paid for maikinge the saide britches   iiij d
paid for halfe A yarde of harden for iij pockattes for the   40
fovlles cootes   ij d
paid for pointes to thc ffovlles cottes   vj d

...

f 159v *(4 week December)*

...

paid for iij payer for showes to the ffovlles   iij s vj d

...

1581
Chamberlains' Account Books TW: 543/16
f 160 *(1 week January)*

...

paid for iij sharte collor*es* for the ffovlles   xvj d   10

...

f 162v *(2 week February)*

...

paid to the iiij waytes for theare q*uartriche*   xxvj s viij d   15

...

f 163

...

paid to wedowe belsaye for hir quartriche for kepinge Iohn   20
watson the ffovll   xx d

...

f 163v *(3 week February)*

...   25

paid for ij payer of showes to ij of the foolles   ij s iiij d

...

f 164v *(1 week March)*

...   30

paid for A payer of showes to edwarde errington the foull   xij d

...

f 165 *(2 week March)*

...   35

paid for sollinge A payer of showes to Iohn watson the fovll viij d

...

f 165v* *(3 week March)*

...   40

paid for A bagge to edward errington the ffooll   iij d

...

f 166v *(1 week April)*

...

paid for A horse to Iohn hodshon chamberlayne to durham
ridinge to by the ffolles cottes & for his charges   ij s

...   5

paid for iij payer of showes to the folles   iij s iiij d
paid for A payer of hose to Iohn watson the foll & for
A payer of gloves   xviij d
paid for A payer of shorte hosse to edward errington the
foll   xij d   10

...

f 167 *(2 week April)*

...

geven in rewarde by Mr Maior to my Lorde bartholomewes   15
player*es*   x s

...

f 168v *(1 week May)*

...   20

paid for 7 yardes of lynn clothe for ij shartes to the folles at
11 d A yarde & for maikinge   vij s iiij d

...

Masons' Ordinary (1669 copy): Enrolment Books   25
TW: 544/72
f 52 *(1 September)*

...And that the said felowship and occupation of Masons and
their Succsesou*rs* of the same felowship att all times hereafter   30
for euer whensoeuer the generall plaies of this towne of newcastle
antientlie called the Corpus Christi plaies shall be plaied shall
decentlie and comelie assemble themselues together and att the
Corpus christi
playes
charge of the said fellowship and occupation for the time being
shall in the best manner and wise they can cause to be sett forth   35
and plaied among other plaies of the said towne the plaies
antientlie Called and Named the buriall of o*u*r Lady Saint Mary
the virgin and for euery one of the said fellowship and occupation
of Masons according to the antient order of the same felowship
and occupation of masons to Attend and waite upon the saide   40
plaie except Sickness or other lawfull cause be impediment to
him upon paine euerie one of the said felowship and occupation

that is soe absent shall paie to the use of the said fellowship and
occupation of Masons the some of ij s. vj d....

1582
AC *Tanners Accounts: Brand MS 18*
NCL: L942.82 N536 B
nf

payd to the Mynstrelles   20 d.

1589
Joiners' Ordinary (1669 copy): Enrolment Books
TW: 544/73
f 4 *(28 March)*

...And that the said Wardens and ffellowshipp of Ioyners and
their successors att all times hereafter whensoever it shall be
thought necessarie and convenient by Mr Maior the Aldermen
and Sheriffe of this Towne of Newcastle aforesaid to comand to
be sett forth and plaied or exercised any generall playe or Marshall
exercise within the said Towne of Newcastle aforesaid That then
the said Wardens and ffellowshipp of Ioyners shall Decently and
comely assemble themselves together to attend and waite upon
the said Playes or other Martiall exercise according as other
ffellowshipps within the said Towne shall be charged to doe and
att their charges sett fourth to be plaed or exercised in the best
manner they can amongst other ffellowshipps and occupacions
of the said Towne such parte of the same plays or exercises as
shall be appointed unto the said Wardens and ffellowshipp by
the Maior Aldermen and Sherif of Newcastle aforesaid for the
time being upon paine every one of the said ffellowshipp that is
absent except sicknesse or other such Lawfull Cause as the
Wardens and ffellowshipp of Ioyners aforesaid or the most parte
shall allowe shall pay for every his Default to the said Wardens of
the said ffellowshipp Two Shillings Sixpence...

to Attend their
play

30 / Sherif *at edge of folio, perhaps* Sheriffe *originally*

1590
Chamberlains' Account Books TW: 543/18
f 167v *(2 week October²)*

...

paid for Ledder to the fovles shone   xij d   5

...

f 168

geven in rewarde to the earle of hardforthes player*es*   xl s   10
geven in rewarde to the earle of worceter*es* player*es*   xxx s

...

f 169 *(3 week October²)*

...   15
paid for [⟨...⟩] boot ∧ ⌐hyer⌐ to the maggestrates to
whickham   xviij d
paid to the mynstrelles at whickham in rewarde   iij s x d

...
                                                                         20
f 169v *(4 week October²)*

...

paide for mending the fovles showes   xij d

...
                                                                         25
f 171 *(1 week November)*

...

paid to the iiij waites for thear q*uarter*   xxvj s 8⟨.⟩

...
                                                                         30
f 171v *(2 week November)*

...

geven in rewarde to my Lord of essexs tvmbler*es*   xl s

...
                                                                         35
f 172

...

paid for iiij yardes d of russat for A coot to Allan the
fovle at 16 d   vj s
paid for 4 yardes d of whit cotton for lynnynge his cott ij s vij d   40
paid for maiking his coote and for harden   xxiij d

...

f 172v *(3 week November)*

...

paid for 3 yardes d of white cotton for A petticott for
Allon the fovle, 2 s j d & for maiking   ij s viij d

...   5

paid for A payer of showes to Allan the
fovle   ij s

...

f 173 *(4 week November)*   10

...

paid for 2 payer of hosse to the fovles Allan &
lawson   iij s

...

                                                                                          15

f 175v *(3 week December)*

...

paid for vj yardes d of white cotton for A petticote
to Allan the fovle at 8 d & for maiking   v s

...   20

f 176 *(4 week December)*

...

paid for A payer of hosse to Iohn Lawson the fovle,
& for A belte and A payer of gloves   ij s ij d   25

...

1591
Chamberlains' Account Books TW: 543/18
f 176v *(1 week January)*   30

...

paid for A payer of shone to Iohn Lawson the fovle
& mending his old showes   ij s vj d

...

                                                                                          35

f 177 *(2 week January)*

...

paid for iij yerdes q*uarter* of cotton for A petticote to Iohn
Lawson the fovle & for maikinge   ij s vij d

...   40

f 179v *(2 week February)*

...

paid to the iiij waites for thear q*uarter*   xxvj s viij d

...

f 180

...

paid for mending Iohn lawsones cott the fovles 2 tymes &
for skenne thread to his coot & mending his stock⟨.⟩nges   xxij d
paid for A payer of hosse to Allan the fovle   xv d
paid for A payer of showes to hym   ij s

...

f 181v *(1 week March)*

...

paid to *(blank)* bakar for keping Io*hn* lawson the fovle   xvj d

...

f 182 *(2 week March)*

...

paid for keping Iohn lawson the fovle this
weike   xvj d

...

f 182v *(3 week March)*

...

paid for keping Iohn Lawson the fovle this
weike   xvj d

...

f 183 *(4 week March)*

...

paid for keping Iohn Lawson the fovle this
weike   xvj d

...

f 183v *(1 week April)*

...

geven in reward to my Lord Darcyes player*es*   xl s

...

9 / stock⟨.⟩nges: *original letter converted (ascender deleted), but result illegible*

f 184 *(2 week April)*

...

paid for 2 payer of hosse to the 2 folles	iij s
paid for 2 shart bandes to Iohn Lawson the fovle	xij d

...

paid for A belt to Iohn Lawson the fovle   iij d

f 184v

...

paid for iij yardes of brode popingloye grean for A cott to Iohn Lawson the fovle at x s A yarde	xxx s
paid for A yarde of read stamell for gairding the said coote	xj s
paid for iij yardes d & d q*uarter* of brode grean for A cott to Allan the fovle	xxiiij s ij d
paid for A yarde d of stamell cairsaye for gairding the cott	vj s
paid for x yardes of white cotton for lynnyng thear cott*es*	v s x d
paid for j yarde d of graye culler cairsaye for A payer of britches to Iohn lawson the fovle 3 s & maiking	iiij s
paid for skene thread & harden for *yer* cott*es*	iij s j d
paid for maiking the fovles 2 cottes	x s
paid for pointes to the fovles cott*es*	iiij d

...

f 185 *(3 week April)*

...

paide for ij paire of showes to the ij fooles   iiij s

...

f 185v

...

paide for ij lether skynnes & a dozen pointes to Iohn
lawson the foole   xviij d

...

f 186 *(4 week April)*

...

paide to georg fuster surgant for letting Iohn lawson foole
bloud   viij d

...

f 188 *(3 week May)*

...

paide to the iiij waites for their quarteriches   xxvj s viij d

...

     5

f 188v

...

paide for ij shartes to Iohn Lawson the foole ⌈& for
making⌉   iiij s ij d

...

     10

f 189 *(4 week May)*

...

paide for 7 yardes of hardne to be shartes to allon the
foole and to ij poore childer   iiij s j d   15

f 191 *(2 week June)*

...

paide for a paire of hose to lawson the foole   xx d
paide for a paire of shose to him   ij s   20
paide for soling and healing ij paire of hose to Io*hn*
lawson   iiij d
paide for mending of his cote   vj d

...

     25

f 192v *(1 week July)*

...

paide for iij yardes of straken 8 d A yearde to be Allon
the foole ij shartes and for ij shart banndes   iij s

...

     30

f 193

...

paide for lether for mending Iohn lawson the foole showes   viij d

...

     35

f 194v *(4 week July)*

...

paide for iiij sharte bandes to Allon the foole   xvj d

...

     40

10 / ij d *apparently, but* i *badly formed, written over another letter or figure*

f 195

...

paide for A yeard of brode clothe to Iohn lawson the foole
to be A Ierken & a paire of bretches comaunded by mr
maiore   x s viij d   5

...

f 195v *(1 week August)*

...

paide for cotton to line Iohn lawson the fooles Ierken   xij d   10
paide for buttons and lyninge Clothe   iiij d
paide for making his Ierken and britches   xviij d

...

paide for a dozen pointes to Io lawson foole   iiij d

...   15

f 196 *(2 week August)*

...

paide for a paire of hose to Allon the foole   xvj d
paide for a paire of showes to Allon   ij s   20

...

f 197v *(4 week August)*

...

paide to the iiij waytes for their quarteriches   xxvj s viij d   25

...

f 198

...

paide for a paire of showes to Iohn t⟨.⟩ lawson foole   ij s   30
paide for a paire of hose to Iohn lawson   ij s

...

f 199 *(1 week September)*

...   35

paide for ij new shartes to Iohn lawson the foole   v s iiij d
paide for sewinge of his shartes   iiij d
paide for mending the fooles showes   vj d
paide for skowringe of his coate   vj d

...   40

30 / t⟨.⟩: t *followed by what looks like the upper part of* h

geuen in rewarde to the queenes ma*ies*ties plaiers graunted
by mr maior   v li.

...

f 200 *(2 week September)*   5

...

geuen in reward to the earle of worcesters plaiers com*manded*
by mr   xl s

...

                                                                    10

f 203v *(3 week October[1])*

...

paide for keeping hogmagoge this year   vj s viij d

f 204   15

...

paide for a paire of hose to allon the foole   xvj d
paide for a paire of showes to — Allon   ij s
paide for lether to mend Io*hn* lawson the fooles showes   viij d

...   20

f 205v *(4 week October[1])*

...

paide for a paire of showes to allon foole   ij s
...   25

paide for iij[xx] yardes and one of brode clothe
for the sergauntes lyveries and for will*i*am
Iacksons lyuerie at 8 s – 8 d a yeard / 26:8:8:
mor xvj yardes iij q*uarter* for the waites the   xxxiiij l v s x d
plum*er* & the pauer at 7 s. 6 d. a yearde :6:5:7:   30
mor for cariadge canvas cordes & certeficat :
1:[4] ⌐11¬ :7

...

paide to the waites att the Auditt dynn*er*   vij s iiij d
...   35

f 215 *(2 week October[2])*

...

paide for ij paire of hose to the 2 fooles   ij s viij d

8 / mr *for* mr maior

paide for ij paire of showes to the 2 fooles   iiij s

...

f 217v *(1 week November)*

...

paide to the iiij waytes for theire q*uarter*iches   xxvj s 8 d

...

paide for a paire of showes to allon the foole   ij s

...

f 219 *(3 week November)*

...

paide for 2: yardes 3 q*uarter* of white cotton for a
peticot to Iohn lawson the foole 22 d and for mak*ing*   ij s iiij d
& butons
paide for lether to Iohn lawson for mending his show*es*   viij d

...

paide for 3 yardes of harne to be a shart to allo*n* the
foole 21 d and for makinge 3 d   ij s

...

f 220 *(4 week November)*

...

paide for a paire of hose to Allon the foole   ij s
paide for a paire of showes to Iohn lawso*n* the foole   ij s

...

f 222 *(3 week December)*

...

paide for a paire of showes to Iohn lawson   ij s

...

f 223 *(4 week December)*

...

paide for j yarde d q*uarter* of brode clothe to be a paire of
bretches to Iohn Lawson the foole v s 4 d a yeard   vj s j d

...

f 223v

...

paide for making a paire of bretches to Io*h*n lawso   viij d

...

paide for a paire of hose to Iohn Lawson   xx d

...

paide for pointes to Iohn lawsons bretches   iiij d

...

5

AC   *Coopers' Accounts: Brand MS 10*
NCL: L942.82 N536 B
nf

A.d. 1577. Item geiven to the Mynstrells   8 d. also 1591   10
                                                        occurs —

1592
Chamberlains' Account Books   TW: 543/18
f 225 *(2 week January)*   15

paide for a paire of new soles to allon
showes   xij d

...

20

f 226 *(4 week January)*

...

paide for a shart baund to Allon the foole   vj d

...

25

f 227 *(1 week February)*

...

paide for lether to mende Iohn lawson the fooles
shows   xij d

...   30

f 227v *(2 week February)*

...

paide to the 4 waites for their q*uarter*iches   xxvj s 8 d

...   35

f 228v *(3 week February)*

...

paide for a paire of showes to Allon the foole   ij s

...   40

f 229v *(1 week March)*

...

paide for a paire of gloues to — lawson the fole   iiij d

...

    5

f 230v *(2 week March)*

...

paide for a paire of showes to Allon the foole   ij s
paide for a paire of — carsey hose to him   xvj d

...

    10

f 234v *(2 week April)*

...

paide for a new hatt to Io*hn* lawson the foole   iij s iiij d

...

    15

f 235* *(3 week April)*

...

paide for 2 yeardes d of brode clothe rattes culer
to be a paire of pretches and a Ierken to Iohn   xij s vj d   20
Lawson the foole att v s p*er* yearde
paide for a yeard d of canuas to be a dublett to
Iohn Lawson the foole 2 s. 4 d and for iij yeardes   iiij s iiij d
of white cottonn for the lyninge of his dublett
paide for a yeard of harne for lyininge to his dublett   vj d   25
paide for making a Ierken a paire of bretches and a
dublett to Iohn lawson the foole   ij s. viij d.
paide for a lether belt to him   vj d.
paide for vij yeardes of sheep coloure cairsey to be a
side cotte to Allon the foole ij s p*er* yeard   xiiij s   30
paide for vj yeard*es* of white cotton to line his cote   iij s iiij d
paide for a yearde d of hardne to line his cote   ix d
paide for makinge of Allon his coate   xvj d
paide for vij yeardes of brode white cottonn to be a
petticote to Allon the foole viij d a yeard   iiij s viij d   35
paide for making Allons petticote   viij d
paide for a capp to the foole Allon   iiij d
paide for a shart baund and 2 lether lases to Allon
the fooles 2 cotes   iiij d
paide for buttons to Iohn lawsons cotes   vj d   40

31 / vj *converted from* iij

paide for a paire of hose to Iohn lawson   xx d

...

paide for a dozen d of pointes to Iohn lawson   vj d

...

      5

f 236v *(4 week April)*

...

paide for a seruice booke to Iohn lawson
foole   iij s

...   10

paide for a pair of soles to allon showes   x d

...

f 239 *(3 week May)*

...   15

paide to the iiij waites for their q*uarter*iches 6 s. 8 d
a peec*e*   xxvj s viij d

...

f 239v   20

...

paide for cloth*e* to be a shart band to Io*h*n
lawson   xvj d

...

      25

f 240v *(4 week May)*

paide for v yeardes of lin clothe for to be 2 shart*es*
to Io*h*n lawson the foole att xj d a yearde   iiij s vij d
paide for the making of his 2 shartes   iiij d   30
paide for v yeardes of harnde to be shartes to allon
the foole and george spence com*manded* by mr maior   iij s
paide for the makinge of their shartes   iiij d

...

paide for a paire of showes to allon the foole   ij s   35
paide for a paire of hose to him of carsey   xvj d

...

f 246 *(2 week July)*

...   40

paide to robert askew for plainge of his flute   xij d

...

f 248 *(4 week July)*

...

geuen in reward to my lord *(blank)* plaiers com*m*anded
by mr maior   xviij s

...   5

f 250v *(2 week August)*

...

paide for 2 paire of showes to the 2 fooles   iij s

...   10

f 251v *(4 week August)*

...

paide to the 4 waites for their q*uarter*iches   xxvj s viij d

...   15

f 252v

...

paide to 3 musions w*h*ich [was] ⌈did⌉ plaie[d] att wedowe
shafto when the 24^tie was att dynner their   iij s   20

...

f 253v *(1 week September)*

...

paide for 2 paire of hose to the 2 fooles   iij s   25

...

f 254v *(2 week September)*

...

paide for 2 drumes w*h*ich plaied in the feilde when my   30
lord pr*e*sident did take muster of this towne   ij s
paide to 2 men w*h*ich plaied one the drumes   xij d
paide to j w*h*ich plaied of a floute one the same day   vj d

...

                                                                                                      35

f 256v *(4 week September)*

...

paide for lether for soling Io*h*n lawson the fooles showes   x d

...

paide for 2 yeardes d of hardne to be a shart to allon   xvj d   40
paide for a shart baund to Allon the foole   iiij d

...

f 257v *(1 week October[1])*

...

paide for a paire of showes to Iohn lawson the foole   xx d

...

f 258 *(2 week October[1])*

...

paide for 2 yeardes d of brode clothe to be a Ierken and
a paire of bretches to Iohn lawson the foole   xiij s iiij d
paide for 2 yeardes of blackett ⌈cottin⌉ for lyninge his
ierken   xvj d
paide for makinge of his bretches and Ierken   xxij d
paide for 2 dozen haire buttons to his Ierken   iiij d
paide for a dozen pointes to his bretches   ij d

...

f 258v

...

paide for a banquett to the auditors in Iohn blithmans: 53 s
paide for wine & musicke their vij s. paide for a bankett to
the auditors: xl s. paide for wine & musick their
xvj s x d   xj l. xj s
paide for a banquett to the auditors in wedowe raines: v l.
paide for wine & musick theire xiiij s ij d / Soma totalis

...

f 259v *(3 week October[1])*

...

paide for keeping hogmagogg this yeare   v s viij d

...

f 260v

...

paide for a banquett to the auditors in Iohn carrs for good
chere 40 s & for wine & musick theire: 39 s   iij l. xix s

...

f 261

...

paide to mr Iohn oldam att london for iij[xx] and
j yeardes of brode clothe for the sergauntes &
william Iacksons lyuereis att viij s viij d per

yearde: 26 l. 8 s. 8 d. more paide for xvj yeardes   xxxiiij l ix s ij d
3 q*uarter* for the waites the plumer and the pauer:
att: vij s vj d p*er* yearde: 6. 5. 7. more paide
for cariadge canuas cordes and: certificate:
1 .15 Soma totalis paide is   5
...

f 264 *(4 week October*[1]*)*
...
paide for a paire of blew hose to Io*h*n lawson: 20 d and   10
for a paire of showes to him 18d in all   iij s ij d
paide for a paire of hose to allon: 16 d and for a paire of
showes to him. 18 d in all   ij s x d
...
paide for 2 sheepe skynnes to be a paire of lether lyning*es*   15
to Iohn lawson the foole   xiiij d
...

f 264v
...   20
paide for wine to mr maiore and his brethren att
thauditt dynner in Io*h*n pearsons   v s
paide to the waites for playing mussicke att the
Auditt dynner   v s
...   25

f 113v *(2 week October*[2]*)*
...
paide for sollinge allon the fooles showes   x d
...   30

f 114v *(4 week October*[2]*)*
...
geuen in reward to my lorde darcies plaiers   xx s
...   35

f 115v *(1 week November)*
...
paide to the 4 waites for their q*uarter*iches   xxvj s 8 d
...   40

f 116v *(2 week November)*

...

paide for a paire of showes to a*ntony* hall & one
other paire to allon the foole 18 d a paire   iij s

...   5

117v *(3 week November)*

...

paide for lether to Io*hn* lawson the fooles
showes   xviij d   10

...

f 120 *(2 week December)*

...

paide for a hatt to Iohn lawson the foole   iij s   15

...

paide for 2 shartes to allon the foole   iij s iiij d
paide for sewinge theis 2 shartes   iiij d

...
                                                                                         20

f 120v *(3 week December)*

...

paide to mr brucke in p*ar*te of paymente of vj l.
13 s. 4 d for mendinge the organs of sainte   xl s
N*ich*olas churche letten to him in the whole   25

...

paide for 2 lether skynnes 2 pockettes & a dozen
lether l pointes to Io*hn* lawson the foole   ij s ij d

...

paide for 2 shart bandes to allon the foole   x d   30

...

Tanners Accounts: Brand MS *18*
nf   35

mor geven ∧ ⌐to⌐ the Mynstrells the Morrow after
the feast day   6

1593
Chamberlains' Account Books TW: 543/18
f 122v *(2 week January)*

paide for a paire of grene cairsey hose to Iohn lawson	xx d	5
...		
paide for a paire of showes to Iohn lawson	xviij d	
paide for a paire of hose to allon: 16 d & a pair of sho	ij s x d	
...		10

f 123v *(3 week January)*

...		
paide for 2 shart bands to Iohn lawson	viij d	
...		15

f 124v *(1 week February)*

...		
paide for 4 yeardes d of blacke frees to be cloths to Iohn lawson the foole: att 14 d a yearde	iiij s viij d	20
paid for a iearde of brode clothe rates culler to be a Ierken to him att v d a iearde	v s iiij d	
paid for 4 ieardes of black cotton to be lyning: 8 d yeard	ij s viij d	
...		25

f 125v *(2 week February)*

...		
geuen in reward to my lorde ogles plaiers	xx s	
...		30

f 126 *(3 week February)*

...		
paide for mending allon the fooles showes	iiij d	
...		35
paide for making a peticote to Iohn lawson the foole	iiij d	
...		

f 128v *(3 week March)*

...		40
paide to the 4 waites for their quarteriches	xxvj s 8 d	
...		

paide to mr brucke in full paymente of vj l. 13 s 4 d for
mendinge the organs of sainte N*icholas* churche   liij s iiij d
...

f 129v *(4 week March)*   5

...

paide to a ioiner for mending the organs in st N*icholas*
churche   viij d

...

paide for a new knyfe to Iohn lawson foole   iiij d   10
...

f 130

...

paide for makinge of Ioh*n* lawsons the fooles clothe w*hich*   15
was made in the j weke of fabr*uary* laste & for lyning &   iij s
buttons

...

f 131 *(2 week April)*   20

...

paide for 4 shart bandes to Iohn lawson the foole   xviij d
...

paide for 2 paire of showes j paire to Iohn lawson and ane
other paire to allon the foole 18 d p*er* yeerd paire   iij s   25

...

f 132 *(3 week April)*

...

paide for 2 paire of hose one paire to allon & a nother paire   30
to Iohn lawson the foole att 20 d p*er* paire   iij s iiij d

...

paide for a paire of gartins a paire of gloues and a
dozen lether pointes to Ioh*n* lawson the foole   x d
...   35

f 132v *(4 week April)*

...

paide for 7 ieardes of reed russatt to be a cotte to allo*n*   xvij s
paide for 6 ieard*es* of white rugg to line his cote w*ith*all   iiij s   40
paide for j ieard of lin to lyne the ou*er*bodies of his cote   ix d
paide for makinge of his cote and of his capp   ij s

paide for 6 ieardes of white rugg to make him a peticote   iiij s
paide for makinge of his petycoate   viij d

...

paide for 2 yerdes of rates culler clothe to be Iohne
lawson a paire of bretches & a Ierken 5 s vj d a ieard   xj s   5
paide for 3 ieardes of white cotton to be lyning   xxj d
paide for 3 yeardes of white rugg to be him a
peticote   ij s
paide for makinge him a dublett a paire of bretches &
a Ierken: 4 s for lyn & hardne to the dublett: 2 s for   vj s iiij d   10
buttons to his Ierken 4 d

...

paide for 2 lether skynnes & 2 lether pocktes to Iohn
lawsons   xxij d

...   15

f 133v *(1 week May)*

...

geuen in reward to my *lord* admiralles plaiers and my *lord*
morleis plaiers beinge all in one companye   xxx s   20
...

f 135 *(3 week May)*

...

paide to the 4 waites for theire q*uarter*iches   xxvj s viij d   25
...

f 136 *(4 week May)*

...

paide for a q*uarter* of browne canuas to be Io*hn* lawson   30
a dublett 2 s. 9 d & for pointes to him 3 d some:3 s.   iij s
...

f 137 *(1 week June)*

...   35
p*ai*d for the releif of Io*hn* lawso*n* foole lying sicke of a
sore legg com*manded* by mr maiore to be paide him weeklie   ij s
...

f 137v   40

...

paide for v ieardes of lin clothe to be Iohn lawson the foole

2 shartes: att x d p*er* iearde: 4 s. 2 d for sewinge   iiij s vj d
theme: 4 d
paide for the releif of Iohn lawso*n* lying sicke
of a sore legg   ij s
...   5

f 138v *(3 week June)*

...

paide for 2 paire of showes to Io*hn* lawson the
foole   iij s 4 d   10
paide for a paire of hose to Io*hn* lawso*n* the foole   xx d
paide for a shart band to allon the foole   iiij d

...

p*ai*d in reward to mr brucke for a plaie & other sportes to
him & his brethren plaied com*manded* by mr maior to be   x s   15
p*ai*d

f 140 *(1 week July)*

...

paide for lether for mendinge Iohn lawson the fooles   20
shoues   xviij d

...

f 145v *(3 week August)*

...   25

paide to a tabron*er* for playing att the shore for
making mr ma*ior* & his brethren merie: 2 s vj d &   iij s vj d
for ale to mr maiore: 12 d in all

...

     30

f 146

...

paide for 2 paire of showes to the 2 fooles lawso*n* &
allon   iij s
...   35

f 146v *(4 week August)*

...

paide to the 4 waites for their q*uarter*iches   xxvj s viij d
...   40
paide & geuen in reward to my lorde worcest*er*s plaiers   iij l.

...

f 147

...

paide for 2 paire of hose to the 2 fooles 2 s. & 14 d   iij s ij d

...

5

f 148 *(1 week September)*

...

paide & geuen in reward to the erle of successx*es*
plaiers   xl s

...   10

f 149 *(2 week September)*

...

paide for a shart & a shart band to allon the foole   ij s vj d

...   15

paide to the erle of successx plaiers in full paymente of
iij l. for playing a free play com*manded* by mr maiore   xx s

...

f 150 *(3 week September)*   20

...

paide & geuen in reward to the quenes ma*iest*is
plaiers   iij l.

...

                                                                            25

f 152v *(1 week October[1])*

...

paide to mr Iohn oldam att londo*n* for iij^{xx} j yeardes of
brodes clothe for the sergaunt*es* & *willia*m Iacksons
lyuerie att viij s viij d p*er* iearde 26: 8: 8: more   30
paide for xvj ieardes 3 q*uar*ters for the waites   xxxiiij l. ix s ij d
the plumer and the pauer att 7 s 6 d p*er* iearde
vj l. v s vij d more paide for cariadge canuas
cordes and certyficate j l. xvs / some in all
with charges p*ai*d is   35

...

f 153 *(2 week October[1])*

...

paide for keeping hogmogogs cotte this yeare   vj s viij d   40

...

f 155 *(3 week October[1])*

...

paide for the loodging of Iohn lawson foole beding
this iear   xx s

...   5

paide for a paire of showes to Allon the foole   xviij d

...

f 158 *(4 week October[1])*

...   10

paide the waites for playinge Musicke att dynner   v s

...

paide for 2 paire of hose j paire to allon the foole
and a paire to george spence att xviij d & xvj d p*er*   ij s x d
paire   15

...

paide for v ieardes of black frees to be Io*hn* lawson
foole britches & Ierken: vj s v d for 2 ieardes of
cotton for to be lyninge: 14 d for makinge &   ix s ix d
buttons: 2 s 2 d in all   20

...

paide for a paire of showes to Iohn lawson foole   xviij d

...

paide for sewing 2 shartes to Iohn lawson the foole   iiij d
paide for a paire of hose and showes to thomas doddes   25
foole   ij s
paide for lether pockettes & pointes to Iohn lawsons
clothes   viij d

...   30

f 59 *(1 week October[2])*

...

paide for a paire of hose to Iohn lawson the foole   xx d

...   35

f 59v *(2 week October[2])*

...

paide and geuen in rewarde to my lord darcies plaiers   xx s

...

paide georg barker for soling allon the fooles showes   viij d   40

...

f 61v *(4 week October²)*

...

p*ai*d for d a bend of lether for mendinge Io*hn* lawsons shows   ij s

...

paide for lether for mendinge allon the fooles showes   viij d   5

...

f 62v *(1 week November)*

...

paide for 3 ieard*es* d of harne to be a shart to   10
allon   ij s

...

f 63v *(2 week November)*

...   15

paide & geuen in reward to my *lord* muntegles
plaiers   xx s

...

paide for a belt to Iohn lawson the foole   iiij d

...   20

f 65 *(4 week November)*

...

paide to the 4 waites for theire q*uarter*iches due att
allhallowmas last beinge behinde and vnpaide   xxvj s 8 d   25

...

paide to the clarke of sainte Nicho*la*s churche for ringing
their billes the 17 daie of nouem*ber* for ioie of o*ur*   ij s vj d
ma*ie*sties raign
paide for ringing all hallowe churche bells likewise   xx d   30
paide for ringinge sainte Iohn church bells lik   xvj d
paide for ringinge sainte andro churche bells
lik   xvj d
paide to *willia*m lassles & ro*bert* askewe for playing one
the drum & floote w*ith* the gunners the 17 daie of   v s   35
nouem*ber* for y*er* pains

...

f 65v

...   40

paide for 2 paire of showes j paire to Iohn lawso*n* and
ane other paire to allon the foole: 20 d p*er* paire   iij s 4 d

...

f 68v *(4 week December)*

...

paide & geuen in rewrde to my *lord* ogles plaiers
com*mand*ed   xx s

...   5

f 69

paide for v ieardes d of reed russatt to be a cote to allon
the foole: ij s iiij d the iearde   xij s x d   10
paide for makinge of his cote and buttons   xx d
paide for a paire of hose & showes to allo*n* 20 d p*er*
paior   iij s iiij d

...

paide for 4 ieardes of clothe to be Iohn lawson a paire   15
of bretches & a Ierken 3 s vj d p*er* iearde   xiiij s
paide for 4 ieardes of cotton to be him a peticote   ij s viij d
paide for makinge his bretches ierken & petticote   xx d
paide for buttons to his coates   ij d
paide for pointes pockett*es* & skynns to lawson   ij s   20
paide for a pairc of hose & showes to him   iij s viij d

...

1594
Chamberlains' Account Books TW: 543/18   25
f 70v *(2 week January)*

...

paide for v ieardes of cotton for lyning allon the fooles
cl*othes*   iij s 4 d

...   30

f 73 *(1 week February)*

...

paide for lyninge to a capp for Iohn lawson foole   vj d

...   35

paide for solinge allon the fooles showes   x d

...

f 74v *(3 week February)*

...   40

paide to the 4 waites for their q*uarter*iches   xxvj s viij d

...

f 76 *(4 week February)*

...

paide for a shart to allo*n* the foole and for sewing itt   ij s 4 d

...

f 77 *(1 week March)*

...

paide for a paire of new shoues to allon the foole   xx d

...

f 78 *(2 week March)*

...

paide for a paire of hose to allon the foole   xx d

...

f 79v *(4 week March)*

...

paide for 2 ieardes & a q*uar*ter of silkrussatt brode clothe
to be Iohn lawson a paire of bretches & a Ierken: xij s ix d
5 s 8 d p*er* ieard
paide for v ieardes of lin clothe to be Io*hn* lawso*n*
2 shartes   v s
paide for sewinge of his 2 shartes & washing theme   iiij d
paide for a paire of new showes to Iohn lawson   xx d
paide for a paire of showes to thomas doddes the foole   xiiij d

...

f 80v *(1 week April)*

...

paide for a paire of hose to Iohn lawson   xx d

...

f 81v *(2 week April)*

...

paide for 2 ieardes d & d a q*uar*ter of brode clothe
blacke and grene to be thomas doddes the foole a   x s viij d
cote: 5 s 6 d p*er* ieard
p*ai*d for a q*uar*ter & d of reed kairsey for gardinge of
his coate   xxij d
paide for 3 ieardes of white cotto to be lyning to his
cote   ij s iij d
paide for makinge of thomas doddes the fooles coate   iij s 4 d

paide for lyninge to the bodie of his cote & for skene
threde   viij d

paide for v ieardes of reed russatt to be allon the fole
a cote   ix s ij d

paide for makinge of allon the foole his coate   xvj d   5

paide for lyninge to the bodie of his coate d a
ierd of lin   v d

paide for vj ieardes of white cotton to be allon a
petycote   iij s vj d

paide for makinge of the foole his pettycote   viij d   10

paide for a new hatt to Iohn lawson colourede   iij s

paide for makinge Iohn lawson a dublett: 2 s. 6 d for
flockes to his dublett: 4 d for buttons & skene threed: iij s j d
3 d in all

paide for makinge him a paire of britches & a ierken &   15
for buttons   xx d

paide for lyn & hardne to Iohn lawsons
dublett   ij s iiij d

paide for lyninges pockettes & pointes to Iohn lawsons
bretches   ij s   20

paide for a paire of showes to allon the foole against
ester   xx d
...

f 84 *(4 week April)*   25
...
paide for 2 paire of soles to Iohn lawson
showes   xij d
...
                                                                                 30

f 85 *(1 week May)*
...
paide for canuas to be Iohn lawson a dublett   ij s viij d
...
paide for a paire of soles to allon the fooles   35
showes   x d
...

f 86 *(2 week May)*
...   40
paide for mendinge 2 paire of showes to Iohn lawson   iiij d
...

f 88 *(4 week May)*

...

paide for A paire of showes to Allon the foole   xx d

...

5

f 89 *(1 week June)*

...

paide for a paire of hose and showes to Iohn lawson   iij s viij d
paide for a paire of showes to thomas doddes the foole   xiiij d
paide for a paire of hoase to allon the foole   xx d   10

...

f 89v *(2 week June)*

...

paide for a shart band to allon the foole of skott*es*   15
clothe   viij d

...

f 92v *(1 week July)*

...   20

paide for a paire of soles to allon the fooles showes   x d

f 95v *(1 week August)*

...

paide and geuen in rewrde to my *lord* muntegles plaiers   xl s   25

...

f 96v *(2 week August)*

...

paide for 2 paire of hose and showes to Iohn law & allo*n*   v s   30

...

f 98 *(3 week August)*

...

paide for a paire of hose to Iohn lawson foole   ij s   35

...

f 99v *(4 week August)*

...

paide for lether for mending of Io*hn* lawsons fooles   40
shows   xij d

...

f 102v *(3 week September)*

...

paide for 5 ieard*es* of lin clothe to be Iohn lawson 2 shartes   v s

...

f 103v *(4 week September)*

...

paide for a paire of soles to allon the fooles showes   x d

...

paide for a paire of hose showes & a shart to thomas dod*es*   10
fool   iiij s vj d

...

paide and geuen to peter rutlishe waite of this towne was att
his dep*ar*ture frome newcastle to london: com*manded*   vj s viij d
he beinge in want   15

...

f 104v *(1 week October[1])*

...

paide for sewinge of Iohn lawson foole 2 shart*es*   iiij d   20

...

f 105v *(2 week October[1])*

...

paide to *m*r oldam of londo*n* for 63 ieard*es* of new   25
cullerd brothe cloth for w*illia*m Iackson & th*e*
officers: 8 s 8 d p*er* ieard: 27. 6. 4. more for 16
ieard*es* of new cullerd cloth for the waite*s*   xxxiij l. 14 s 7d
plum*er* & pauer: 7 s. 6 d p*er* iearde: 6. 5. 7 for
canuas corde & packinge itt: 2 s 8 d. some in all is   30

...

paide for keepinge hogmago*es* koate and him self in
licknes: 6 s. 8   *(blank)*

...

f 106

...

paide for a paire of hose & showes to thomas dodd*es*
a naturall   ij s viij d

...   40

paide for musicke to the auditors att theire banquett   v s

...

f 108v *(4 week October¹)*

...

paide to Iohn lawson foole: 10 s   x s

...

5

f 110

...

paide for a banquett to the staites in mr maiors ... the wait*es*
playinge musicke: 10 s....

paide for vj ieard*es* & a q*uar*ter of scearsnett of corde   10
⌈to: ro*bert* fennick⌉ w*hich* caried the auncient
before the staites 5 s 4 d p*er* iearde 33 s 4 d   iij l. viij s x d
for 35 l d of powder w*hich* was shott when they
cam: 35 s. 6 d

paide to ro*bert* askewe for playinge wit*h* his fife before   15
the drume   xvj d

...

paide to the waites for playinge musick at thauditt
dynn*er*   v s

...   20

f 110v

...

paide for 3 sewd sharte band*es* to Iohn lawson the
foole   xviij d   25

...

paide for hose and showes to Iohn lawson allon and
thomas dodd*es* the fooles: eyther of theme a paire of
hose & showes   viij s vij d

...   30

f 2v *(1 week October²)*

...

paide to a boie for playinge of a drum befor ye stat*es* of
fland*er*   xij d   35

...

f 3v *(2 week October²)*

...

paide to thom*a*s richeson tailor for makinge 23 shift*es* of app*er*ell   40
to those w*hich* had theme grauntide before michlem*a*s as apperes
by his bill & their names who had theme viz ... allon foole a longe

cote thom*a*s dodd*es* foole a peticote : &c:...

...

f 4 *(3 week October²)*

...

payde for vj ieard*es* of white cotto*n* to be allon foole a
peticote   iij s vj d

...

f 5 *(4 week October²)*

...

paide to Iohn lawson foole toward*es* mending of his sore
legg   xij d

...

f 6 *(1 week November)*

...

paide to the 4 waites ro*bert* askew: Iarrerd heron
georgio hero*n* and abraham farren: for y*er*   xxvj s viij d
q*uarter*iches: 6 s 8 d p*er* peece

...

f 8 *(3 week November)*

p*a*id for lether for mending allon the fooles showes   viij d   25

...

paide for 28 yerdes of graie and reed russatt to be
cloths to the p*er*sons heareafter followinge: i6 d p*er*
yerde:... for makinge a pety cote to allon and a
paire of hose: 1 s. 10 d....

...

f 9 *(4 week November)*

...

p*a*id for 2 yerd*es* d of hardne to be allo*n* the foole a
shart & sewing   ij s

...

f 10 *(1 week December)*

...

paide for 2 shart band*es* to allo the foole   vj d

...

f 11 *(2 week December)*

...

paide for 2 paire of showes j paire to lawson & other
dodd*es*   iij s viij d

...   5

AC *Saddlers' Accounts: Brand MS 18* NCL: L942.82 N536 B
nf *(30 May)*

Spended in Iohn Stoke House for the fellowshippe the 30   10
daye of Maye 1594

...

more payde to the myntreles   6–8

1595   15
Chamberlains' Account Books TW: 543/18
f 13 *(1 week January)*

...

paide for 3 paire of showes j paire to allon j paire to the
foole captheton j paire to and*er*son com*manded*   ij s viij d   20

...

f 15v *(4 week January)*

...

p*ai*d for lether for Iohn lawson the fooles   25
showes   xij d

...

f 16 *(1 week February)*

...   30

paide for 4 yerdes of reed russatt to be t*homa*s dodd*es* the
foole cloth   vj s viij d

...

f 17 *(2 week February)*   35

...

paide for a paire of hose & showes to allo*n* the
foole   iij s 4 d

...

f 18 *(3 week February)*

...

paide for 10 yerd*es* of fine white cott*on* to be lyninge for
the ou*er*boids of Io*hn* nicols & allon fooles cloathes   vj s viij d
8 d p*er* yerd   5

...

paide for a shart to allon foole & for sewinge   xxij d

...

f 19v *(1 week March)*   10

...

paide to the 4 waites for theire q*uarter*iches   xxvj s viij d

...

f 23v *(1 week April)*   15

...

paide for lether for mendinge Iohn lawso*n* fooles
showes   xvj d

...

paide for 12 yerd*es* d of reed rassatt to be clothes to   20
Iohn lawson & allon the fooles: aginste easter 22 d   xxij s viij d
p*er* yerde

...

f 26 *(4 week April)*   25

...

paide to mr Brooke for mendinge the organs of saint
nichol*a*s churche the wiers beinge all broaken   xx s

...
                                                                                          30
f 27 *(1 week May)*

...

p*ai*d for 6 paire of showes to theis p*er*sons
follow*ing* Iarrerd dods a pair w*illia*m dent
gent*leman* Iohn lawso*n* foole georg spence foole   x s ix d   35
allon foole & to ro*bert* pattison a fatherls child:
aginst est*er* last

...

4 / ouerboids *presumably for* ouerbodis

f 27v

...

p*ai*d for a paire of gloues & gartris to Iohn lawso*n* foole   x d

...

f 29 *(3 week May)*

p*ai*d to the 4 waites for theire q*uarter*iches 6 s 8 d p*er*
peec   xxvj s viij d

...

f 30v *(1 week June)*

...

paide for lether to Iohn lawson the foole his showes   xij d

f 31

...

paide for 7 yerd*es* & a q*uart*er of brode clothe to be
*willia*m dent & Iohn lawson clothes aginste   xliij s vj d
whittsonndaie: 6 s p*er* yerde

...

p*ai*d for vj yerd*es* of lin to be Iohn lawson 2 shartes 10 d
p*er* yerde: 5 s & for sewinge of theme 2 shart*es*: 6 d   v s vj d
paide for a new colloured hatt to the same lawson   ij s viij d

...

f 31v

...

paide for a paire of hose to thomas doddes a natur*all foole   x d

...

f 32v *(2 week June)*

...

paide for 3 shart band*es* to Iohn lawson the foole   xviij d
paide for a paire of showes to thomas doddes the foole   xxij d   35

...

f 33 *(3 week June)*

...

paide for 7 yerd*es* of white cotton to be allo*n* a petycote   40
& lyninge for the vpp*er* bodie of his coate: 7 d p*er* yard   iiij s j d
p*ai*d for ... Ierken britches Buttons & lyning to lawson

2 s for mak*ing* a dublett lyn stentinge & buttons to
lawso*n*: 3 s 6 d for mak*ing* allons cote a cap & lyninge:
22 d ... for 2 skynns & mak*ing* lawso a peticot 22 d to
the foole of captheton a pee & a paire of bretches w*ith*
a capp: 5 s for 3 q*uarters* of cairsey to garde his clothes: 5
2 s 6 d...

f 33v

...for a cote mak*ing* to thomas dodd*es* & a capp garded 5 s   10
for 3 q*uarters* of cairsey to gard the cap: 2 s. 6 d for
mak*ing* him a peticote 6 d...
paide for 8 paire of nether stock*es* to theis p*ersons*: w*illia*m
dent t*homas* nicholso*n* foole antony hall Io*hn* nicholso
thomas doddes allon george spence a fatherles wench   xij s   15
ro*bert* pattiso*n*
...

f 34 *(4 week June)*
...   20
paide for a paire of showes *t*o thoms dodd*es*
fool   xvj d
...

f 40 *(2 week August)*   25
...
paide for lether for mending Io*hn* lawso*n* fooles
showes   viij d
...
                                                                                               30
f 41 *(3 week August)*
...
paide to the 4 waites for their q*uarter*iches   xxvj s 8 d
...
                                                                                               35
f 42v *(4 week August)*
...
paide for 2 paire of hose j pair to lawso*n* & anoth*er* to
allo   iij s ij d
paide for a paire of showes to allon the   40
foole   ij s
...

f 43v *(1 week September)*

...

paide for 2 shart*es* to Iohn lawson foole & for sewing
theme   v s 4 d
paide for a paire of showes to the same lawson   xxij d   5

...

f 44v *(2 week September)*

...

paide for 2 shart bandes to allon the foole   vj d   10

...

f 46v *(4 week September)*

...

paide for 3 shart*es* of lin clothe to allo foole & for   15
sewing the*m*   iiij s

...

f 47 *(1 week October*[1]*)*

...   20

paide for 64 yerd*es* of brode blacke clothe for to be
*willia*m Iackso*n* & the office*r*s liu*er*ies att: 8 d 8 d p*er*
yerde: 27. 14. 8 d more for 16 yerdes: for the waites
the plum*er* & the pau*er*: 7 s. 6 d p*er* yerde: 6 l...
...   25

f 47v

...

paide to george hodshon tailor for keping hogmagog*es*
cote in lik   vj s 8 d   30
p*ai*d to him for keepinge the same cote vnp*ai*d last yeare vj s 8 d
...

f 48v

...   35
paide for lether for mendinge Iohn lawson fooles showcs   xij d

...

22 / 8 d 8 d *for* 8 s 8 d

f 49v *(2 week October[1])*

...

paide for 2 shart band*es* to Iohn lawson the foole   vj d

f 51 *(3 week October[1])*   5

...

p*ai*d for 2 yerd*es* of black brode clothe to be Iohn lauso*n*
the foole: brytches & Ierken: 6 s p*er* yeirde   xij s
p*ai*d for lyninge to his Ierken 6 d for 2 skynns to line his
bretches: 16 d for buttons: 3 d for 2 pockett*es* 6d for   iiij s j d   10
makinge of his clothes: 18 d s*u*ma in all p*ai*d

...

f 52 *(4 week October[1])*

...   15

p*ai*d for 2 paire of showes j paire to Iohn lawson:
22 d & the oth*er* paire to thomas dodd*es* a naturell fool: iij s ij d
16 d s*u*ma
paide for 4 yerd*es* of reed russatt to be thomas dodd*es*
foole clothes 8 s for j yerde & d a q*uarter* of cairsey   20
to garde his cote & cap w*ith*all: 2 s for makinge his
cote and his capp: 5 s for 7 yerd*es* of cotton to be   xx s ix d.
him a petycote & for lyninge his cote 4 s j d for
makinge his petycote: 6 d for a paire of stokins to
him: 14 d s*u*ma   25

...

f 54 *(5 week October[1])*

...

paide for 2 yerd*es* of lin to be *thomas* dodd*es* foole a   30
shart and for sewinge ytt   xx d
paide for 2 paire of stockins j paire to antony hall and
a no ther paire to Io*hn* lawson   iij s

...

                                                                       35

f 54v

...

p*ai*d to the waittes for playinge musick att thauditt dyn*er*   v s
paide for musicke att m*istr*is shaftoes din*er*   ij s

...   40

f 266v *(1 week October²)*

...

paide to Iohn lawson foole   x s

...

     5

f 271v *(3 week October²)*

...

paide for a paire of showes to allon the foole   ij s

...

    10

f 272v *(4 week October²)*

...

paide for 3 yerdes & a d of hardne to be a cou*er* for
one of the townes drumes   xxj d

...

    15

f 273v *(1 week November)*

...

paide to the 4 waites for theire q*uarter*iches   xxvj s 8 d

...

    20

f 275v *(2 week November)*

...

paide for makinge a cou*er* for j of the townes
drums   xij d   25

...

f 278v *(1 week December)*

...

paide for lether for mending Iohn lawso*n* showes   xij d   30

...

f 281 *(4 week December)*

...

paide for 4 yerdes & a d of graie russatt to be thomas   35
nicholso foole of captheto*n* a pee & a paire of britches
7 s 6 d w*ith* a hoode & a paire of stockins: p*ai*d for   x s
reed kairsey to gairde theme 6 d p*ai*d for mak*ing* theme
2 s

...

    40

1596
Chamberlains' Account Books TW: 543/18
f 282 *(1 week January)*

...

paid for v yerd*es* of reed sussatt to be allo*n* clarke   5
the foole clothes: geuen to him before michlemas &   x s
vnp*ai*d till nowe 2 s
paide for makinge his cote & a capp to the foole   xij d
paide for hardne to line the bodies of his coate   iiij d
paide for vij yerd*es* of whitte cotton: 4 s j d to be allon   10
clarke foole a petycote and for lyninge the q*uar*ters   iiij s vij d
of his cote: for mak*ing* of his pety cote: 6 d. s*u*ma: p*ai*d

...

p*ai*d for makinge 22 sut*es* of app*ar*ell to theis p*er*sons
followinge grauntid in mr andersons maioraltye:...   15
for a paire of hose to allo*n* foole: 14 d

...

f 282v *(2 week January)*

...   20

paide to a man w*hich* baited a bere one the sandhill before
mr maiore in rewarde geuen him for his paines com*m*anded   x s

...

f 284 *(1 week February)*   25

...

paide and geuen in rewarde to my lorde oagles Plaiers   xx s

...

f 285 *(3 week February)*   30

...

paide for x paire of showes to theis p*er*sons following
geuen aginst christenmas: henrie dent a paire 2 s Iarrad
dodd*es* a paire 2 s thomas Swinburne foole of captheton
a paire 2 s Iohn lawso*n* a paire 2 s george spenc a pair: xx s   35
2 s peter aiden a paire 2 s allen clarke foole a paire:
4 s bartr*am* fenckle a paire: 2 s 4 d thomas dodd*es*
foole a paire 20 d s*u*ma

5 / sussatt *for* russatt

f 286v *(1 week March)*

...

paide for lether for mendinge Io*hn* lawso*n* & Iarrerd dod*es*
show   xviij d

...   5

f 289v *(1 week April)*

...

paide for a sharte bande to Iohn lawson   iiij d

...   10

f 290v *(2 week April)*

...

paide for a shart to thomas dodd*es* the foole & sewing ytt   xviij d
paide for vj yerd*es* of lin to be Iohn lawso*n* shart*es* & for   15
sewinge of theme   v s vj d
paide for 2 sharte band*es* to Iohn lawson   xviij d

...

paide for gloues & point*es* to Iohn lawson foole   viij d
paide for a shart & a shartband to allon the foole   ij s iiij d   20

...

paide for vj yard*es* of lin to be Iohn lawso*n* shart*es* and
sewing   v s vj d

...

                                                                                                          25

f 292v *(1 week May)*

...

paide for 2 yerd*es* of brode clothe: 10 s 8 d for 2 skins
& pockett*es* 2 s for linnge to his ierken 10 d for threed   xv s ij d
& buttons 4 d for mak*ing* them 16 d. to Iohn lawson   30
paide for a paire of hose to him   ij s 4 d
p*ai*d for 5 yerd*es* & a d of reed russatt to be allo*n*
foole a coate 11 s for 4 yerd*es* & a d of cotto*n* for
lyninge: 2 s 7 d for v yerd*es* & a d of cotto*n* to be   xix s 4 d
him a petticote: 3 s 3 d for mak*ing* of his 2 coates   35
& his hoode: 2 s 6 d
paide for a paire of hose to him   xvj d
paide for 4 yerd*es* & a d of reed russatt to be dodd*es*
foole a coate: 9 s for 4 yerd*es* of cotto*n* to line itt:
2 s 4 d for 3 q*uar*ters of reed [russatt] Carsey to   40
garde itt: 3 s 4 d for white skene: 4 d for 5 yerd*es*   xxiij s 8 d
of cotto*n* to make him a petycote: 3 s for makinge
of his 2 cottes and his hoode 4 s 4 d s*u*ma

...

paide for 2 paire of hoose to allon & doddes 16 d per
paire   ij s viij d
paide for 3 paire of more stockens: bartram fenckle a
paire antonie hall a paire Iohn lawson a cullerd paire: v s ij d   5
2 s 2 d

...

paide for a yerde & a d of reed russatt to be Iohn
lawson a paire of bretches: 3 s for skins & pockettes: v s viij d
[d] 2 s for making 8 d   10

...

f 293v *(2 week May)*

...

paide for 4 paire of showes Iarrerd doddes j paire 2 s   15
Iohn lawson a paire 2 s doddes the foole a paire 20 d   vij s viij d
allon a pare 2 s

...

f 294 *(3 week May)*   20

...

paide to the 4 waittes of the towne for yer
quarteriche   xxvj s viij d

...

                                                                               25

f 294v

...

paide for a hatt to Iohn lawson. 3 s 8 d for lether to
shows   iiij s 8 d
...   30

f 296 *(1 week June)*

...

paide for a nell of canvas to be Iohn lawson a
dublett: 2 s 6 d for stenting hardne to ytt 5 d   35
for 3 yerdes of cotton to line ytt: 21 d for flockes: vj s
4 d for threede & buttons: 4 d for makinge ytt:
18 d. suma paid

...

f 297 *(2 week June)*

...

paide for 2 paire of showes j paire to william dent
2 s 4 d & thother paire to Iohn lawson: 2 s. aginst   iiij s 4 d
whitsunday   5
...

f 297v *(3 week June)*

...

paide for lether for Iarrerd doddes showes & Iohn lauson   ij s   10

...

f 298v *(4 week June)*

...

paide for a paire of hose to Iohn lawson   ij s 4 d   15

...

f 299v *(1 week July)*

...

paide for 2 shart bandes to Iohn lawson   xx d   20

...

f 300v *(2 week July)*

...

paide for lether to Iohn lawsons showes   xij d   25

...

f 303v *(1 week August)*

...

paide for a paire of hose to allan   xvj d   30

...

paide for a paire of shoes to Allon the foole   ij s

...

f 307 *(4 week August)*   35

...

paide to the 4 wates for quarter   xxvj s viij d

...

f 307v   40

...

paide for a paire of hose to Iohn lawson   ij s viij d

paide for a paire of shose to Lawson   ij s
paide for 2 paire hoes to william Dent & Doddes
the foole   ij s viij d
...

5

f 310 *(2 week September)*
...
paid for a shert to allon the foole & sewinge   ij s vj d
...

10

f 313* *(1 week October[1])*
...
paid for keepinge hogmagogge kot this yeare   vj s viij d
...

15

f 313v
...
paide and geuen in rewrde to robert askew waite lyinge
sicke his wife and children commanded   vj s viij d
...   20

f 315 *(2 week October[1])*
...
paide for 4 shartes to Iohn lawson & william dent with
sewing   xiij s 4 d   25
...
paide for lether to Iohn lawsons showes   xij d
...

f 316v *(3 week October[1])*   30
...
paide and spent by thauditors with the 24⟨...⟩ with a
bankett att mistris shaftoes for wine and good chere   xiiij l.
paide and geuen to the musicke their att dynner   xij s
...   35

32 / 24⟨...⟩: 24tie

Chamberlains' Account Books TW: 543/19
f 4 *(1 week October²)*

...

paide to Iohn lawson mr maiores foole yerl*ie* p*ai*d   x s

...   5

f 5v

...

paide for a shart to thom*as* dodd*es* foole &

sewing   ij s vj d   10

...

f 7 *(3 week October²)*

...

paide to Iohn lawson foole for his beddinge and   15
washinge yerlie paide due att michlemas laste   xx s

...

f 8 *(4 week October²)*

...   20

paide for 3 yerd*es* of white cotton to be Io*hn* lauso*n*
a peticol   iij s vj d

...

f 9 *(1 week November)*   25

...

paide to the 4 waites for y*er* q*uarter*iches   xxvj s 8 d

...

f 10 *(2 week November)*   30

...

paide for a pare of hose & showes to allo*n* the
foole   iij s 4 d
paide for leth*er* for mending Iohn lawson his
showes   xx d   35

...

f 12 *(1 week December)*

...

paide to the wait*es* for playinge musicke at thauditt   40
dyn*er*   v s

...

(2 week December)

paide and geuen in rewarde to a skott*es* poyett
com*manded*   v s

...   5

f 13 *(3 week December)*
...
paide for 2 yerd*es* & j q*uar*ter of brode clothe silk*es*
culler to be Iohn lawson bretches & Ierken: 6 s   xiij s vj d   10
p*er* yerde
paide for 3 q*uar*ters of skie cull*er* carsey to be
him a paire of stockins & for a cap to him   ij s vj d
paide for 2 skynnes & pockett*es* to his clothes   iij s
paide for v yerdes of checker cullerd clothe to be   15
thomas doddes foole a coate: 2 s 6 d p*er* yerde   xij s vj d
paide for ix yerd*es* of white cotton to be him a
peticol as also d a yerde & d a q*uar*ter of skie
cull*er* carsey for his stockins   v s x d
paide for skynns & pockett*es* for dodd*es* his clothes   xij d   20
paide for x yerd*es* of white cotton to be allo*n* a peticol   v s
paide for 3 q*uar*ters & d a q*uar*ter of skie cull*er*
carsey to be allon a paire of stockins   xxj d

...
p*ai*d to Iohn lawson for goinge an eraund to ye   25
white house   iiij d
...

f 13v* *(4 week December)*
...   30
paide for a paire of showes to Iohn lawson   ij s
paide for a paire of showes to thomas dodd*es* foole   xx d
all this showes was bestowd in rewarde aginst
christenmas
...   35

1597
Chamberlains' Account Books TW: 543/19
f 15 *(2 week January)*
...   40
paide by Iames graie to j abrahame *(blank)* father
his sonne being one of the townes wates & deed att

leedes he hauing the townes cunisente: & in reward   iij s 4 d

...

f 15v *(3 week January)*

...   5

paide for 2 pare of showes j pare to george bouell
and an other paire to allon the foole   iiij s

...

f 17 *(1 week February)*   10

...

paide to the 4 wates for their q*uarter*iches   xxvj s viij d

...

paide for cloute leth*er* to Io*hn* lawson Iarrerd dodd*es*
thomas gibson & george bouell their showes   iiij s   15

...

f 23v *(1 week April)*

...

paide to Thomas Richardson tayler for makeinge 24   20
gounes to the poore   xxiiij s
paide for makeing Iohn Lawson his cote &
butanes   vij d.

...

paide for makeing Iohn Lawson a Ierkin, & a pare   25
of briches and a pare of short hose and lineing and
buttanes to them   ij s. iiij d
paide for makeeing 2 cottes & j pare of Briches &
harden to line them and buttanes   ij s. v d.

...   30

paide for 2 cottes to Allon & 2 petticotes to Allo*n*
and for lyneing and buttens to them   v s. iij d.
paide for makeeing Thomas Dodd*ees* a cotte & a
petticote & a pare of short hose & a capp & lyneinge
to th*em*   iij s. j d.   35

...

f 24

...

paide to Iohon Lawson for goeinge 3 tymes to the   40
White house   xviij d.

...

f 24v* *(2 week April)*

...

paide more for 6 yearde*es* of blacke russat p*er* xviij d
a yarde for Allones coate   ix s.

...   5

more for a pare of ded soled showes to Iohn
lawso*n*   ij s.

...

more for a paire to Allon dd soled   ij s.
more paide for soleinge of Iohn Lawsones   10
showes   xij d.
paide for 2 paire of stokeinges to Iaret Dodd*es* &
Iohn Lawso*n*   v s
more for ix yardes and D. of white cottane p*er* x d
ayarde for Alland younge   vj s viij d.   15

...

f 25

paide for 5 yeardes of lynn to be Iohn lawson a   20
shirte   v s.

...

paide for a locke to the doore where Allon
dwelte   viij d.

...   25

f 25v *(3 week April)*

...

paide for sewinge 2 sharte*es* to Iohn lawson   vj d.
paide for 2 bandes to Iohn lawson   xij d.   30

...

f 26v *(4 week April)*

...

paide & giuen in rewarde to one of my lord Admyralles   35
menne att mr maiores com*mand*   xx s.

...

f 29v *(3 week May)*

...   40

paide to the 4 weates for there q*uar*triges   xxvj s viij d

...

f 31 *(4 week May)*

...

paide for 2 skines & 2 poketes to Iohn lawson   *(blank)*

...

5

f 31v

...

paide for 2 yardes of brode clothe clay culer 6 s p*er*
yarde to Iohn lawson   xij s.
paide for a showes to him   xx d   10
paide for 2 yardes 3 qarteres of white cottane & for
a nell & d quarter canues   iij s. v d.
paide for a yarde & a quarter of russat   xviij d

...

15

f 32v *(1 and 2 week June)*

...

paide for a pare of showes & soleinge of a pare to
Iohn Lawson   iij s
...   20
paide for a pare of showes to thomas Doddes & for
lether   iij s.

...

f 34v *(3 week June)*   25

...

paide for makeinge a dublite to Iohn Lawson & for
flokes & harden & buttanes & thride to the bota*n*holes   iiij s xj d
...
paide for 3 pare of duble soled showes. j pare to Iohn   30
lawson. j pare to w*illiam* Dente. j pare to tho*mas* gilson   vj s.
...
paide for skines for lyneinge Iohn lawsons briches   xij d
...
paide for a hatt to Iohn lawson   iij s viij d   35

...

f 35 *(4 week June)*

...

paide for a pare of white hose to Allon yownge   xvj d.   40

8 / 6 s: s *converted from* d

paide thomas Doddes to byeing him a pare of hose   xvj d.
...

f 37 *(1 week July)*
...   5
more paid for lether to Iohn Lawsones showes   xij d
...

f 38 *(2 week July)*
...   10
paide to Iohn lawson for runinge of arandes   ij s
...

f 41 *(1 week August)*
...   15
paide for [for] 2 yardes & a quarter of brode popen
Ioae greene 8 s per yarde & for ayarde of stamle
Carsie 5 s per yarde more for 10 yardes of white
cottane 6 d per yaird 10 s & for a quarter of the   xxx s iij d
same stammell Carsey & a quarter of brode greene   20
carsiey 2 s for Thomas Doddes apparill the some is
...
paide for apare of netherstockeinges & 2 shirtebandes
to Iohn lawson   iij s viij d.
...   25

f 42 *(2 week August)*
...
more paide for makeinge thomas Doddes a cott & a Capp   vj s.
more for makeinge him a petticote   viij d   30
paide for lyneinge for the bodie of the cotte   iiij d.
paide for makeinge of gardes to his cotte   x d
...

f 44 *(4 week August)*   35
...
paide to the 4 wates there quartridge   xxvj s viij d
...

f 44v   40
...
paide for makeinge Allone the foole a cote and a capp   ij s.

paide for harden to lyne the booddie of the cotte   iiij d.
paide for makeinge him a petticotte   xij d.
paide more for 2 shirtes clothe & makeinge of them to
Allon   iiij s.
...   5

f 47 *(2 week September)*

...

paide for vij yardes & a q*uar*ter of karsie to be Allan
Younge apparrill ij s vj d p*er* yarde ys   xviij s. j d ob.   10
paide more for iiij yardes of wheete cottane 7 d p*er* yar   ij s iiij d.
more paide to him for 7 yardes of wheete ruge 9 d p*er* yar   v s iiij d.

...

giuen to Iohn Lawson att mr maiores his appointment for
runninge of Arandes   vj d.   15
...

f 48 *(3 week September)*

...

paide for 2 shirtes to Iohn lawson & makeinge of then   vj s vj d   20
...

f 51v *(1 week October[1])*

...

paide for a parre of yallow stockeinges to Iohn lawso*n*   ij s iiij d   25
...

paide for a parr of showes to Iohn lawson   ij s.
...

paide for aparr of showes to Allon the foole   ij s
...   30

f 54 *(2 week October[1])*

...

paide Iohn lawso*n* foole for Runinge of Arandes att mr
maiores his appointment   vj d   35
...

f 57 *(4 week October[1])*

...

paide Iohn Oldam cytizen & clotheworker of london senior   40
for iiij yardes of clothe. to mr *willia*m Iackeson towne

Clarke. 10 s p*er* yarde. 40 s ... for 16 oth*er* yardes & 3
querters to the plumner the waittes & the pauer. 7 s 6 d
p*er* yarde. 6. 5. 7....

...

f 61 *(2 week October²)*

...

paide for a parr of showes to thomas Doddes the foole   ij s
paide for a parr to Iohn Lawsonn the foole   ij s

...

f 65 *(1 week November)*

...

paid   paide to the iiijº waites for ther qvertridges   *(blank)*

...

f 66v *(2 and 3 week November)*

...

paide for canddelles to the cou*r*te of the crounatio*n* daie
att neight   xx d.
paide to the companiy of mr maiores shipp for letting of
gounnes. of the crounatio*n* daie   vij s
paide mr Anthoniyes children w*hi*ch was giu*e*n them in
rewarde. by mr maiore. for ther paines takeinge in   xl s.
playinge of musike of the crounatio*n* daie

...

f 70v *(3 week December)*

...

paide Iohn Lawsonn foole runninge of aranndes aboute
the townes bussines for his charges   iiij s
paide for a parr of stockeinges to Allonn the
foole   xviij d

...

f 72 *(4 week December)*

...

p*ai*d Rickabies weife for washeinge Iohn Lawsonnes
clothes yearlie graunted hir for & in consideracoun
of his paines   xij s

...

1598
Chamberlains' Account Books TW: 543/19
f 75 *(3 week January)*

...

paide for one parr of showes to Iarrett Doddes   ij s   5

...

paide for one parr to Allonn the foole   ij s

...

paide for one parr of showes to Iohn Lawsonn foole   ij s
paide for sollinge Iohn Lawsonnes his showes   xij d   10

...

paide for one parr to littell Doddes the foole   xviij d

...

f 75v   15

...

paide for one parr of hose to Iohn Lawsonn the
foole   [xvj d] ij s
paide for one parr of hose to littell Doddes the foole   xvj d
paide for one parr of hose for Allonn the foole   xvj d   20

...

f 76v *(1 week February)*

...

paide for lether for mendeinge Iohn Lawsonnes showes   xvj d   25

...

f 77v *(2 week February)*

...

paide to the iiij⁰ waittes ther quartridge   *(blank)*   30

...

f 79v *(4 week February)*

...

paide for 2 shirtte bandes to Iohn Lawsonn th foole   viij d   35

...

f 91 *(2 week May)*

...

paide the 4 waittes ther quartridge due att allhallowmes last   40
past   xxvj s 8 d./.

...

f 91v *(3 week May)*

...

paide to the iiij° waittes ther quartridge   *(blank)*

...

5

f 95 *(2 week June)*

...

paide for one parr of showes to Iohn Lawsonn the foole   ij s
paide for one parr of showes to Allonn the foole   ij s/

...   10

paide for j parr of showes to littell Doddes the foole   xviij d/.

...

f 96v *(4 week June)*

...   15

paide for 2 parr of showes j parr to Iarrett Doddes j
parr to Iohn Lawson   iiij s/

...

f 97v *(1 week July)*   20

...

paide wche was given in rewarde vpon mr Maiores his warraunte
to waittes who Came to be hiered to be town waites   x s/

...

25

f 99 *(3 week July)*

...

paide for 2 shirtte banndes to Iohn Lawsonn the foole   xvj d/.
paide for 3 shirttes & for makeinge of them to Iohn
Lawsonn the foole   viij s   30

...

f 103v *(4 week August)*

...

paide to the iiij° Waittes for ther quartridge   *(blank)* 35

...

f 105 *(1 week September)*

...

paide for 2 parr of showes j° to Iohn Lawsonn the foole   40
j° to Nicolson beedle   iiij s/.

...

f 106 *(3 week September)*

...

paide for 2 yeardes & d of brode greene clothe: 8 s. 6 d p*er*
yeard to make a Coatte to Thomas Doddes the foole   xxj s vj d.
paide for one yearde & a q*uart*er of reed d Carsey to   5
garde yt   v s. x d/.
paide for 4 yeardes & d of Cottam to lyne itt 8 d p*er*
yearde   iij s
paide for skeene threedde to stiche his Coate   viij d/
paide for harden to lyne the boddie of his Coate   vj d/   10
paide for j° yearde of Cottame to make a petticotte
to him   v s. x d.
paide for makeinge his Coatte his petticoatte & his hude   vj s 8 d./
paide for 6 yeardes & d of cheecker 2 s 4 d p*er*
yearde to be a coate to Allon the foole: 15 s.   15
02 d. for 6 yeardes of Cottame to lyne the Coatte:
8 d p*er* yeard: 4 s. for 7 yeard*es* of Cottam to   xxvij s viij d/
make him a petticoate 8 d p*er* yeard: 4 s. 8 d.
for harden for lyneinge the bodie of his coate:
6 d. for make*ing* his Coatte his petticoate &   20
Capp: 3 s. 4 d. suma paide ys
paide for 2 yeardes & q*uart*er of brode Clothe: vj s p*er* yearde
to be Irckin & briches to Iohn Lawsonn the ffoole   xiij s vj d/
paide for lyneinge & Buttannes to his briches ⌈Irckin⌉ :
10 d. for 2 shippe skinnes & pockettes to his briches: iiij s/   25
18 d. for make*ing* his Clothes 20 d. suma

...

f 106v

...   30

paide wche was given to waittes who came to be hierd
for towne*es* waitt*es*   ij s/.

...

f 110v *(2 week October[1])*   35

...

paide for sollinge Iohn Lawsonnes his showes   xij d/

...

f 111 *(3 week October[1])*   40

...

paide Thomas Dawltonn for lether d*eliuere*d to Iohn Lawsonn

att diuerse tymes for mendeinge his showes   iij s
...

f 111v

...   5
paide for 2 parr of showes j parr to Iarrett Doddes & jᵒ parr
to Thomas Doddes the foole   iiij s/

...
paide for one parr of hose to Iohn Lawsonn foole   ij s
...   10
paide for a nother parr of hose to Iohn Lawsonn green
culleerd   ij s/
...

f 112 (4 week October¹)   15

...
paide for one parr of showes to Allon the ffoole   ij s/

f 112v

...   20
paide for 3 yeardees & d of secken to make a dublett
to Iohn Lawsonn: 3 s. 6 d. for 3 yeardes of white
cottam to lyne itt 1 s. 9 d. for stynteinge harden   vij s 3 d/
to stynte itt: 5 d. for makeinge his dublett : 16 d.
for buttanes 3 d. suma is   25
paide for one parr of hose to Allonn the ffoole   xvj d
paide for one parr of hose to Thomas Doddes the
foole   xvj d/
...
paide wche was given in rewarde to the waittes of Bostonn   30
att the command of Mr Maiore   ij s vj d/
...

f 116 (1 week October²)

...   35
paide wche was given in rewarde to the waittes of Boston ij s vj d
...

f 120v (1 week November)

...   40
paid   paide to the 4 waittes for ther quartridge   (blank)
...

f 127 *(4 week December)*

...

paide for one parr of showes to Iarrett Doddes: 2 s.... jº parr
to Iohn Lawsonn foole: 2 s & one parr to Thomas Doddes foole:
2 s....   5

...

paide for 2 parr of solles for Iohn Lawsons his showes   xij d/

...

1599   10
Chamberlains' Account Books TW: 543/19
f 128 *(1 week January)*

...

paide for jº parr of showes to Iohn Lawsonn ffoole   ij s/
                                                                                          15
...

f 130 *(4 week January)*

paide to Rickobies his weife for beddinge to Iohn Lawson
the foole & for washeinge his clothes wche was due att   xx s/.   20
michel*mas* last

...

f 131 *(1 week February)*

...   25

paide att mr maiores his com*mand* to my Lorde willabies
players   xl s./

...

f 132 *(3 week February)*   30

...

paide for ledder for mendeinge Iohn Lawsons his showes   ij s/

...

f 132v   35

...

paide to the: 5 waitts in p*ar*te of paymente of: *(blank)* due
to them att Alhallowmes & Candelmes last past beinge   l s./
2 q*uar*ters wages

...   40

38 / 1 *for* 50

f 133 *(4 week February)*

...

paide to Thomas Richeson tailor ... for mak*einge* Iohn
Lawson Ierkine briches & waist ∧ ᶜˡoate: 1: 10:... for
2 parr of stockeinges to Thomas Doddes foole for mak*einge*   5
them: 6 d

...

f 135v *(3 week March)*

...   10

paide for 2 yeardes a q*uar*ter of brode clothe to be
Irckin & briches to Iohn Lawson the foole: 5 s. 4 d
p*er* yearde: 11 s. 11 d. for 2 skines to lyne his
briches: 1: 3: for harden to his Irckenne & buttans: xvij s 5 d/
10 d. for 2 pockeates: 6 d. for 3 yeardes of cottam   15
to be a waiste coate to Lawson: 2: 11: suma is

...

paide for 2 parr of stockesinge*es* to Thomas Dodde*es*
foole   iij s iiij d/
...   20

f 136 *(4 week March)*

...

paide for ledder for mendeinge Iohn Lawsons his showes   xij d
...   25

f 137v *(1 week April)*

...

paide wche was given to my Lorde Staffordes players
com*manded* by mr maior: xx s/   30

...

f 140v *(3 week April)*

...

paide for 3 parr of showes *videlice*t: one parr to Iohn Lawsonn   35
foole one parr to Iane Readeheade & one parr to *willia*m Dente
2 s p*er* p*arr*   vj s/

...

6 / 6 d: *6 converted from 3*
18 / stockesingee*s*: *second* s *blotted, perhaps cancellation intended*

paide to the 5 waites for one q*uarteres* wages due att
Candelmes last   l s/
...

f 143v *(3 week May)*   5
...
paide to the ⌈5⌉ 5 waites for ther q*uar*tridge   *(blank)*
...

f 144v *(4 week May)*   10
...
paide for one cullerred hatt to Iohn Lawson foole   iiij s/
...

f 145   15

Paide for 2 yeardes & a q*uar*ter of brode clothe for
Iohn Lawson foole to be him Irckeinge & briches
5 s 4 d p*er* yearde: 12 s. for harden to his Irckeinge   xij s xj d/
buttans & threede: 11 d. suma totallis is   20
...

f 146 *(1 week June)*
...
paide to Iohn Lawson foole wche was granted vnto him att   25
michelmes last past in rewarde by mr maior his bretheren   x s/
& xxiiijtie
...

f 146v *(2 week June)*   30
...
paide for 2 parr of showes one parr to Tho*mas* Doddes foole &
one parr to William Dente: att 2 s. p*er* parr is   iiij s/.
...
                                                                     35
f 147 *(3 week June)*
...
Paide to Iames Graie for 2 yearde*es* & a halfe of
brode popenioye green to be a coate & a Capp:

2 / l *for* 50
7 / 5 *converted from* 4; *superscript 5 added to clarify correction*

for Thomas Dodd*es* ffoole: 1: 4: 2: for one
yearde of oringe cullerred Carsey for a Petticoate
for him: 4 s. 8 d. for 4 yeardes of white cottam
for lyneinge his Coate 7 d p*er* yearde: 2 s. 4 d. for
one d q*uar*ter of branche cullerred carsie & one   5
q*uar*ter & a naile of oringe culler Carsie: 2 s. 1 d.   xlviij s. iij d/.
more for one q*uar*ter & a naile of brode popenioe
green for gardeinge his Coate 3 s. for 6 yearde*es*
& d of rugg for a nother petticoate for him:
4 s. for Makeinge his Coate petticotes & capp: 10
6. 8: for threed to stiche the gardes: 1 s. for j°d
ₐ ⌐yerd⌐ lynin clothe for lyneinge the bodie of
his coate 6 d. suma

...
                                                                                        15

f 147v

...

paide to Thomas Richeson tailor for makeinge Iohn
Lawson Ircken & briches & 7 coates to 7 poore
wedowes granted to them by mr maior his bretheren   viij s vj d/   20
& the xxiiij^tie att michelmes last

...

f 150 *(2 week July)*

...   25

paide to the Kinge of skotes his musicion*ers* playeinge
before mr maiore his Bretheren in rewarde   xxs./.

...

f 151v *(4 week July)*   30

...

Paide to mr E chr*is*tofer Gaillor of london for the townes
liuereyes as followethe: videli*cet*:... for: 16 yeardes 3
q*uar*ter*s* of newe cullerred clothe to the plummer the
waite*es* & the pauer att. 7 s. 6 d p*er* yearde: 6 li. 5 s.   35
07 d....

...

f 153 *(2 week August)*

...   40
paide for one parr of showes to Iohn Lawson
foole   ij s iiij d

paide for one parr of showes to Thomas Doddes foole   ij s/
...

paide for one parr of stockeinges to Iohn Lawson foole   iij s/
...

f 154 *(3 week August)*

...

paide for ledder for mendeinge Iohn Lawsons his showes   iij s/
...

f 154v *(4 week August)*

...

paide to the 5 waittes ther q*uar*tridge   xxxiij s 4 d
...

f 155

Paide for 6 yerdes of russatt att 20 d p*er* yerde to be
a Coate for Allon the foole: 10 s. for 5 yerdes of
Cottam to lyne itt: 3 s. for harde⌈n⌉ for the bodies: xix s. ix d.
6 d. for 6 yerdes Cottam for his Petticoate: 4 s for 3
yerdes of harden to be him a shirte & for sewinge itt:
2 s. 3 d. suma
Paide to Thomas Richeson tailor for makeinge a Coate &
a Petticoate for Allon: foole: 2 s. 6 d...

...

f 157 *(2 week September)*

...

paide to Thomas Recheson for makeinge a dublet & a petticoate
for Iohn Lawson the foole   ij s vj d./

...

Paide for 4 yerdes of secken to be a dublet to Iohn
Lawso*n* foole: 4 s. 8 d. for 4 yerdes of Cottam: 2 s.   xj s j d/
8 d. for stintinge & Buttons: 9 d. for one waiste
coate to him 3 s. suma totallis is

...

f 157v *(3 week September)*

...

paide att mr maiors com*mand* to my Lorde of Cumberland
his musicions   iij s iiij d./

...

paide for one parr of showes to Allon the
foole   ij s iiij d./
paide for one parr of hose to Allon the
foole   ij s   5

...

f 159v *(1 week October*[1]*)*

...

paide for 2 shirtes to Iohn Lawson foole & for   10
makeinge them   vj s viij d./

...

f 160v *(2 week October*[1]*)*

...   15

Paide to my Lorde Willabies musecions playinge before
mr Maior   iij s viij d/

...

f 161v *(4 week October*[1]*)*   20

...

paide to wedowe Rickobie for washeinge and Beddinge to
Iohn Lawson foole due att Michelmes. yearlie   xx s./

...
                                                                     25

f 162

...

paide for one parr of showes ... to Doddes the foole: 2 s. 4 d.
... for one parr to Iohn Lawson foole: 2 s. 4 d....

                                                                     30

f 162v

...

paide for one parr of stockeinges to Iohn Lawson foole:
one parr to Thomas Doddes foole, & one parr to   v s vj d./
Anthony hall: 22 d p*er* parr is   35

...

f 165v *(1 week October*[2]*)*

...

paide wche was given to the Earle of Penbroughe players   40
in rew*ard*   liij s iiij d./

...

f 169 *(1 week November)*

...

paide to the 5 Waites ther Quartridge   *(blank)*

...

                                                                                              5

f 170 *(3 week November)*

...

paide wche was given by mr maiors appoyntment to my
L*ord* morley his ⌈player⌉ men   xx s./

...   10

f 171v *(2 week December)*

...

paide to Thomas Richeson for mak*ing* 2 parr of stockinges to
Thomas Doddes & Allon the ffoole & vnpaide   vj d./   15

...

***Goldsmiths, Plumbers, Pewterers, Glaziers, and
Painters' Company Book*** TW: 940/3
f 3* *(15 March)*   20

CHR*IST*US Iesus Salvat nos March day
                    1598   15

An Invoic of all the player*es* apperrell/ p*er*tanyng to the   25
Goldsmyth*es* plum*mer*es puderer*es* Glacie⌊*res*⌋ & paynter*es*
Bye beard*es* to the kyng*es* thre & for the messenger—one with
theyr head hayres
It*em* the Cappes & thre septer*es* & thre crownes
It*em* on sterre & twey crownes   30
It*em* box with o*ur* ordenarie & our Playe boik

...

AC ***Tanners' Accounts: Brand*** *MS 18*
NCL: L942.82 N536 B   35
nf

Imprimis paid to the Menstrels on our Rekninge
day at nyght   2 sh.

1600
Chamberlains' Account Books TW:543/19
f 173 *(4 week January)*

...

paide for Candells to the courte to mr maior & mr Deane   5
seeing the schoollers plaie commaunded by mr maior   ij s. viij d/

...

f 175 *(3 week February)*

...   10

paid   paide to the five Waites ther quartridge   *(blank)*

...

paide to George Myburne tailor for makeing hose:
stockinges briches & Capp for william Iackson who   iiij s./
plaide the Clowne in the plaie Commaunded by mr   15
maior to paie

...

f 178v *(4 week March)*

                                                                           20
Paide for one parr of showes ... to Thomas Doddes foole:
2 s. 4 d.... for jº parr to Iohn Lawson foole· 2 s. 6 d.... for
jº parr to Allon the foole: 2 s. 4 d....

...

Paide wche was given to the Earle of Lincolne & my   25
Lorde Dudleys ther players in rewarde by mr Maiors   xl s./
Commaundiment

...

f 179   30
...

paide to Iarrett Hearon & Iohn Hawkins two of the
townes waites ther quartridge wche was due att   xiij s. iiij d/
Alhallowmes last past

...   35

f 179v *(1 week April)*

...

paide to Allon the foole in releife   xviij d

...   40

f 180

...

Paide for iij⁰ yeardes of popingoe greene Clothe to be
a Coate and a Cap to Thomas Dodds foole att 8s. 6 d.
p*er* yearde is: 25 s. 6 d. for j⁰ halfe ell of stamell for   5
gardeing his Coate & his Capp: 7 s. 3 d. for 4 yerdes
of white Cottam for lyneing his Coate: 2 s. 4 d. for   xlvj s. iij d./
vj⁰ yeardes of Cottam for to be him a petticoate:
3 s. 6 d. for thrid for sticheing the gardes: 1 s. for
makeing his Coate petticoate & Capp: 6 s. 8 d.   10
soma is
Paide for 5 yeard*es* of russat to be a Coate for Allon
the foole: 10 s. for 4 yeardes of Cottam for lyneing
his Coate: 2 s. 4 d. for vj⁰ yeardes of Cottam for his
petticoate: 3 s. 6 d. for one yearde of Clothe for   xviij s vij d/   15
lyneing the Boddie of his Coate & Dodd*es* his
Coate: 9 d. for makeing his Coate & his petticoate:
2 s. soma is

...
                                                                            20

f 180v

...

paide for Clothe to be Clothes to the boyes who plaide
the Commodie   vj s. j d/
...
                                                                            25
paide to the 5 waites ther quartridge due att Candelmes
last   xxxiij s. iiij d/
...

paide wche was given to Iohn Lawson foole wche was granted
vnto him att michelmes last by mr maior & the xxiiij^tie   x s./   30
...

f 181 *(2 week April)*

...

Paide for ij⁰ yeardes of sad brode Coales Clothe for   35
Iohn Lawson foole for to make him Irckeing & briches:
12 s. forr iiij⁰ ⌜4⌝ yerd*es* of Cottam: 2 s. 8 d. for   xvj s. x d.
Buttons: 2 d. for makeing his Cloth*es*: 2 s. soma

...

paide for j⁰ yearde 3 q*uar*ters of white Clothe to be   40
a petticoate to Iohn Lawson att j s ix d p*er* yearde   iij s. vj d/
& for makeing of itt: 4 d. soma

...

paide for jᵒ parr of hose ... to Thomas Dodd*es* foole:
14 d. for jᵒ parr to Iohn Lawson: : 20 d. for jᵒ parr
to Allon younge foole: 18 d....

f 182v *(3 week April)*   5
...
paide for ledder for mending Iohn Lawsons his
showes   xij d
...
                                                                       10
f 185 *(3 week May)*
...
paide to the five waites ther quartridge   xxxiij s. iiij d/
...
                                                                       15
f 186 *(4 week May)*
...
Paide for one parr of blew hose to Thomas Dodd*es* foole: 20 d
for jᵒ parr to Iohn Lawson foole: 20 d. for one parr of hose to
Allon younge foole: 20 d....   20
Paide to Thomas Cockrell Cordiner ... for jᵒ parr of showe*es* to
Iohn Lawson foole 2 s. 4 d. for one parr of showes to Allon
younge foole: 2 s. 4 d.... for one parr to Thomas Dodd*es* foole
2 s 4 d...
                                                                       25
f 187* *(1 week June)*
...
paide to Thomas Turner for vj li. of Candell*es* wche was
deliu*er*ed vnto William Iackson when the boyes [laste]   ij s./
playde in the Courte   30
...

f 193v *(1 week August)*
...
Paide to mr Banck*es* for his paines taken in playeing w*i*th   35
his horse before mr maior & his Bretheren Commaunded   xl s./
by mr Maior to paie
...

f 195v *(4 week August)*   40
...
paide to the five waites ther q*u*artridge   xxxiij s. iiij d./
...

f 197v *(1 week September)*

...

paide to Thomas Cockrell Cordiner for one parr of showes to
william Dent: 2 s 4 d for jo paire to Thomas Dodd*es* foole: 2 s.
4 d.... Allon foole jo paire: 2 s. 4 d....   5

...

Paide for jo parr of blew stocking*es* to thomas Dodd*es* foole:
20 d jo parr to Allon the foole: 16 d....

...

                                                                                       10

f 201 *(1 week October[1])*

...

Paide wche was given to a ffrenchman a fune ambule or
rope walker playing before mr maior the aldermen w*i*th   l s./
others in the Manners com*mande*d to paie   15

...

Paide wche was given to the Earle of Huntington his
Players in rewarde   xx s./

...

paide to Dorrathie Bonner for 4 yerdes ½ of russat att   20
22 d p*er* yerde to be a Coate to Allon the foole: 8 s. 3 d.
for 5 yerdes $\frac{2}{1}$ of white russat to be him a petticoate: xvij s. iiij d/
5 s. 1 d. for vjo yerdes of lyning to be him a shirte:
4 s. soma is

...   25

f 202v *(3 week October[1])*

...

paide to Iohn Stoute cordiner for jo parr of showes to
Allon the foole   ij s./   30

...

f 203 *(4 week October[1])*

...

Paide for makeing a Coate & a petticoate ⌈to Allon⌉ & ⌈for⌉   35
harden to the bodies of his coate 22 d.... for jo parr
of Cullered stocking*es* to Allon the foole: 20 d....
paide for one parr of new showes to Thomas Dodd*es* foole   ij s.

...

14 / l *for 50*

f 204* *(5 week October[1])*

...

Paide for one new blew Coate to william Jackson
seriant att Mace wche he had stolne foorthe of the
marchant*es* Courte att ch*rist*ofermm*es* playing the   5
Comidie of Terence before mr maior his bretheren   xxxvj s viij d/
& others 20 s. for a rap*er* and a paire of silke
imbroudered hangers, wche was loste att the
same tyme: 13 s 4 d.: for a duble silke sypers
w*hic*h was loste: 3 s. 4 d. soma com*manded*   10
by mr Maior

...

paide ... for j° parr of stockinge*s* to Thomas Dodd*es*
foole: 19 d....

...   15

f 205

...

paide for makeing a shirte to Allon the foole   vj d/
...   20

1601
Chamberlains' Account Books TW: 543/19
f 279 *(3 week May)*

...   25

Paid to the wayt*es* for their quartridge   xxxiij s iiij d
...

Paide for a Shirte for Allon the foole   xviij d
...

                                                                                             30

f 284 *(3 week July)*

...

Payde for a payer of Shooes for marshall the foole   xij d
more for a shirt to marshall the foole   xij d
...   35

f 285 *(2 week August)*

...

Payde for a payre of Shoes & a payre of hose to Tho*mas*
Dods the foole   iiij s iiij d   40
...

f 286 *(4 week August)*

...

Paid to mr Cooke late vsher of the gram*m*er schole for
halfe a qu*a*rters wages & for his paines in makeinge of a   xl s
plaie befor mr maior, & his brethren   5

...

Payd to Iohn Robinson vid*elicet* for ij yardes, & iij
quarters of motlay to be Cappe Ierkin, & Breches to
marshall the foole at ij s iiij d p*er* yard vj s v d for   ix s j d
lyneinge to his Ierkin, & Breches xij d & for   10
makinge therof xx d totallis

...

f 286v *(1 week September)*

...   15

Payde to Iohn Robinson for cloath, & other charges
for a Cote to Dods the foole vid*elicet* for ij yardes, &
iij *quarteres* of popinIaye greene at ix s p*er* yarde
xxiiij s ix d, more for j yearde of stam*m*ell Kayrsaye
iiij s viij d, more for v yardes & a halfe of whyte rugge   xlij s v d   20
iij s ix d, more for ij yardes, & a halfe of whyte Cotton
xvij d for makinge his cote, his petticote & his
cappe vj s viij d more for a quarter of skene thread to
stiche on the guardes viij d, more for harden to lyne
the boddyes of his cote vj d totallis is   25

...

f 287

...

Payd to five Waytt*es* for their quartridges due at Lam*m*as   30
last   xxxiij s iiij d

...

Payde for the townes Lyvereyes, viz. for iiij° yardes
of Cloath for the towne clarke his seconde gowne
xl s more for lxij yardes of Newe Cooller for the   35
sergeaunt*es* Lyvereyes wherof the plum*b*er had
iij yardes, & a halfe at viij s viij d p*er* yarde   xxxv li. viij s v d
xxvj li. xvij s more xvj yardes, & iij quarters
for the waytt*es* at vij s viij d p*er* yard vj li.
viij s. v d, more for a Baskett to kepe the   40
cloath clene iij s totallis is

...

f 287v *(3 week September)*

...

Payd to Iohn Robinson Tayllor viz.... for ij yardes of
broadcloath at v s. iiij d p*er* yarde to be Ierkin, & breches
to Iohn Lawson x s viij d more for harden to lyne the   5
same xviij d more for buttons to the Ierkin, & for
makinge the Ierkin, & breches ij s...

f 290v *(4 week October[1])*

...   10

Paid for ij paire of Shooes j paire to Ierrard Dods, &
annother paire to Allon the foole   iiij s.

...

f 291v   15

...

payd to [Iarrat] ⌐Thoms¬ Dodds ∧ ⌐fowle¬ for A payr of
showes   ij s

...

                                                                     20

1603
Merchant Adventurers' Book of Orders   TW ₁ 988/2
f 52v *(10 November)*

> At A Court holden the xth of Nouember Anno   25
> Dom*in*i /1603/ Anno.[y] Regni Regis Iacobi

Whereas greate Disorder and abuses, haue been Comitted and
practised by manie of the Apprentices belonginge the bretheren
of this fellowship of m*er*chant*es* aduenturers, as well in their
comm*on* and outward behauior, toward*es* their Superiors and   30
betters, as also in excessive extraordinarie and costlie app*er*ell,
to the [yll] evill example of others of better quallitie and Cariage,
ffor reformac*io*n whereof, yt is orderid and enactid this p*re*sente
daye, by the Gouernor, Assistent*es*, wardens and said ffellowship, 35
that from hence forth no brother or sister of the same, shall
p*er*mitt or suffer, his or [their] her Apprentice or apprentices,
to daunce, dice, carde, Mum, or vse anye musick, eyther by night
or daye, in the streetes neyther to weare anie vndecent app*er*ell,
but plaine and of clothe, vnder x s the yarde, or fustian of or   40
vnder iij s the yeard,...

Visit of James I STC: 17153
np*

...

    On Saterday the 9. of Aprill, his Maiestie prepared towards
New-castle. But before his departure from *Withrington*, he   5
Knighted M. *Henry Withrington*, M. *William Fenicke*, and M.
Edward Gorge. After which taking his leaue with Royall curtesie,
he set forwards towards *New-castle*, being 16. miles from
Withrington.
    To passe the occurrentes by the way, being not very materiall,   10
when his Maiestie drew neare to *New-castle*, the Mayor, Aldermen,
Counsell, and best Commoners of the same, beside numbers of
other people, in ioyfull manner met him. | The Mayor presenting
him with the sword and keyes with humble dutie and submission.
Which his Highnesse graciously accepting, he returned them   15
againe: Giuing also to his Maiestie in token of their loue and
heartie loyaltie, a purse full of Gold. His Maiestie giuing them full
power and authoritie vnder him, as they lately held in her Maiesties
name: Ratifying all their customes and priuiledges that they were
possessed of, and had a long time held. And so passing on, hee   20
was conducted to the Mayors house, where he was richly
entertained, and remained there three dayes.

...

1605   25

Housecarpenters' Meeting Book TW: 903/1
nf*

...

paid for tastinge the drincke ⌐Cuthbart mode¬	vj d
paid for wine	iij s 30
paid for mvsicke	viij d

...

1606

Chamberlains' Account Books TW: 543/21   35
f 179v *(3 week October[2])*

...

Payed to Iohn pott*es* for showes the last yeare as p*er*
bill apeare*es* viz ... Tho*mas* dodes j paire ij s vj d.... Iohn

13 / *catchword* The

Lawson a paire ij s. vj d.... thomas dod*es* a paire
ij s. vj d....
...

f 180v *(1 week November)*   5
...

Payd to Cuthbert Bayley for ij payer of stocking*es* to
*willia*m Dent & Iohn Lawson   v s.
Payd for a windinge & for buryinge of allon the foolle   v s. ij d.
...   10

Tanners' Accounts: Brand MS *18*
NCL: L942.82 N536 B
nf
                                                                         15
paid for a Pound of Suger att Diner   20 d.
paid to a pypper   3 d.
for a Quarte of wyne   8 d.

1607   20
Chamberlains' Account Books TW: 543/21
f 185 *(4 week February)*
...

Pay*e*d for shooe*es* for the poore folke*es* viz.... tho*mas* dod*es*
a pair ij s. vj d.... marshall a paire ij s. vj d.... Iohn Lawso*n*   25
a paire ij s vj d...
...

f 187 *(3 week March)*
...   30

Payed to Anthonny halle for a paire of boot*es* for
Adrian halle viij s & [to Ad⟨...⟩] to marssall the   x s vj d.
foole a pair of shooe*es* ij s. vj d
...
                                                                         35

(4 week March)

Payed w*hich* was giuen to the Lord dudley*ees* plaiers   L s.
...

---

9 / windinge *apparently, but carelessly written*
32 / Ad⟨...⟩: Adrian halle

f 188 *(2 week April)*

...

Payed to the wait*es* beinge vj in nomber for ther ½ yere*es*
fee dewe at candlemas last at xl s. p*er* q*u*artere*es*   iiij li.

5

f 189 *(3 week April)*

...

Payed to Anthony nicholson for iiij payre of shooe*es* to
Iohn Stoke thomas dod*es* foole Io*h*n [s⟨...⟩ke] bullocke   x s.
grace dewe   10

...

f 190 *(4 week April)*

...

Payed to w*illia*m haddiricke for cloth*es* for the towne as p*er*   15
bill apere*es* viz for tho*mas* dod*es* the foole viij yeard*es* of
broat graye friese at ij s. viij d yeard xviij s. viij d. more for
him a yeard & a halfe & halfe a q*uar*ter of red Carsey at
v s. p*er* yeard viij s j d. ½ mor for him vij yeard*es* of whit
cotton for his petticon at xij d p*er* yead vij s. mor for   20
lininge of his coat v yeard*es* of whit cotton at viij d. p*er*
yeard. iij s. iiij d. dd ... more for Iohn Lawson ij yeard*es* of
broad silke russett collor at v s. ⌈vj d⌉ p*er* yeard xj s. ix d.
                              ^
more ffor marshall the foole v yeard*es* of motley at ij s.
viij d. p*er* yeard xiij s. iiij d....   25

...

Payed for a paire of stocking*es* for a cripple ij s.
iiij d for a paire of george carre ij s. & for   v s. vj d.
lether to Io*h*n Lawson to mend [⌈lether⌉] his
shooe*es* j s. ij d   30

...

f 191 *(2 week May)*

...

Payed for pipping*es* for mr maior & his brethren   vj d.   35

...

f 191v *(3 week May)*

...

Payed to Cuthbert Bayley in full of his bille*es* for the   40

---

9 / s⟨...⟩ke: stocke   20 / petticon: c *apparently written over* s

poore folke*es* gowne*es* as p*er* his bille*es* appeare*es* viz....
more for ij yeard*es* of white to be Io Lawson a wast
cote at xx d. p*er* yeard ... for makeinge at cote & a
petticote to tho dod*es* the foole vij s. vj d. for makinge
a sute to mashall ⟨..⟩ foole ij s. iiij d. for makinge at   5
sute to Io*hn* Lawson ij s. iiij d.... for makinge a
wast cote to Io*hn* Lawson vj d.... for skeane to sticth
the garde*es* of tho*mas* dode*es* Coate...

f 192v *(1 week June)*   10

...

Payed to Cuthbert Bayley as p*er* bill appeare*es* viz
for ij shirt*es* for Io*hn* Lawso*n* vj s. vd. for iiij yeard*es*
of hardon to Line tho*mas* dod*es* cote & pettycott &
Io*hn* Lawson*es* & marshalle*es* cloase ij s. viij d. for   15
skean to stitch the gard*es* of tho*mas* dod*es* Coat j s.
for buttone*es* to Io*hn* Lawsone*es* & marshalle*es*   xxv s. ij d.
closse vj d. for makinge tho*mas* dod*es* cote & hate
vj s. viij d. for makinge his petticote xij d. for
makinge a to tho*mas* ffenwicke mr maior*es* porter   20
ij s. for makinge a sute to Io*hn* Lawson ij s. for
makinge a sute to marshall ij s. for makinge at
coat to Anthony god send as p*er* Som*m*a

...

Payed to Anthony nicholson for iiij paire of shooe*es* for   25
tho dod*es* a payre for tho*mas* ffenwicke a paire for marshall   x s.
a payre for bartram ffenkell a payre

f 194v *(4 week July)*

...   30

Payed to *willia*m hadericke for cloath as p*er* bill
appeare*es* tho*mas* dod*es* iij yerd*es* & ½ of broad
green at x s. p*er* yeard xxxv s. for a yeard & iij
q*uar*ter*es* of Red karsey at v s p*er* yeard viij s. ix d.
for vij yeard*es* of broad white cotton at xij d. p*er*   35
yeard vij s. more for v yeard*es* of whit cotton to
line his petticott at viij d. p*er* yeard iij s. iiij d....

f 195*

                                                                                 40

Payed for 3 yeard*es* & a q*uar*ter of black silke Russett
for Iohn Lawson at vj s. p*er* yeard xiij s. vj d. for ij

yeard*es* of broad silke Russett at vj s p*er* yeard for   v li iiij s ij d
marshall xij s. Soma

...

Payed to Cuthbert Bayley as p*er* bill apearee*s* for a payre of
stocking*es* for *willia*m dent ij s. vj d.... for a payre to Iohn   5
Lawson ij s. vj d. for a payre to tho*mas* dod*es* ij s. vj d....
for shirt*es* for Iohn Lawson iij s. ix d....

...

Payed to tho*mas* Swanne for a payre of Shoooe*s* for Iohn
Lawson   ij s. vj d.   10

...

f 196v *(3 week August)*

...

Payed for 7 paire of shooee*s* for tho*mas* dod*es* a   15
payre ij s. vj d. for marchall a payre ij s vj d
for a payre for Io*hn* Lawson ij s. vj d....

...

Payed to the vj wait*es* for one q*uart*ere*s* wagee*s* dewe at
candlemas last   xl s.   20

...

Payed to thomas Swan for a payre of shoooe*s* to Io*hn*
Lawson   ij s vj d

...

                                                                              25

f 198 *(1 week September)*

...

Payed for a free playe to the Lord vriee*s* servaunt*es*   xl s
Payed w*hi*ch was giuen to the player*es* w*hi*ch had the
baboonee*s*   xl s.   30

...

f 199 *(3 week September)*

...

Payed to peter foster for lether d*eliuere*d to Io Lawson &   35
tho*mas* dod*es* by the chamberlainee*s* appoyntment   ij s.

...

f 199v

...

                                                                              40
Payed for ij shirt*es* for tho*mas* dod*es*   vj s. vj d.
Payed for iij band*es* for tho*mas* dod*es*   iij s.

Payed for ij band*es* for Io*hn* Lawson   ij s.

...

f 200v *(2 week October*[1]*)*

...

Payed for iij payre of stockei(.)*ges* for Io*hn* Lawson thomas
& marshall   vij s vj d

...

f 202 *(4 week October*[1]*)*

...

Payed to the vj wayt*es* for ther ½ year*es* stipent dewe at
Lammas Last at 6 s. viij d. p*er* peece   iiij li.

...

f 208v *(4 week November)*

...

payed to the wayts for ther q*uar*ters wayges dew at Allhallow
mase last   xl s

...

f 211 *(3 week December)*

...

payd to Rob*er*t Kell for makinge the poor folkes gownes
as p*er* bill appeareth ... for making marshells Closes
vj s viij d ... for makinge a frese Cote for Thomas Dodes
vj s viij d for makinge a pettye Cote for Thomas Dodes
xij d for makinge a cap and mittens for him xvj d...

Coopers' Accounts: Brand MS 10 NCL: L942.82 N536 B
nf

Impremes for the Mynstrelles   15 d

1608
Chamberlains' Account Books TW: 543/21
f 212v *(4 week January)*

...

payd for a poplye playe at mr Maiors   vj s

...

f 216v *(2 week March)*

...

payd w*hich* was given to the players for a free playe by
mr Maior apoyntment   ij li.

...   5

f 217

...

payd w*hich* was giuen to the players by sundry of the
common counsell for wyne mony   v s   10

...

f 218 *(3 week March)*

...

payd to the eight waytes for a q*uar*teredge dew at Candolle   15
mase last past   xl s

...

f 218v *(4 week March)*

...   20

payd to Iohn Potts Cordinarye as p*er* bill appeareth for
showes to the poor folkes ... Tho*mas* Dodes a payre ij s vj d
... Rober Marsholl A payre...

f 226 *(3 week May)*   25

...

payd to the waytes beinge viij in nuber dew at St Tellenmas
last past   xl s

...

                                                                        30

f 226v

...

payd for mending marsholl the fowle showes   xij d

...

                                                                        35

ff 231-1v *(3 week June)*

...

payd to Symond Bembricke in full of this bill for the poore
folkes Gowenes as by his bill appeareth ... for towe yeardes and
a halfe of Brode Cloath to be marshell clothes at vj s p*er* yeardes   40
apeace xv s — for Carsay to garde his cape j s – vj d for cottom
to line his cape vj d in all iij s for vj yeardes of Lynne to be

marshell towe shartes j s p*er* yearde makinge vj d iiij sherte[⟨.⟩]
baⁿdes ij s towe pare of shorte Hose xiij s for iiij sheape skines
to line marchelles brithes ij s – viij d pocketes vj d v yeardes of
cottom to Lyne his Gerkine iij s – iiij d — Butenes vj d in all
vij s l … for viij yeardes of white frease to be dodes the foole A   5
cote ij s p*er* yeard for a payr of shorte hose to hime ij s vj d in
all xviij s – vj d for x yeardes of white Cottom to Lynne his Coate
j s p*er* yearde for ij yeardes of harne to line his Bodies xj s iiij d
for towe yeardes & a halfe of Carsaye to garde his cape & Coate
v s p*er* yeard for skeynes to stytche his cape & cote j s – iiij d   10
for halfe a yeard of ffrease to be hime A payre of myttines xiiij s
vj d for A pare of shorte hose for foole dodes ij s – vj d…

f 234v *(1 week July)*

…   15

payd to Symond BenBicke in full of all his billes for the poure
folke as by his bill appearethe for to be dodes the folle a cote
iiij y*eardes* and aquarter of Popingoye Greane at viij s — p*er* the
yeard j l – xiiij s — for to Lyne his Cote and be hime a peticote
x y of white coteme at xiiij d p*er* yeardes xj s – viij d for iij   20
y*eardes* of harne to line his cotes & slewes ij s for skine to slyghte
his Coate & cape ij s for ij y*eardes* of Reade stamell to garde his
Coase & Cape at vj s – iiij d p*er yeard* x s – viij d for viij y of
motley to be marchell Clothes and Cape at ij s [⟨.⟩]iiij d p*er*
y*earde* j l. j s. iiij d for lininge to line his Clothes butenes &   25
pocketes iij s – iiij d for towe pare of hose to dodes and marchell
the foule v s…

f 243v *(4 week August)*

…   30
payd which was giuen to the wattes of Hallefax by
mr maiores appoyntmente   xij d
…

f 244   35

…
payd to The wattes ffor ther quarteredge dew at lamess   xl s
…

16 / all: *second* l *written over* h
20, 23 / y *for* yeardes; *no abbreviation mark*
23 / Coase: s *written over* t

f 246 *(2 week September)*

...

payd to Hughe masson sarvant at masse which he disbursed
by mr maioree his appoyntment to the waites of Lenn and   xj s
to poore Soldieres   5
...

1613
Goldsmiths, Plumbers, Pewterers, Glaziers, and
Painters' Company Book   TW: 940/3   10
f 16v

...

Item more payd at our Companye meattinge   0-j-8
Item more spent at our meattinge another tyme   0-1-4
Item paid for the museccke   0-2-0   15
Item more spent vpon our last meatting daye   0-4-0
...

1615
Chamberlains' Account Books   TW: 543/22   20
f 266 *(1 week November)*

...

Payed to the Waittes for ther halfe yeares ffee due
at Michelmas last past   iiij l.
...   25

f 269 *(4 week December)*

...

Payed which was giuenn to the queannes playeres   xl s
...   30

1616
Chamberlains' Account Books   TW: 543/22
f 275v *(2 week May)*

...   35
Paied to the Waites for ther halfe yeares ffee due the
25 of March last past   iiij l.

f 277

...   40
Paied to Iohn Lawsonn which was granted vnto him by
Order of Common Counsell   x s
...

f 278v *(1 week June)*

...

Paied wch was giuenn to Marchell the ffolle in Reward
by Order of Common Counsell   x s

...   5

f 280 *(2 week July)*

...

Paied for the Sargantes waittes and plumeres Leueres
this yeare   xlvj l.   10

f 282

...

Paied to Iohn Lawson in p*ar*te of paymente of his
wadges   x s   15

...

f 285 *(1 week September)*

...

Paied wch was giuenn to the waittes at Lynn for 3   20
Seuerall Tymes   xx s

...

f 286v

                                                                      25

Paied to Iohn Coucke for Clothes to Errington the ffouell
this yeare   xl s iij d
Paied for the Mackinge of his Clothes   vj s viij d

...

                                                                      30

f 292 *(4 week October¹)*

...

Paied to the waittes for ther halfe yeares ffee due at
Michelmas   iij l.

...   35

f 293v

...

Paied to Edward Hall for 2 paire of stookenes to Errington
the ffouell   iij s viij d   40
Paied for 2 shertes and a paire of Stockenes to Bartram
ffenckell and Erringto the ffoulle   ix s ij d

...

f 299 *(3 week November)*

...

Paied Which was giuenn to the Trumpetter   v s

...

f 300

...

Inprim*is* to Iohn Lawsonn   xxx s

...

1617
Chamberlains' Account Books TW: 543/22
f 307v *(2 week June)*

...

Paied to Roberte Riddell ffor Cloth ffor the Sairgaunte   15
waittes and plumeres Leueres and for Clothe to   xliij l xvj s ij d
pore wedowes gounes

...

f 308   20

...

Paied to the waittes for theire Halfe yeares ffee
due the 25 of March last paste   iij l. vj s viij d

...

f 308v

...

Paied wch was giuenn to Iohn Lawson in p*ar*te of
paymente of his ffee   xx s

...   30

1622
Barber Surgeons and Chandlers' Minute Book
TW: 786/1
f 30 *(17 June)*   35

...

Beinge our head meting daye dispursed for our
breakfaste   ⌜xv s⌝

...

more at leanard Carres spent with the Consent of   40
the Companye   v s
to the musicke   v s

dispoursed to the musick at Iohn Clarkes   iij s

...

for the mitions dinners at Iohn Clarks   ij s
dispursed at Leanards Carres / In wine and
tobacco annd to the musicke   xiiij s   5

...

1623
Masters and Mariners' Account Book (Trinity House)
TW: 659/446   10
nf *(month ending 22 July)*

...

It*em* ffor: o*ur* Suppers of S*ai*nt peters ∧ ⌐eaven⌐ wine:
musycke & all: 002 00 00
...   15

1624
Masters and Mariners' Account Book (Trinity House)
TW: 659/446
nf *(month ending 2 February)*   20

...

It*em* To: the: Musytians: for Musycke vpo*n* ye
electio*n* day   000 10 00

...

It*em* ffor: all charges conserninge ye feaste as   25
vyttaylls wyne & beare & whatt soever ells   012 15 08
except Musycke & bread for ye poore w*hi*ch ys
beffore sett downe

...

                                                                        30

(month ending 19 July)

...

It*em* ffor: o*ur*: feaste of Sainte: peter: eaven att
Iane mawes: as vyttaylls, wyne & musycke: 002 03 01
...   35

Barber Surgeons and Chandlers' Minute Book
TW: 786/1
f 33

...   40

Impr*imis* at our diner on our metinge

3 / mitions *for* musitions

day to the musseck	00–05–00
mor for ther diners	00–02–06
for wishinge the linendge	00–02–06
to the maydes	00–01–00
to the power	00–02–04
spent at George mitcoiffe in wine	00–06–08
more spent In beare[r]	00–03–04
at mitsumor spent In wine	00–04–04
to the mussecke	00–02–06
...	

1625
Masters and Mariners' Account Book (Trinity House)
TW: 659/446
nf *(month ending 7 February)*
...

Item ffor: musycke vpon the Election daye:	00 10 00

...

1626
Masters and Mariners' Account Book (Trinity House)
TW: 659/446
nf *(month ending 30 January)*
...

Item for our Dineres on the Liction day	004 10 00
...	
Item for the musick	000 04 00

...

1627
Barber Surgeons and Chandlers' Minute Book
TW: 786/1
f 42
...

Imprymus that was left vnpaid of our head metting	
day and ˄ ⌐that⌐ we spent when Nickolas Bryan	03 li.–08 s–00
was maid fre	
more paid then to the musike and when Thomas	
marchell was fre	00–05–00
...	

Masters and Mariners' Account Book (Trinity House)
TW: 659/446
nf *(month ending 5 March)*

...

Item to museck on the Elxsion day   000 05 00   5

...

1628
Barber Surgeons and Chandlers' Minute Book
TW: 786/1   10
f 45

...

Item payd for our dynners of our heaid meittinge daye
in Rob Spores   1-0-0
...   15
Item for the Mussicks Dynner   3-0
Item geuen to the mussick   5-0
...
Item of midsomer euen for our Suppers   12-0
...   20
Item to the mussick   2-6
...

1629
Saddlers' Minutes Book N: ZAN M13/A3   25
nf
...
Ittem giuen to the muisike with the Consent of
the most parte of the Company   01 s-00 d
...   30

1631
Chamberlains' Account Books TW: 543/24
f 285 *(1 week December)*
...   35
Paid the Waites being 6. in parte of their ½ yeares
stypend due the same tyme   iij li.
...

37 / the same tyme: *Michaelmas 1631 (from earlier entry)*

Paid Thomas Tonstall for playing on the organs his ½
yea stypend due the same tyme   xiij s. iiij d

...

1632   5
Chamberlains' Account Books TW: 543/24
f 287v *(4 week February)*

...

Paid the Organist for repairing the Organs in St
Nicholas Church   iij li. vj s. viij d.   10

...

f 288v *(4 week April)*

...

Paid the Waites being .6. at 10 s per man their stipend   15
due for ¼ at Michelmas 1631   iij li.

...

f 292 *(1 week June)*

...   20
Paid the waites being .6 at xx s per man their ½ yeares
stipends due at Lady day 1632   vj li.

...

f 292v   25

...

Paid the waites being .6. at: 34 s per man for their
liueries   x li. iiij s.

...

                                                                           30

f 293

...

Paid Gawan Preston shoomaker for shooes for the
foole and poore people deliuered since March 1631   xxviij s. vj d.
as per note   35

...

f 295 *(4 week July)*

...

Paid which was giuen by direccion of Mr Maior and the   40

---

2 / the same tyme: *Michaelmas 1631 (from earlier entry)*

Aldermen to Robert Mawpous one of the Townes waites   xx s.
when he was sicke

...

f 296v *(4 week August)*   5
...
Paid him more for cloth and trimming and
making of Wil*lia*m Erringtons Coate petticoate   iiij li. xiij s. iiij d
and stockings as p*er* note
...   10

Masters and Mariners' Account Book (Trinity House)
TW: 659/446
nf *(month ending 23 April)*
...   15
Itim given to the Church toward*es* the repeare
of the Orgines   001 00 00
...

1633   20
Housecarpenters' Meeting Book   TW: 903/1
nf*

...
p*a*id for musick   ij s
...   25

1634
Chamberlains' Account Books   TW: 543/26
f 129v *(3 week November)*
...   30
Paid the waites for their service at St Nicholas church due
at Mich*elmas* 1634 for a whole yeare   v li.
...
Paid the waites being .6. at xx s p*er* man   vj li.
...   35

f 130

...
Paid Iohn Nicholas for playing on the organs of St
Nicholas church   iij li. iij s. iiij d.   40
...

7 / him: *John Pithy, chamberlain (from previous entry)*

1635
Chamberlains' Account Books TW: 543/26
f 131 *(1 week January)*

...

Paid which was giuen by consent of Mr Maior and   5
Aldermen to the kings players   xx s.

...

f 135v *(1 week July)*

...   10
Paid the Waytes being 6 at xx s p*er* man   vj li./

...

Paid Iohn Nichols for playing on the organs of
St Nichol*as*   [v] iij li vj s viij d

...   15

f 139 *(1 week September)*

...

Paid Timothy Cooke Drap*er* for cloth d*eliuere*d for the waites
and Marshalls liueries as p*er* note   xj li. xviij s iiij d   20

...

f 141v *(2 week October[1])*

...

Paid Iohn Nichols in p*ar*te of his ½ yeares stip*en*d due   25
at Michaelmas 1635   xl s

...

Paid Edward Wood Draper for cloth and cotton for the
fooles coate   [⟨.⟩] Liiij s v d

...   30

Masters and Mariners' Account Book (Trinity House)
TW: 659/446
nf *(month ending 5 January)*

...   35
Itim paide to the mewsicke att the Election diner   000 i0 00

...

nf *(month ending 2 February)*

...   40
for wine and victualls when the bretheren had

---

29 / [⟨.⟩]: *probably* [x]

their dinner at Raphe Lomax his   05 i5 06
house vpon the great reckoninge daie
to the musicke that daie their   00 07 06
...
                                                                        5

nf *(month ending 20 July)*

...

paid for wine and victalls as p*er* note of
p*er*ticulers when Captaine pett [⟨..⟩]   07 05 i0
was entertained at Tri*nity* house   10
giuen the Musicke at that tyme   00 i0 00
...

1636
Barber Surgeons and Chandlers' Minute Book   15
TW: 786/1
f 87 *(13 June)*
...

May 28   Item spent on our head meting day in wine   00+10+08
1635   ...   20
          giuen to the musicke and for there dinners   00-03+06
          spent on midsomer euen in wine by consent   00-12 00
          giuen to the musicke   00-04-00

...

                                                                        25

1638
Masters and Mariners' Account Book (Trinity House)
TW: 659/446
nf *(month ending 29 January)*
...   30
p*ai*d Eliz*abeth* winn in p*ar*t payment of the Eleccon
daie dinner and the dinner after the   i0 00 00
p*er*fectinge the ᴧ ⌐last⌐ yeares accompts
p*ai*d the Towens Mizsitiens that daie   00 i0 00
...   35

Bakers and Brewers' Account Book N: ZAN M17/51
nf

...

Impr*imis* for wine att Will*ia*m Mitchisons on St Clement   40
day 1637   00 i6 00

Item to the Musick the same day   00 io 00
...

1639
Butchers' Meeting Book TW: 859/1   5
nf *(19 February)*

...

ffor the ffree supp*er*   3:06:06
To the Musick   0:03:00
...   10

Bakers and Brewers' Account Book N: ZAN M17/51
nf

...

Paid to the Musick   00:10:00   15
...

Visit of Charles I Nalson: *An Impartial Collection I*
p 218

...   20

The King
comes to *Dur-
ham*

        From thence he advanced to *Durham*, where Dr. *Morton* the
Bishop magnificently entertained His Majesty with all the
demonstrations of Welcome and Loyalty for several days, while
the Levies of Horse and Foot were compleated in that County,
and upon their march from *Durham* His Majesty passed forward   25
to *Newcastle*, where he was likewise by the Magistrates received
with great testimonies of Duty and Affection, and magnificently
Entertained; His Majesty to manifest the sense he had of their
kindness was pleased to confer the honour of Knighthood upon
Mr. *Alexander Davison* the then Mayor, *Thomas Riddell* Esq; the   30
Town Clerk, and the Son of Sir *Thomas Riddell* the Recorder.
...

1640
Barber Surgeons and Chandlers' Minute Book   35
TW: 786/1
f 113 v

disbursd at our entrance for the Musicke at
Iohn halls   00-03-00   40
...

1641
Bakers and Brewers' Account Book   N: ZAN M17/51
nf

...

Im*primis* for wine att Richard Tothericks the 23°.   5
of Nouember 1640   01:16:06
Item to the Musick   00:10:00

...

Barber Surgeons and Chandlers' Minute Book   10
TW: 786/1
f 119 col b*

...

                                                     l   s   d
Item giuen to the musicke   00–03–00   15

...

APPENDIXES, ENDNOTES, GLOSSARY

APPENDIX 1
Undated Document

Tailors' Records (copy, 1731?) Black Gate: M 13 / D 10
f 8*

An order that the playes of Tayllers shalbe played upon Corpus
Cristus daye when as the playes is played amiabely and to   5
Assemble tham to gether in thare plaice accustomed & thare to
chose the xij and all other officers &c.

Cancelled Allso it is orderede and agreede that all the Tayllers now being
and in the tym coming & shal be dwellinge in the sam Towne of
Newcastele shall agre and loue together as loving bretheren of   10
that fellowshipe shall gether tham selves together in thare plaice
accoustomed in the sam Towne of Newcastele upon Tyne & shale
every yeare upon Corpus Cristus day when that the playes is
played amiabely assemble tham selves gether in thare plaice
accoustomed and playe thare playes upon thare owne coste &   15
charges after thare order with thare Stewards.

1677 Waits' Ordinary

This ordinary, although of late date, is included in the edition because it gives information about the Newcastle waits, not found in any other source, which may well be relevant to the pre-1642 period. It is given complete (other ordinaries used in the edition are excerpted), and therefore it may also serve the reader as a specimen ordinary of a Newcastle company.

Enrolment Books TW: 544/74
ff 25v–7 *(18 September 1677)*

To all christian people to whom these presents shall come and
cheifely to whom the knowledge thereof shall appertaine wee *Sir*   5
Ralph Carr knight Maior the Alldermen and Sheriffe of the Towne
of Newcastle upon Tine in the County of the Towne of Newcastle
upon Tine doe send greeting in our Lord God euerlasting. Whereas
the Company of Waites and Musecioners of the said Towne are and
haue beene time out of mind an antient Company incorporated   10
ancient ordinary [by] by the name of the ffellowshipp of waites and musetioners
lost. and they haueing Casually lost their [⟨...⟩] said ordinary by which
they were soe encorporated (as is asserted to us) Know yee that
wee the said Maior Alldermen and Sheriffe upon the humble
petion of Robert Wood John Bell Thomas Morre Edward Harbert   15
& Thomas Sweeting members of the said societie taeking the
premisses into our serious Consideracion doe by these presents
grant order establish & decree in Manner and forme following.
ffirst that the said Robert Wood John Bell Thomas More Edward

15 / *second* o *of* Wood *written over* r
17 / si *of* Consideracion *written over* d *and several following letters written over other*
letters
19 / *second* o *of* Wood *written over another letter*; r *of* More *written over another letter*

Herbert Thomas Sweeting shall be one society and ffellowshipp
called and knowne by the name of the ffellowshipp or Company
of Waites & Musecioners in the said Towne of Newcastle upon
Tine aforesaid and that they and their Successors of the said
ffellowshipp or Company soe much as in us lyeth | according to   5
the antient Customes liberties and Lawes of the said Towne shall
be reputed taken and accepted for euer to be a ffellowshipp or
Company and shall haue a perpetuall Succession within the said

Incorporated   Towne and County and liberties thereof as other societies and
ffellowshipps within the same Towne haue and that the said   10
Thomas Moore and Edward Harbert shall be Stewards for one
whole yeare next ensueing the date of these presents and att a
Conuenient place by the said ffellowshipp to be agreed on
yearely foreuer the said ffellowshipp or society upon the ffeast

head meeting   day of St. Iames the Apostle in *euery* ˄ ⌐yeare if it⌐ fall not to be   15
day.   upon the Lords day and if it be then the next day after two
persons of the said ffellowshipp & Company shall be elected and
Chosen by the said Bretheren of most part of them as in their
discretions they shall [f⟨..⟩] thinke most meet to be stewards of
the said ffellowshipp to rule and gouerne the said fellowshipp for   20
the then next ensueing yeare And further wee the said Maior
Alldermen and Sheriffe doe by these presents order and appoint
soe much as in us lieth for us and our Successors that the said
ffellowshipp of waites and Musecioners shall and may from
hencforth for euer by the name of the Steward and ffellowshipp   25
of waites and Musecioners of the Towne and County of Newcastle

power to   apon Tine prosecute suc and Innpleade and be prosecuted Sewed
sue &c.   and Impleaded to be answered and to answer in all manner of
actions Suites and Demands whatsoeuer within the Courts of
Newcastle upon Tine and County of the Same and that the Said   30
Stewarde and ffellowshipp of waites and Museconers or maior
part of them and their [⟨..⟩] Successors for euer shall haue power
and authority to make among themselues such lawfull orders acts

to make lawes.   and lawes as by them shall be thought fitt and Conuenient for
the well quiett and orderly Gouernment of themselues and the   35
transgressors and offendors of or against the said orders acts or
lawes to punish by reasonable fines or penalties of Money as in
the discretion of the said Stewards and ffellowshipp of waites
and Musecioners shall be thought fitt and the transgressors and
offendors in such Case upon refuseall pay the fine or penalty soe   40

27 / Innpleade *for* Impleade

to pay fines

sett on him or them to be utterly remoued and putt of and from
the said ffellowshipp of waites and Musecioners soe to remaine
remoued untill such time as he or they hath or haue willingly
submitted & reconciled himselfe to the said society or ffellowshipp
of waites & Museconers and allsoe payd his or their [e⟨.⟩] fine or   5
fines soe sett and Imposed apon him or them as a aforesaid and
allsoe that euery one of the said ffellowshipp of waites &
Museconers whensoeuer he or they shall be warned by the
Stewards of the said ffellowshippe or either of them or any other
person by their or any of their appointment to come to any   10

to come on
summons

meeting or assembly of the said ffellowshipp of waites and
Museconers either for the makeing or establishing good Lawes &
orders amongst themselues for their well and quiett Gouerment
or for any other businesse Concerneing the said ffellowshipp of

fines for absence
& shortt.

waites and Musecioners ⌜or⌝ any of them shall accordingly repaire   15
att the time hour and place appointed | by the Stewards for the
time being or either of them upon the paine and penalty of
Sixpence to be paid by euery brother of the said ffellowshipp of
waites and Museconers who shall willfully neglect to come and
upon the paine and penalty of threepence to be paid by euery   20
brother of the said ffellowshipp of waites and Musecioners that
shall Come to such assembly after the houre and time appointed
as aforesaid the said paines and penallties to be paid to the said
Stewards of the said ffellowshipp and Socitety for the time being
upon demand to ⌜the⌝ use of the said ffellowshipp of waites and   25
Musecioners for euery time soe offending. And wee the said
Maior Alldermen and Sheriffe doe further order and appoint that
whatsoeuer Brother of the said ffellowshipp of waites and
Museconers att any time of their assemblies or Conuentions shall

fine for words

by vnciuill words reproach and reuile any brother of the Said   30
ffellowshipp of waites and Musecioners such person and persons
shall forthwith pay to the said stewards or one of them demanding
the same to the use of the said ffellowshipp for euery such offence
the sume of two shillings sixpence And that euery brother of the
said ffellowshipp of waites and Musecioners which att any time   35

for strokes &c

of the said assemblies and Conuentions shall strike Smite or beate
any brother of the said ffellowshipp of waites and Musecioners
shall forthwith upon demand made by the said Stewards for the
time being or either of them pay to the use of the said ffellowshipp
for euery such offence the sume of Six Shillings Eight pence and   40
the party beaten to be left to his remedy att Law for his damage
and further wee the said Maior Alldermen and Sheriffe by these

*pre*sents for much as in us lieth doe order that when any person[s]
or persons are or shall be admitted ffree in or amongst the said

Moneys for
freedome

ffellowshipp of Waites and Muse*ci*oners shall pay to the Stewards
for the use of the Company upon such admission to be free
amongst them the sume of Tenn Shillings if he or they Come in   5
by ser*ui*ce to any brother of the said ffellowshipp and in Case he
Come in by patrymony as the sonne of any brother of the said
ffellowshipp then to pay on his admission six shillings eight
pence. And in Case he Come in att the orders Comand and
direction of the Maior and Alldermen of the said Towne for the   10
time being or any seauen of them whereof the maior to be one
then upon his admission In and amongst the said Company which
orders & Comands the said ffellowshipp are hereby enioyned to
obserue and obey then to pay to the Stewards for the use of the

Maior &
Ald*er*men to
appoint freemen
among them /

said ffellowshipp twenty Shillings and none to be admitted to the   15
benefitt aduantage & priuiledge in and amongst the said Company
but such as haue serued or Come in by patrimony as aforesaid
unlesse the Consent approbac*i*on orders & Comands of the said
Maior and Alldermen be first had and obtained in manner and
form aforesaid and further wee the said Maior Alldermen and   20
Sheriffe by these *pre*sents doe order and appoint that noe
Stranger or other person comeing to this Towne professing the

Strange*r*s to be
licensed by the
Maior /

science of a Musician shall be sufferd to teach use or exercise the
aforesaid scienc*e* ⌃ ⌈fo*r*⌉ his benefitt and aduantage untill he be
first licensed and allowed by the Maior of this Towne for the   25
time being upon paine of twenty Shilling. for e*u*ery time soe
offending to be paid for the use of the said ffellowshipp. And
that noe stranger or other person professing the said art shall be

Strange*r*s
offending
to pay 6 s. 8 d

Suffered to play att any wedding or feast or any other meeting
within the said Towne and County or liberties thereof unlesse   30
such stranger or other person be allowed by the Maior for the
time being upon paine of e*u*ery one offending herein for e*u*ery
such offence to pay six shillings Eight pence to the use aforesaid
and that noe fidler piper Dancer upon Ropes and others that
pretends to haue skill in Musicke nor any such as goe about with   35
mo⌈c⌉cons or shewes shall att any time here after be suffered to
practize in this Townes or liberties thereof without the license of

ffidl*er*s &c.
offending to
pay x s

the Maior of the Said Towne for time being first had & obtained
upon paine of e*u*ery one offending herein to forfeit tenn Shillings
to the use aforesaid | And wee the said Maior Alldermen and   40
Sheriffe by these *pre*sents as much as in us lieth doe for the better
maintenance and Incouragement of the said waites & Musi*ci*oners

and that they may the better Continue to be men of Skill and
Knowledge in Musicke) order and appoint that [if] att any
marriage within this Towne & liberties therof the persons to be
married or ∧ ⌜any⌝ of their freinds be disposed to haue any
musicke that they shall haue the Waites before any other and if   5
any other doe serue att such Marriages by the license and Consent
of the Maior for the time being they shall allow & pay to the said
waites three shillings fourpence for euery such marriage upon
the paine & penalty of tenn Shillings to be paid by euery such
person soe licensed to serue att such marriages for euery time   10
they shall offend herein in the non payment of the said sume to
the use aforesaed all such paines and penalties sume and sumes of
money are and shall be had obtained recouered and gotten by
action of debt in the Courtor Courts to be held in the Guildhall
of the said Towne or in such other manner and forme as the   15
Maior and Alldermen shall appoint nominate and direct.
Prouided allwayes yat the said waites and Musecioners and their
successors shall for euer hereafter be ready and attendant on [of]
all occasions to doe and performe their duty in all matters and
Clauses whatsoeuer belonging & appertaineing to the science and   20
Imployment and obseruant and obedient to all such orders
Comands and directions as shall or may be giuen by the said
maior Alldermen otherwise this present grant and authoritie and
all things therein Contained shall utterly cease determine and be
uoid whensoeuer itt shall seeme fitt and expidient to the said   25
Maior Alldermen or any seauen of them whereof the Maior to be
one soe to expresse and declare & publish the same And wee the
Said Maior and Alldermen Sheriffe doe order and appoint that if
any Contrauorsy shall arise twixt any Brethren of the Said
ffellowshipp or any other person whatsoeuer about any fines or   30
other things relateing to their ffellowshipp science or Imployment
that upon application or Complaint of the parties greiued to the
Maior and Alldermen and the deliberate heareing thereof
whattsoeuer shall be determined by the said Maior and Alldermen
they shall yeild their conformity thereunto. In Wittnesse whereof   35
wee the said Maior Alldermen and Sheriffe haue hereunto sett
our hands and Caused the seale of Maiorallty of the said Towne
of Newcastle upon Tine in such Cases used to be hereunto affixed
[In] the Eighteenth day of September in the Nine and twentith
yeare of the raigne &c. Annoque Domini 1677   40
                    Ralph Carr maior

Marginal notes:

None but the waites to play att mariages vnlesse licensed

if licensed to pay 3 s. 4 d

euery offender x s

Waites to be diligent other =wise ordinary to be void.

Maior & Aldermen Judges of their contrauersies

3 / i of this written over e   17 / t of their written over s

APPENDIX 3
Table of Saints' Days and Festivals

Only saints' days and festivals referred to in the text are listed. No attempt is made to record all variant spellings.

Allhallowmas, Hallowmas	1 November
Candlemas	2 February
Corpus Christi Day	Thursday after Trinity Sunday
Lady Day	25 March
Lammas	1 August
Michaelmas	29 September
Midsummer Day	24 June
St Clement's Day	23 November
St Ellenmas (St Elyngmes, St Tellenmas, Saintelmas)	3 May
St James' Day	25 July
St John the Baptist's Day	24 June
St John the Evangelist's Day (St John before the Latin Gate)	6 May
St Loy's Day (ie, St Eligius)	25 June
St Peter's Day	29 June
St Thomas' Day	21 December
Whitsunday	7th Sunday after Easter

Endnotes

4–5   544/72   f 64v
Collated with N: ZAN M13/A3a, f 1. 544/72 has been chosen as the base text because it is earlier, based on an original document, and more accurate.

5   ZAN M13/B33 A f 180
After the first sentence of the ordinary, there is no further reference to the procession or play, although one would expect such a reference in an ordinary of a date as early as 1438. There is however a reference to the duty of 'all Skinners now dwelling in this Towne or repairing to dwell in the said Towne' to 'Amicably Yearly upon I Tuesday next after the Feast of St Michaell the Archangell [their head meeting day] ... Meet and Assemble themselves together in their accustomed place of meeting...' (ff 180-1). Variants of the formula 'amicably yearly' are used in several ordinaries in the context of the procession and play; see, for example, the Tailors' Ordinary of 1537 (p 22, l. 35) and the Curriers, Feltmakers, and Armourers' Ordinary of 1545 (p 23, l. 18). The expected reference to the procession and play in the Skinners' Ordinary may have been introduced by this formula, and the transcriber (presumably John Potts) may have left it out because he mistook the second occurrence of the formula for the first.

7–8   544/72   f 51v
The purpose of the meeting in the Carlolcroft is uncertain. The head meeting day of the company was St John's Day in May (6 May), and on this day too, according to their ordinary, the members of the guild were required to assemble at 6 am in the Carlolcroft.

8–9   988/1   f 3
Another version of this order is entered on f 4 (at the back of the book) in the same volume. The f 3 version is chosen as the base text because it is part of the first enrolment of acts of the company. Both versions have been crossed out by diagonal lines in ink (but not the second act on f 3, p 9, ll. 8–15). On f 3, final 'm' and 'n' frequently end in a flourish, here deemed otiose. On f 4, there are several otiose macron marks.

12   543/212   f 25v
The word '*sergeant*' is expanded from the abbreviation ff^{gt} which occurs often in the 1508–11 section of the Chamberlains' Accounts. The abbreviation is used in the accounts as a designation for several named individuals who were paid wages or fees, notably one John Yong, whose duties

included the levying of obligations, presenting of fines, etc. John Yong is mentioned, as 'a sergeaunt att the mace' of Newcastle, in a record of Star Chamber litigation of 1510 (I.S. Leadam, *Select Cases before the King's Council in the Star Chamber*, vol 2, 1509–44, Selden Society Publications 25 (London, 1911), p 70). The 1516 Star Chamber decree (see Introduction, pp ix–x) indicates that sergeants at mace were elected annually in Newcastle. The form '*ſyanſ*' for '*sergandes*' occurs in the accounts for 8 April 1511 (p 16). But the abbreviation may be for 'servant,' not 'sergeant,' as the word 'servant' was commonly used for 'sergeant' at this time (OED servant, sense 2c), cf 'sarvant at masse' in the Chamberlains' Accounts for 2 week September 1608 (p 148, l. 3).

14 543/212 f 71
The next heading in the MS is also for 18 May; presumably, one of the two headings is erroneous. The sequence of the headings is 11, 13, 14, 15, 16, 18, 18, 22, 24, 25 May. Nowhere else in these accounts is the same date found in consecutive headings.

15 543/212 f 84
The payment is presumably for dancing before the mayor; see the entry for 28 June 1510.

19–20 ZAN M13/A3b(2)
A few otiose brevigraphs occur. The noun 'ingreetness' ('Ingreetnesses,' l. 25) is otherwise unknown, but there is a verb 'engreaten' meaning 'make great, aggravate (an offence)' and a derived verbal noun 'engreateninge'; see OED under 'engreaten.' The mark of abbreviation used signifies 'er' and 'ri' as well as 're' elsewhere in the document. The word used in the same place in the similar Tanners' Ordinary is 'Inquietnesses' (p 18, l. 12), but it does not resemble the present form.

20 940/1
Letters and words missing in TW: 940/1 are supplied from TW: 861/1, a 17th-century copy of 940/1 which follows the original closely, though it does not keep all of the original spellings.

21–3 98/1/3 mb 1–2
The ordinary is dated not by the date given near the beginning (8 October 1536) but by that at the end, the date of the signing and sealing of the document.

23 151/1/1
Several otiose flourishes occur.
    The section omitted after 'Robert Lewen Mayor' gives the names of other civic officials, and the date of the document (incorporating a fulsome reference to Henry VIII), is given as 'the *(blank)* day of the Monethe of *(blank)* in the xxxvj[th] yere of the reign of ... Henry the viij[th].' The date in the heading of the edition, however, is that found at the end of the ordinary, the date of the signing and sealing of the document: 'the ffirst Day off Octobre in the xxxvij[th] yer of the reign of king Henry viij[th].' The year 1545 is part 36 Henry VIII, part 37 Henry VIII. Robert Lewen was mayor from Michaelmas 1544 until Michaelmas 1545.

23–4 988/1 f 34
The account for this year is given complete except for dating headings and signatures.

24–6   988/1   f 27
Another version of this act is found in the Merchant Adventurers' Book of Orders 1554–1627,
TW: 988/2, f 4. It begins as follows:

An Acte Conceryng the Apperell and behauoure of
Apprentices mayd in Nouember Anno Domini 1554o
fforso Muche as at this present there is gret disorder as well in the excessyue
Apperrell as other mysbehauoures of Apprentices, as in wearyng ∧ ⌜garded⌝
cotes, Iagged hose lyned or drawn out with sylke, cut shoes, daggers cros the
backe / As also vsyng of dyce; cardes; mummyng; daunsyng; typplyng in
alehouses with other lyke suche [b] mysbehauors so that these theyr
mysbehauors and Insolent doynges; ar rather fytt for ragyng Ruffyanes then
decent for honest Apprentices ffor Reformatyon wherof it is Enacted
accorded and Agreed the xxiiij^th day of Nouember Anno 1554 by mr
Cuthbert Ellysone Gouernoure thassistennteswardons andwhole felowshippe;
that from hensforth no brother therof shall permyt or suffer his Apprentice;
to daunce; dyce; carde; or Mumme; or vse any gytterns by nyght in the
streates; or suffer his Apprentice to weare [within] any cutt hose; cotes or
other Apperrell which shalbe garded; stytched; welted; or layde with layce or
[dwa] drawne out with sarsnett, taftay, either any kynde of sylke cutt
shoes, cut or pounced Ierkyns or any other suche curyous Apperrell/...

Cf also the act of 1603, p 139.

41–2   543/14   f 178
Lammas (p 42, l. 4) was one of the annual fair days in Newcastle (by grant of King John).

55   543/15   f 295v
The word 'tydes' is not certain, as the first two letters are written in the bowl of the tail of an 'h'
from the preceding line (as is, for example, the word 'to' in an interlineation in the fifth item for
4 week May 1568, f 294), and are difficult to make out. However, what looks like the top of the
fine, slightly curved vertical stroke of the scribe's 't' is visible, and there is a cross-stroke which is
like the bar of a 't' leading to a 'y'. There is also a trace of what appears to be the tail of a 'y'
leading up to the beginning of the following 'd'. The word is found elsewhere in the accounts, as
in an entry for 1 week August 1566, f 247: 'Item paid to a laborer for gatheringe of stonnes
frome befor the ⌜new⌝ kye vj tyddes at iij d the tyd.' The dictionaries do not record the form,
but it may be a variant of 'tod' meaning 'load,' sometimes 'a load of a definite weight' (OED
tod, sb.2, sense 2).
    The word 'lyinge' is also not certain, though the first letter, with bowl not quite closed, does
look more like other 'l's' than other 'b's' in this hand. If 'lyinge iij tydes' is the correct reading,
the meaning is presumably 'laying three loads,' with reference to the spreading of coarse material
such as sand over the road surface so as to give the pageant vehicles more stability when they are
set down; cf the Chamberlains' Accounts entry for 1 week August 1568 (p 55). The verb 'lie' is
sometimes used transitively, instead of 'lay' (OED lie, v.1, sense 15). Sixteenth-century Newcastle
records, including the Chamberlains' Accounts, refer constantly to 'the New Quay,' only rarely to
'the Quay'; probably the New Quay is the main quay, to the east of the Sandhill. Of course, this
entry does not imply that plays were performed on the New Quay.

55   543/15   f 297
(Thomas) Rudderfurthe appears regularly week by week in the accounts in this volume, carrying
('leddinge') sand and stones to the paver. 'The Head of the Side' was the usual name for the upper
end of the steep street called the Side, where the slope of the hill begins to level out below St
Nicholas Church.

57–8   Dept. of Palaeography and Diplomatic D.R.III.2   f 123v
'This examinate' is Henry Brandling, brother of Sir Robert Brandling, who was four times mayor
of Newcastle. Henry is arguing that although Sir Robert desired to make a will in 1568, the year of
his death, he never did so, and that therefore the court should accept a document dated 1 January
1562 as Sir Robert's last testament, despite the objections of others. Early in his deposition Henry
states that he reported his conversation with Mr Tankerd and Mr Salvayn to Sir Robert on Trinity
Sunday, ie, the Sunday after Whitsunday. If the Friday on which Sir Robert died was the Friday
after Trinity Sunday, ie, the day after Corpus Christi Thursday, then the 'ix or xij dayes or
therabout' may be explained as 'about nine or twelve days before Sir Robert's death,' which would
describe Whitsunday. Madeleine Hope Dodds (*Archaeologia Æliana*, 3rd series, 11, 46) and others
regard this passage as evidence that the Newcastle Corpus Christi plays were performed the day
after Corpus Christi. But the phrase 'after the plays' is vague, and as used here need not imply that
the plays were on the same day as the dinner to which Christopher Chaitor was invited.

58   544/72   f 46
The Cooks' Ordinary of 1575 has been entered twice in the Enrolment Books, in 544/72, ff 45v–6v,
and 544/73, ff 54–5. The differences are insignificant. A note in 544/72, f 45v, below the heading
'Coaques Ordinary,' explains: 'Thorough mistake enrolled afterwards Libro quarto folio 54o'; and
there is another note in 544/73, f 54, below the heading 'Cookes Ordinary': 'Thorough mistake
enrolled heretofore Libro Tertio, folio 45o.' 544/72 has been chosen as the base text because it
is the earlier enrolment, undated, but coming between enrolments dated 1668 and 1669. The
544/73 enrolment is dated 14 January 1673. At the end of the 544/72 version there is a note, in
the same hand as that of the enrolment date in 544/73: 'Januarij 14th. 1673 Examined.'

70   543/16   f 165v
Fools might hold a bladder or a bag in their hands instead of a bauble. See Stephen Hawes, *Pastime
of Pleasure* 3488–91 (quoted by Welsford, *The Fool*, p 123):

> To vs came rydynge on a lytall nagge
> A folysshe dwarf nothynge for the warre
> With a hood, a bell, a foxtayle and a bagge,
> In a pyed cote...

82–3   543/18   f 235
The figure 'vj' (p 82, l. 31) is clear, with the 'v' converted from 'ii,' but the scribe may have intended to convert original 'iij' into 'v,' not 'vj.' Five yards of cotton costing 3 s 4 d would give
a price of 8 d per yard, which is the price of white cotton in two other items in this entry.

113   543/18 f 313
There is a doodle, like a jigsaw-puzzle piece in the shape of a rounded letter 'H,' in the left-hand margin beside the 'hogmagogge' item.

115   543/19 f 13v
The two fools are last in a list of nine people who were given shoes for Christmas.

117   543/19 f 24v
Perhaps 'ded' and 'dd' are for 'doubled' (ie, double). See another item in the same entry, 'more for a pare to george bouell 3 [ie, triple] soled showes ij s.' Double-soled shoes were common; see the entry for 3 week June 1597, p 118.

132   940/3 f 3
The page, like several others at the beginning of the book, has been ruled with pairs of parallel lines across the top and down the sides. The heading takes up the central space between the parallel lines at the top of the page. The lettering of the heading is formal but variable: 'XPS Iesus Salvat nos' is in large lettering in purple ink; 'March day 15' is in smaller lettering, in black ink with a greenish tinge; '1598' is in black ink; a simple scroll-like decorative motif is used. The entries below are in a rather rough cursive script. Despite the variety of ink and lettering, there is nothing on the page incompatible with the date 1598. The item is followed by a list of names and occupations of members of the company which extends to the foot of the page. Some of the names in this list are also found in entries for the year 1599 on the next page.

135   543/19 f 187
William Jackson was town clerk (pp 120–1) and a sergeant at mace (p 137).

137   543/19 f 204
The Chamberlains' Accounts entry for 3 week February 1600 (p 133) also shows William Jackson to be an actor.

140   STC: 17153
John Stow and Edmond Howes, in *The Annales, or Generall Chronicle of England* (London, 1615), p 819, give an account of the visit of James I, the first part of which is evidently taken from *The True Narration*, with some slight compression of wording. After the phrase 'and remained there three dayes,' the *Annales* account continues as follows:

> Sunday the tenth of Aprill, his Maiestie went to the Church, before whome
> preached the Byshoppe of Durham: Munday hee bestowed in viewing the
> Towne, the manner and beautie, the Bridge and Key, being one of the fayrest
> in all the North partes. Besides hee released all prysoners, except for treason,
> murther, and papistrie, giuing summes of money for the release of manie that
> lay for debt. So ioyfull were the Townes-menne of Newcastle of his MAIESTY
> being there, that they thankefully bare all the charge of his house-holde, during
> the time of his abode with them.

140   903/1
Presumably the payments for wine and music relate to a dinner, though the context gives no further indication.

143–4   543/21 f 195
The figure 3 (p 143, l. 41) is clear, but the calculation is for two and a quarter yards. The sum of £5 4 s 2 d includes the previous item on f 194v.

155   903/1
Four items further on in the account there is a reference to 'the feaste' at which the music may have been performed, but the context gives no further indication.

159   786/1 f 119 col b
The Barber Surgeons and Chandlers' Minute Book has a further list of expenses for two dinners on f 9, as numbered from the back of the book, but no year date is given. Under the heading 13 June occur two successive entries: 'more geuen to the musecke 4–0' and 'more payd for ther diners 2–0.' Under the heading 25 December is: 'Dis bourst by the Consent of the Compony at Georg Horslyes for wine and to bakoy and musike –9–6' (with '6 d' written above the '–9–6'). The name George Horsley is found in several other entries in the Barber Surgeons' Minute Book, from 1619 to 1636.

Endnotes Appendix 1

163   M13 D10 f 8
There is a scattering of otiose macron marks over various letters. The order is undated, but it is preceded in the MS by an order dated 1560 and followed by several orders dated 1587, or 6 June 1587. As the arrangement of orders in the book seems to be generally chronological, a date between 1560 and 1587 is indicated.

Glossary

The glossary is selective; only words and phrases likely to be unfamiliar to a modern reader, or which occur in an unfamiliar form or sense, are included. It is assumed that the reader is familiar with common spelling alternations in otherwise easily understood words. Where variant spellings of the same glossed word occur, all are entered, under a headword which is normally the first spelling in alphabetical order. However, where this would result in an odd or rare spelling becoming a headword, a more common spelling has been given precedence. Spellings separated from their main entries by more than two intervening entries have been cross referenced.

Manuscript capitalization has been ignored. Only the first three occurrences of each form are given, with page and line numbers separated by an oblique stroke and followed by 'etc' if the form occurs more than three times. If the form occurs in marginalia, this is indicated by a lower-case *m* following the page and line reference.

Works consulted:

Cunnington, C. Willett and Phillis Cunnington. *Handbook of English Costume in the Sixteenth Century* (London, 1954).
Kurath, Hans and Sherman M. Kuhn. *Middle English Dictionary*. Fascicules A.1–0.4 (Ann Arbor, 1952–81).
Wright, Joseph. *The English Dialect Dictionary*. 6 vols (Oxford, 1898–1905).
The Compact Edition of the Oxford English Dictionary. 2 vols (Oxford, 1971).

Abbreviations

adj	adjective	phr	phrase	pr p	present participle
adv	adverb	phrs	phrases	pp	past participle
attrib	attributive	pl	plural	sg	singular
gen	genitive	poss	possessive	v	verb
inf	infinitive	pr	present	vb	verbal
n	noun	prep	preposition		
perf	perfect	pron	pronoun		

absence mony *n phr* money paid in fines for absence from guild meetings 23/37

abused *pp adj* misguided 25/16

accordid *pp* agreed, decided 21/32; **acordit** 8/15

adwydyng *see* **auoydeing**

adytt dynnar *see* **auditt dynner**

aggre *v inf* agree, unite, be united (with) 21/7; **agre** 163/10; **agree** 4/20; **aggred** *pp* 21/6; **agreed** 4/19, 8/5, 21/32, etc; **agreede** 163/8; **agreit** 8/15

aldermen *n pl* civic magistrates, next in dignity to the mayor, in Newcastle acting also as justices of the peace 3/10, 4/5, 4/34, etc; **alldermen** 164/13, 164/21, 165/22, etc

alleres *adj pl gen in phr* **at ther alleres costage** at the expense of all of them, at their expense 22/36-7; **att their allers costage** 6/3; **at thair allers costagez** 7/11

althyng *pron* everything 17/24

ambule *see* **fune ambule**

amyt *pp* admitted, permitted 9/10

antik *adj* antique, ancient 20/31

arlles *n* earnest money, pledge, first payment 27/26

assistantes *n pl* senior members of guild (of merchant adventurers) 25/30; **assistentes** 139/35

auditt dynner *n phr* dinner on the occasion of the audit 79/34, 86/24; **adytt dynnar** 48/24; **awdite dynner** 52/3, 57/10; *art and n phr* **thauditt dyner** 107/37, 114/40; **thauditt dynner** 86/22, 100/19

audytt *n* annual examination of civic accounts, hearing in connection with this (?) 37/4

auncient *n* ensign, banner 100/11

auoydeing *vb n* avoidance, elimination 7/24, 18/12; **adwydyng** 19/24; **avoydyng** 21/25

austyns *adj pl in phr* **the freres austyns** the house of the Austin or Augustinian friars 10/22

avoyd *v inf* avoid, eliminate 20/32

awdite dynner *see* **auditt dynner**

awdithe supper *n phr* supper on the occasion of the audit 40/27

awdyt banket *n phr* banquet on the occasion of the audit 48/25

awen *pp* owed 24/18

awn *adj as n* own (lodging) 10/25

bagge *n* bag, bladder (for fool) 70/41

bande *n* neck-band, collar (for shirt) 35/31, 39/2; **bandes** *pl* 35/32, 117/30, 144/42, etc; *see also* **shart band**

bankouttes *n pl* banquets 57/11

banndes *see under* **shart band**

barkers *n pl* tanners of hides 18/19

barwarde *see* **berward**

baund *see under* **shart band**

bayn off the play *n phr* the banns or proclamation of the play 14/21, 14/25; **bayn off the playe** 17/3; **bone of the play** 56/18, 56/19-20m; **bonne of the play** 56/26

beareman *n* bear-keeper who led the animal about for public exhibition 69/16

beddell *n* executive officer of a guild 22/40

beedle *n* apparitor 123/41

beer *n* barley 8/21

behofe *n* benefit 20/18; **behoofe** 19/3

beldyng *pr p* building 13/42

bend *n* band, strip (of leather) 94/3

berward *n* bear-keeper who led the animal about for public exhibition 11/9, 11/14, 15/4, etc; **barwarde** 42/10, 47/23, 52/27; **berrward** 14/33; **berrwerd** 13/20; **berwardd** 16/11; **berwarde** 33/27; **berwerd** 15/3

blackett *pp adj* 'blacked,' dyed black (?) 85/10

blew *n* blue cloth 41/38; **blewe** 34/11

boddie *n* upper part of coat or other garment (*often pl with sg sense*) 124/10, 134/16; **bodie** 97/1, 97/6, 119/31, etc; **booddie** 120/1; **boddyes** *pl* 138/25; **bodies** 109/9, 130/20, 136/36, etc; **bodyes** 65/37; *see also* **ouerbodies, vpper bodie**

bodie *n* corporation, body 4/21; **body** 18/37, 20/10

bone, bonne *see* **bayn off the play**

bouthemen *n pl* boothmen, merchants of corn 23/39

branche cullerred *adj phr* branch coloured, brown (?) 129/5

brasenge *vb n* embracing 25/19

breches *n pl* breeches, kind of short trousers 138/8, 138/10, 139/4, etc; **bretches** 78/4, 80/36, 80/41, etc; **briches** 116/26, 116/28, 118/33, etc; **britcheis** 61/7; **britches** 62/41, 64/24, 66/2, etc; **brithes** 147/3; **brytches** 107/8; **pretches** 82/20

brether *n pl* 'brethren' of the mayor, the aldermen (?) 60/15; **brethere** 38/32; **bretheren** 31/21, 50/38, 128/26, etc; **bretheringe** 44/2; **bretherynge** 40/18, 48/2; **brethren** 86/21, 91/15, 91/27, etc

broad *adj* broad, applied technically to certain fabrics distinguished by their width 142/23, 143/32, 143/35, etc; **broat** 142/17; **brod** 34/38, 41/38, 42/1, etc; **brode** 38/13, 38/15, 39/11, etc

broadcloath *n* a fine woollen cloth of plain weave, two yards wide 139/4; **brod clothe** 43/16, 53/35; **brode cloath** 146/40; **brode clothe** 35/17, 43/12, 68/9, etc; **brodes clothe** 92/29; **brothe cloth** 99/26

brother *n* member of a guild 4/17, 18/23, 22/39, etc; **brether** *pl* 23/4; **bretheren** 139/29, 156/41, 163/10, etc; **brethren** 25/31, 168/29

bye beardes *n phr pl* false beards (?) 132/27

cairsaye *n* kersey, a twilled (ribbed) woollen cloth, usually coarse 50/19, 52/39, 54/15, etc; **cairsey** 82/29, 88/5, 105/5, etc; **carsay** 30/36, 146/41; **carsaye** 28/15, 30/34, 46/3, etc; **carsey** 82/9, 83/36, 110/39, etc; **carsie** 119/18, 129/5, 129/6; **carsiey** 119/21; **cayrsaye** 28/16, 34/14, 34/41, etc; **kairsey** 96/38, 108/38; **karsey** 143/34; **karsie** 120/9; **kayrsaye** 138/19

canddyll *n* candle wax, tallow, etc 14/3; **candell** 55/25

cap *n* cap (especially as distinctive item of fool's attire) 105/2, 105/11, 107/31, etc; **cape** 34/23, 35/1, 39/15, etc; **capp** 82/37, 89/42, 95/35, etc; **cappe** 138/8, 138/23; **capes** *pl*

28/26, 28/27, 30/39, etc; **cappes** 28/17, 132/29

carde *v inf* play cards 25/35, 139/38

cardeng *vb n* card-playing 25/18

cariage *n* deportment, conduct 139/33

care *n* pageant car, pageant vehicle 29/22, 57/22, 57/25, etc; **kare** 55/24, 55/27, 55/31; **carres** *pl* 55/37

carmelistes *adj pl* Carmelite, with reference to the Carmelite friars 10/4

carsay, carsaye, carsey, carsie, carsiey *see* cairsaye

castelles *n pl* upper rims of torches, shaped like castle turrets, hence the torches themselves (?) 56/25(2)

casually *adv* accidentally 164/19

cayrsaye *see* cairsaye

certeficat *n* bill of lading (?) 79/31; **certificate** 86/4; **certyficate** 92/34

chamberlayne *n* officer who receives civic revenues 71/3; **chamberlainees** *pl* 144/36

cheecker *n* cloth of chequered pattern 124/14; *in phrs* **checker clothe** 64/16, 69/27; **checker cullerd clothe** 115/15

clark *n* secretary of corporation 8/28; **clerk** 29/31; *see also* **town clerk**

clarke *n* lay officer of parish church 94/27; **clarkees** *poss* 47/38; **clarkes** 51/29; *see also* **vnder clarke**

clere *adj and adv* (paid) in full, fully 17/24(2), 17/26

cloth *n* cloth, woollen unless otherwise specified 29/18, 99/28, 150/15, etc; **cloath** 138/16, 138/34, 138/41, etc; **clothe** 25/41, 25/42, 30/2, etc

clothes *n pl* clothes 61/11, 64/20, 69/33, etc; **cloase** 143/15; **cloathes** 103/4; **closes** 145/25; **closse** 143/18; **cloth** 102/32; **clothe** 89/15; **clothees** 134/38; **cloths** 88/19, 101/28

clotheworker *n* maker of woollen cloth, a member of the twelfth great livery company of London 120/40

cloute lether *n phr* leather for mending shoes 116/14

coales clothe *n phr* some kind of cloth 134/35

coat *n* coat, sometimes a sleeveless close-fitting garment coming no lower than the waist, sometimes loose, with skirts and sleeves 142/21, 143/16, 143/23; **coate** 78/39, 82/33, 96/39, etc; **coatte** 124/4, 124/13, 124/16, etc; **coit** 50/20; **coite** 49/17, 50/17, 52/38, etc; **coot** 29/19, 73/38, 75/9; **coote** 49/20, 50/21, 50/22, etc; **coott** 34/12, 39/12, 41/39, etc; **cot** 29/20, 34/39; **cote** 109/8, 109/12, 116/22, etc; **cott** 34/14, 34/41, 35/1, etc; **cotte** 34/20, 34/22, 34/42, etc; **koate** 99/32; **kot** 113/13; **coates** *pl* 95/19, 110/35, 129/19; **cootes** 61/22, 64/28, 65/39, etc; **coottes** 28/20; **cotes** 25/19, 25/42, 82/39, etc; **cottes** 28/17, 28/25, 30/36, etc

college *n* body of ecclesiastics, clergy 10/4

comen welth *see* common wealth

comin gilde *see* common guild

cominalltie *n* corporation of town (mayor and burgesses) 21/4; **cominalty** 4/12

common *adj* general 139/31

common assent *n phr* general assent 4/14, 5/3-4, 6/4, etc; **comen assent** 20/10; **commyn assent** 3/17; **comon assent** 7/12; **comyn assent** 21/3

common counsell *n phr* administrative body of a corporate town, in Newcastle originally the twenty-four electors 146/10, 148/42, 149/4

common guild *n phr* corporation of town (mayor and burgesses) 4/6, 4/35, 5/32, etc; **common gyld** 12/15; **commyn gilde** 3/11; **comin gilde** 19/31-2; **comon gyld** 7/5

common wealth *n phr* general good 18/11, 18/15; **comen welth** 19/24, 19/29

commyn assent, comon assent, comyn assent *see* common assent

contrathe *n* country, region 29/38

contynentt *adj* restrained, patient 8/21

coot, coote, cootes, coott, coottes *see* coat

cordinarye *n* shoemaker 146/21; **cordiner** 135/21, 136/3, 136/29

coriors *n pl* tradesmen who coloured and dressed tanned leather 23/14

corn powder *n phr* gunpowder (which was 'corned' or granulated) 55/26

costage, costagez *see under* alleres

cot, cote, cotes, cott, cotte, cottes *see* coat

cotton *n* cotton material 64/18, 65/35, 73/40, etc; **coteme** 147/20; **cottam** 124/7, 124/17, 125/23, etc; **cottame** 124/11, 124/16; **cottane** 117/14, 118/11, 119/19, etc; **cottin** 85/10; **cotto** 96/40; **cottom** 146/41, 147/4, 147/7; **cottonn** 69/29, 82/24, 82/34

councelling *pr p in phr* **councelling himself** taking counsel with himself, deliberating 18/8-9; *see also* incounceyllyng

coupers *n pl* tradesmen who made and repaired casks, tubs, etc 3/12, 3/16

cours *n in phr* **in cours** in (due) order 21/12

court *n* meeting (of members of company) 139/25; **courte** 25/31

courtor courts *n phr pl* quarter-sessions (?) 168/14

cowlling *vb n* polling, cutting the hair 52/9

craftesmony *n* money paid by crafts, *ie*, financial contribution to merchant adventurers' company made by constituent companies of mercers, drapers, and boothmen (?) 23/38

croones *n pl* crowns 57/32

cunisente *n* consent 116/1

cut shoes *n phr pl* shoes with leather slashed ornamentally 25/36; **cutt shoes** 25/20

cuthose *n* hose slashed ornamentally 25/36

daylles *n pl* planks, timbers (of fir or pine) 38/39

dd, ded *see* duble soled

defyned *pp* determined, decided 4/2

deliberate *adj* considered, careful 168/33

denyed *v perf 3 sg* refused 58/9

depending *pr p* awaiting settlement 18/6; **dependyng** 19/16

depose *v inf* make deposition 58/18

determine *v inf* come to an end 168/24

detten *vb n* 'dighting,' making, preparing (?) 57/30, 57/32; **dightinge** 55/8

dobell gloves *n phr pl* gloves made from material of double thickness (?) 41/7

doubtyd *pp adj* redoubted, feared 21/2

doyes *v pr 3 pl* do 3/15

draper *n* merchant of woollen cloth 35/16, 156/19, 156/28; drapers *pl* 23/38

duble *adj* (of a kerchief or band) wound round twice (?) 137/9

duble soled *adj phr* having soles made from material of double thickness, or in two layers 118/30; *perhaps abbreviated in* dd soled 117/9, ded soled 117/6

dublet *n* body-garment, usually close-fitting, worn by men over shirt or petticoat 130/30, 130/33; dublett 82/22, 82/24, 82/25, etc; dublite 118/27

election day *n phr* day on which annual election of principal officers of guild took place 151/22; election daye 152/17; eleccon daie 157/31; elxsion day 153/5; *see also* liction day

election diner *n phr* dinner on election day 156/36

ell *n* a measure of length, 45 inches 134/5; nell 111/34, 118/12

emankes *prep* amongst 8/17

entrance *n* (occasion of) admission to membership of a guild 158/39; entraunce 23/32

feate of marchaundize *n phr* mercantile business 25/27

fellowes *n pl* brethren, members of the same guild 22/34

ffre *adj* possessed of citizenship or guild membership, with attendant privileges 22/14; ffree 19/36, 167/2; fre 9/10, 152/37, 152/39; free 18/22, 167/4

ffreas *n* a coarse woollen cloth with a heavy nap on one side 69/37; ffrease 147/11; frease 147/5; frees 88/19, 93/17; frese 145/26; friese 142/17; *see also* welche fres

ffree supper *n phr* supper held by guild on the occasion of the admission of new members 158/8

ffullers *n pl* tradesmen who beat cloth, to clean or thicken it 7/21

fin monaye *n phr* money collected from fines (?) 53/8

flockes *n pl* a material consisting of the coarse tufts and refuse of wool or cotton, used for quilting garments, etc 97/13, 111/36; flokes 118/28

foice *n* abundance 10/33

fre, free *see* ffre

frease *see* ffreas

free play *n phr* play performed in front of, and without charge to, the general public 92/17; free playe 144/28, 146/3; *see also* poplye playe

freedome *n* (granting of) guild membership 167/4m

freemen *n pl* guild members 167/16m; fremen 23/32

frees, frese, friese *see* ffreas

fres *see* welche fres

fune ambule *n* funambulist, rope-walker 136/13

fustian *n* a kind of coarse cloth made of cotton and flax 139/40

gaird *v inf* trim, ornament with 'guards' (*see next entry*) 52/40, 54/15; gairde 50/20, 61/5, 61/15, etc; gard 34/41, 42/1, 46/4, etc; garde 39/13, 42/23, 105/5, etc; gayrde 38/15, 49/20; gairding *vb n* 76/12, 76/16; gairdinge 65/33; gardeing 134/6; gardeinge 129/8; garding 34/20; gardinge 96/38; garded *pp adj* 25/19, 105/10

gairdes *n pl* 'guards,' bands of decorative material used as borders or trimmings on a garment 61/20; gardees 143/8; gardes 26/2, 39/16, 119/32, etc; guardes 138/24

gappys *n pl* gaps, openings of some kind to facilitate progress of procession (?) 14/9; gayppis 14/15

gartins *n pl* garters 89/33

generall diner *n phr* annual dinner for all the members of a guild 23/3

generall playe *n phr* play mounted by the townspeople 72/21; generall plaies *pl* 62/14, 63/10, 71/31; generall plays 63/24 gerkine *see* ierken

gitterns *n pl* citherns, guitar-like instruments 25/20; gytterns 25/35

glacieres *n pl* makers of glass 132/26; glaciers 21/5

gounnes *n pl* guns 121/22

grean *adj and n* green (cloth) 34/38, 39/11, 46/5, etc; greane 65/31; green 125/11, 143/33; greene 119/20, 124/3; gren 38/13; grene 88/5, 96/36; *see also* popenioae greene

guardes *see* gairdes

gyrtthis *n pl* girths; (encircling) straps 14/2

gytterns *see* gitterns

habitanns *n pl* inhabitants 10/16

haire buttons *n phr pl* buttons made from hair 85/13

hanged *pp* hung with decorations 10/16

hangers *n pl* loops on sword-belt from which sword was hung 137/8

harden *n* a coarse linen fabric made from hards (coarser parts of flax or hemp), or from tow 69/40, 73/41, 76/22, etc; hardne 77/14, 82/32, 84/40, etc; hardon 143/14; harnde 83/31; harne 80/18, 82/25, 94/10, etc

head hayres *n phr pl* wigs 132/28

hierman *n* hired man (not a member of a guild, but hired by a member of a guild?) 22/10, 22/11; hiredman 21/15

hoase *see* hose

hobie horse *n phr* figure of horse, made of wickerwork, etc, and worn by performer 50/37; *see also* horse

hoes, hoies, hoise *see* hose

hoistmens *n pl gen* hostmen's, men who gave lodging to, and conducted the business of, visiting merchants 55/23; ostmen 24/10

hom and a felde *adv phr* 'home and afield,' out and back again (?) 38/39

hose *n pl* breeches and long tailored stockings sewn together to form a single garment; some-times, after about 1550, used for breeches portion only 25/19, 51/17, 71/7, etc; hoase 98/10; hoes 113/2; hoies 52/35; hoise 49/22, 50/6, 50/7, etc; hoose 26/1, 111/1; hos 33/37;

hoses 25/40, 31/1, 57/16; hosse 28/27, 34/23, 60/4, etc; hosses 39/18, 41/34; houses 44/9; housses 45/19; howsses 37/24; hoysse 29/20; *see also* short hose

horse *n* hobby horse 135/36; *see also* hobie horse

iacoppyns *adj pl* Jacobins, Dominicans, friars of the Order of Preachers 10/5

iagged *pp adj* cut ornamentally, slashed 25/19

ierken *n* close-fitting jacket with full skirt, worn by men over doublet 78/4, 78/10, 78/12, etc; gerkine 147/4; ierkin 116/25, 138/8, 138/10, etc; ierkine 127/4; irckeing 134/36; irckeinge 128/18, 128/19; ircken 129/19; irckenne 127/14; irckin 124/23, 124/24, 127/12; ierkens *pl* 25/36

incounceyllyng *pr p in phr* incounceyllyng hym selfe taking counsel with himself, deliberating 19/20; in councillyng hym self 20/37-8; *see also* councelling

ingreetnesses *n pl* aggravations 19/25

innpleade *v inf* sue 165/27; impleaded *pp* 165/28

iustices of peace *n phr pl* inferior magistrates appointed by sovereign's special commission (*in Newcastle, the justices of the peace were the aldermen*) 4/5, 4/34, 18/17; iustice of peas 3/10; iustices of pece 21/1; iustices of pese 7/4; iustices of the peace 5/31, 18/9-10; iustices of the kynges peace 19/21-2

kairsey *see* cairsaye

kare *see* care

karsey, karsie, kayrsaye *see* cairsaye

keill *n* keel-load, the quantity (something over 20 tons?) of coal, etc, carried by a keel (a flat-bottomed vessel used on the Tyne and Wear rivers for carrying coal) 55/14

kest *v perf 3 sg* cast, threw (or vomited, with reference to a fire-eater?) 55/31

koate, kot *see* coat

kye *n* quay 55/14

laid *n pl* loads 53/27

laytyng *vb n* 'letting,' hindering, *in phr* haff

laytyng be prevented 8/22

leccion *n* election, *in phr* gyff leccion vote 9/11

leddinge *vb n* bringing 55/36

lether skynnes *n phr pl* pieces of leather, used in lining garments 76/34, 87/27, 90/13; *see also* sheape skines, skine

letten *pp* allowed 87/25

lettine *pp* handed over (?) 29/8

licknes *n* likeness, effigy 99/33

liction day *n phr* day on which annual election of principal officers of guild took place 152/25; *see also* election day

lik *n* likeness, effigy (?) 106/30

lin *adj and n* linen 83/28, 89/41, 90/42, etc; lyn 29/18, 32/3, 35/29, etc; lyne 30/2, 37/20, 42/31; lynn 51/13, 53/2, 54/22, etc; lynne 146/42

linendge *adj and n* linen 152/3; lynin 129/12; lynnynge 28/19

loodging *vb n* provision (?) 93/3

louppes *n pl* wall-openings, embrasures 10/17

lyinge *pr p* laying 55/15

lyn, lyne *see* lin

lynin *see* linendge

lyninge *adj* linen *or vb adj* lining 78/11

lynkes *n pl* torches 53/25

lynn, lynne *see* lin

lynnclothe *n* linen cloth 58/38

lynnynge *see* linendge

lyttinge *pr p and vb n* dyeing 42/21, 49/18

mache *n* 'match,' cord, etc used for ignition 55/25

markyn *vb n* 'marking,' taking note (?) 58/15

marshall *adj* martial 72/21; martiall 72/25

marshalls *n pl gen* marshals', *ie*, sergeants' (?) 156/20

masse *n* mace 10/10; *see also* sarvant at masse, seriant att mace

mawndy *n* (*attrib*) Last Supper, used of the food served to Christ and the disciples at the Last Supper 29/16

mercers *n pl* merchants of silk and small wares 23/38

mettes *n pl* foods, dishes 10/34

moccons *n pl* 'motions,' puppet-shows 167/36

mode *v perf 3 sg* made 140/29

monthe pence *n phr* monthly payment to merchant adventurers' company made by members 23/34

motlay *n* a worsted cloth of mixed colours giving a mottled effect 138/8; motley 142/24, 147/24

moued *v perf 3 pl* brought to court 18/6; moved 19/16

mum *v inf* act in dumb-show or mummers' play 139/38; mvm 25/35

mummyng *vb n* acting in dumb-show or mummers' play 25/18

mylke & watter clothe *n phr* a kind of cloth of the colour of milk and water, *ie*, bluish-white 61/3; mylke and water clothe 61/12

naile *n* measure of length for cloth, 1/16 yard = 2¼ inches 129/6, 129/7

naturall *adj as n* natural fool, one who is born simple-minded, though he may still be a performing fool 99/39; *in phr* naturall foole 104/29; naturell fool 107/17

neck *n* that part of a garment which covers the neck 41/15; necke 37/22, 39/2, 46/25, etc; *in phr* shart neck 45/26; sharte neke 51/14; *pl* shart nekes 47/29

nell *see* ell

nether stockes *n phr pl* stockings 105/13

netherstockeinges *n pl* stockings 119/23

new colloured *adj phr* neutral-couloured (?) *or adj* new and coloured (?) 104/24

new cullerd *adj phr* new-wool-coloured, neutral-colored (?) 99/25–6, 99/28; newe cullerred 129/34; newe cooller *n phr* cloth of neutral colour (?) 138/35

occurrentes *n pl* occurrences, events 140/10

officers *n pl* sergeants (*see* sargant) 99/27, 106/22

opayn *prep and n in phr* opayn to pay on pain of paying 7/14

ordenarie *n* ordinary or 'charter' of guild, document of incorporation 132/31; ordinarie

4/28, 5/25, 7/21, etc; **ordinary** 3/27,
164/18m, 168/20m, etc
ordenaunce *n* ordering, direction, instruction
7/11; **ordinance** 3/16, 4/13, 5/3, etc;
ordynance 21/13, 23/16; **ordynaunces** *pl* 20/7
ordonnaunce *n* artillery 10/20
organs *n pl* organ 87/24, 89/2, 89/7, etc;
orgines 155/17; **orgons** 11/25, 16/5, 16/18, etc
ostmen *see* **hoistmens**
ouerbodies *n pl* upper part(s) of coat, etc where
it fitted the body 89/41; **ouerboids** 103/4;
see also **boddie, vpper bodie**

pagente *n* a pageant or play in the Corpus
Christi cycle; a vehicle on which a pageant
or play was mounted (but it is not clear that
the latter sense applies in any of the
Newcastle instances) 17/34; **pagiant** 21/16,
23/20; **pajent** 29/28; **pageants** *pl* (*sg sense*)
6/8; **pagions** 18/32, 20/5
pawper *n* paper 55/25
pee *n* coat of coarse cloth worn by men 105/4,
108/36
peticote *n* small coat or waistcoat worn by men
beneath the doublet 88/36, 90/1, 90/8, etc;
paticott 42/28, 42/29; **peticol** 114/22,
115/18, 115/21; **peticot** 80/14, 105/3;
pettecotte 33/40, 33/41; **petticoate** 124/18,
124/20, 129/2, etc; **petticoatte** 124/13;
petticon 142/20; **petticote** 52/33, 74/18,
74/38, etc; **petticott** 64/26, 74/3, 143/37;
petticotte 120/2, 124/11; **pettycote** 52/36,
97/10; **pettycott** 143/14; **pettye cote**
145/27; **pety cote** 101/29, 109/12; **petycoate**
90/2; **petycote** 97/9, 104/40, 107/23, etc;
pettecotes *pl* 69/34; **pettecottes** 69/31;
petticotes 116/31, 129/10
pippinges *n pl* pipings, music (?) or pippins,
apples (?) 142/35
plumber *n* tradesman who sold and/or worked
with lead 138/36; **plumer** 68/12, 79/30,
86/2, etc; **plummer** 129/34; **plumner** 121/2;
plumeres *pl* 149/9, 150/16; **plumers** 21/5;
plummeres 132/26

pocketes *n pl* small bags or pouches, attached
to garments or detachable, used for carrying
purses or other small articles 147/3, 147/26;
pockattes 65/38, 69/40; **pockeates** 127/15;
pockettes 87/27, 93/27, 95/20, etc; **pocktes**
90/13; **poketes** 118/3; **pokettes** 64/23
pointes *n pl* laces or cords with metal tags, used
as fastenings, especially for attaching hose to
doublet or coat 50/8, 50/23, 54/25, etc;
pountes 42/33, 45/25; **punttes** 31/8
pollynge *pr p* cutting the hair of 40/3; **povllinge**
59/12, 68/26; **powling** 33/3, 36/9; **powlinge**
48/17; **powllinge** 57/4; *see also* **poullinge**
popenioae greene *n phr* 'parrot green,' (cloth of)
light green or blue-green colour 119/16–17;
popenioe green 129/7; **popenioye green**
128/39; **popingioye grean** 76/10; **popingoe
greene** 134/3; **popingoye greane** 147/18;
popiniaye greene 138/18
poplye playe *n phr* play performed in front of,
and without charge to, the general public
145/39; *see also* **free play**
poullinge *vb n* cutting the hair 51/32
pounced *pp adj* ornamentally slashed, pinked,
jagged 25/36
pounseng *vb n* ornamental slashing, pinking
26/2
pountes *see* **pointes**
povllinge, powling, powlinge, powllinge *see*
pollynge
poyett *n* poet, storyteller (?) 115/3
premisses *n pl* aforesaid (matters) 164/24
presents *n pl in phr* **these presents** the (present)
document 62/12, 164/11, 164/24, etc
pretches *see* **breches**
princypall *adv* first 9/5
pudereres *n pl* pewterers 132/26; **puderers** 21/5
punttes *see* **pointes**
pyper *n* piper 57/28; **pypper** 141/17

quarter *n* (*sometimes attrib or gen*) quarter;
period of three months of the financial year
13/3, 13/14, 15/15, etc; **quartter** 13/27,
15/37, 16/17, etc; **quarteres** *gen* 128/1,

144/19; **quarters** 126/39, 138/4, 145/18;
quarterees *pl* 142/4

quarter *n* measure of length, especially for cloth:
¼ yard or 9 inches 32/3, 34/40(2), etc;
qarteres *pl* 118/11; **quarteres** 41/32, 46/1,
50/4, etc; **quarters** 34/16, 34/38, 39/11, etc;
querters 121/2

quarteriche *n* quarterage, quarterly payment or
wages 28/4, 30/14, 31/26, etc; **quarteredge**
146/15, 147/37; **quarteryche** 45/31;
quartrich 56/12; **quartriche** 50/30, 50/32,
51/9, etc; **quartridge** 119/37, 122/30,
122/40, etc; **quartryche** 48/35, 48/37, 49/34,
etc; **quartteriche** 40/35; **quateriche** 47/10;
quarteriches *pl* 77/3, 78/25, 80/6, etc;
quartridges 138/30; **quartriges** 117/41;
quertridges 121/14

quarters *n pl* skirts (of coat) 109/11

quear *n* choir 36/31; **queare** 33/16; **quer** 40/30

raper *n* rapier 137/7

rassatt *see* **russat**

rates culler *n phr as adj* rat's colour, *ie*, dull grey
88/21, 90/4; **rattes culer** 82/19

read *adj and n* red (cloth) 38/15, 39/13, 39/16,
etc; **readc** 34/40, 42/22, 61/5, etc; **red**
142/18, 143/34; **rede** 57/21; **rced** 89/39,
95/9, 96/38, etc; **reede** 52/37

reckoninge *vb n in phrs* **great reckoninge daie**
day on which accounts for the year were
made up 157/2; **rekninge day** 132/38–39

recorder *n* chief legal officer appointed by city,
magistrate 21/38, 158/31

resauid *pp* received 23/32; **resceyued** 20/19;
resseived 11/25, 14/32; *in phr* **ressaved of**
taken out of, kept back from (?) 17/23

revested *pp* dressed (in ecclesiastical garments)
10/3, 10/12, 10/23

rod *v perf 3 sg and pl* rode 41/8; *in phr* **rod the
fayr** opened the fair by riding in procession
42/4–5; **rod ye faire** 59/41 *see also* **ryddinge**

rosmare *n* rosemary (spice) 57/29

rossell *n* rosin, resin 55/24

rouffes *n pl* ruffs; circular frills worn at neck or

wrist 27/40; **ruffes** 30/2, 33/36, 35/30

rowll *n* roll, register (of names) 8/26, 8/27

ruge *n* a shaggy woollen material 120/12;
rugg 89/40, 90/1, 90/7, etc; **rugge** 138/21;
rvgge 61/17, 69/30

russat *n* a coarse homespun woollen cloth,
originally of a reddish-brown or neutral
colour 73/38, 117/3, 118/13, etc; **rassatt**
103/20; **russate** 51/15, 61/7, 66/1; **russatt**
89/39, 95/9, 97/3, etc; **russett** 41/30, 41/36,
47/30; *see also* **silke russett**

ryddinge *vb n* riding (of the fair) 59/37; *see also*
rod

sad *adj* dark-coloured 134/35

sargant *n* sergeant, an executive officer of the
law, charged with enforcing judgements,
summonses, etc 30/6; **sairgaunte** 150/15;
sergeant 12/8; *pl gen* **sargantes** 30/6, 43/13,
46/32, etc; **sergandes** 16/20, **sergantes** 56/23;
sergauntes 79/27, 85/41, 92/29; **sergeauntes**
138/36

sarvant at masse *n phr* servant, *ie*, sergeant, at
mace 148/3; *see also* **seriant att mace**

sarveed *see* **serued**

sarvis *see* **seruice**

saylltwyn *n* twine of a kind used in sewing sails,
here used as thread or candle-wick 14/3;
sayltwyne 55/25

scearsnett of corde *n phr* sarcenet (a fine
lustrous silk material) woven from silk
thread (?) 100/10

science *n* craft 167/23, 167/24, 168/20, etc

secken *n* 'sacking' used as dress material, of fine
or coarse quality 125/21, 130/33

**sergandes, sergantes, sergauntes, sergeant,
sergeauntes** *see* **sargant**

seriant att mace *n phr* sergeant at mace (the full
title of a Newcastle sergeant), *ie*, carrying a
mace as badge of office 137/4; *see also*
sarvant at masse

seruandes *see* **servaunt**

serue *v inf* serve, perform 168/6, 168/10

serued *v pl 3 perf* served time as apprentice

165/17; **sarveed** *sg* 22/1; **serv⟨.⟩d** 26/10

seruice *n* service as apprentice 167/6

seruice booke *n phr* book containing forms of
divine service, especially the Book of
Common Prayer 83/8

servaunt *n* servant, subordinate, apprentice
25/14; **seruandes** *pl* 9/2; **servauntes** 25/3,
25/4

servauntes *n pl* members of a company of
players attached to the name of a noble
patron 144/28

serv⟨.⟩d *see* **serued**

service *n* service, assistance 155/31; **sarvis** 52/21

servyng *pr p* serving time (as apprentices) 25/10

sesmony *n* money raised by levy or fine 23/37

sessing *vb n* assessment or levying of financial
contribution 18/34; **sessyng** 20/7

shart band *n phr* neck-band or collar for shirt
83/22, 91/12, 92/14, etc; **shartband** 110/20;
shart baund 81/23, 82/38, 84/41; **sharte
bande** 110/9; **shart bandes** *pl* 76/4, 87/30,
89/22, etc; **shart bands** 88/14; **shart bannndes**
77/29; **sharte bandes** 77/39, 100/24, 110/17;
sherte[⟨.⟩] bandes 147/1–2; **shirtebandes**
119/23, **shirtte bandes** 122/35; **shirtte bannndes**
123/28; *see also* **bande**

shart neck, shart nekes, sharte neke *see* **neck**

sheape skines *n phr pl* sheep skins or pieces of
sheep skin, used in lining garments 147/2;
sheepe skynnes 86/15; **shippe skinnes**
124/25; *see also* **lether skynnes, skine**

sheep coloure *n phr as adj* the colour of
unbleached sheep's wool 82/29

shereff *n* chief administrative and executive
officer, under the mayor, of a borough
which was 'a county of itself' 9/1, 41/9;
sherif 3/10, 62/11, 72/31; **sheriffe** 4/3, 4/32,
5/31, etc; **sheryff** 21/36; **shiref** 20/38;
shireffe 19/21, 19/30; **shereffes** *pl* 9/4

sherte bandes *see* **shart band**

shewinge *pr p* sewing 46/25

shiftes of apperell *n phr pl* suits or sets of
clothes 100/40; *see also* **sutes of apparell**

shipe mony *n phr* duty paid to merchant adventurers' company by owners of ships carrying
wool, skins, or other merchants' goods abroad
from Newcastle 23/35

shippe skinnes *see* **sheape skines**

shiref, shireffe *see* **shereff**

shirtebandes, shirtte bandes, shirtte bannndes *see*
shart band

short hose *n phr pl* stockings reaching only a
short way up the leg 35/2, 116/26, 116/34;
shor hosses 48/22; **short hoses** 45/4; **short
hosse** 34/17, 35/34; **short hosses** 41/32–33;
short houses 47/1, 47/17; **short housses**
45/22; **short hoys** 42/28; **short hoy⟨.⟩** 42/30;
shorte hose 147/2, 147/6, 147/12; **shorte
hosse** 69/35, 71/9; **shorte hosses** 38/17;
shorte hoise 54/19; *see also* **hose**

shortt *n* partial attendance, late arrival (at
meeting, etc) 166/20m

side cotte *n phr* long coat 82/30

sik *adj* such 8/30; **syke** 8/25

silke *n* silk material 25/20, 137/7

silke *n* silk thread 34/42; **sylke** 35/8

silke russett *n phr* a kind of material originally
of russet or neutral colour 143/41, 144/1;
silkrussat *adj* of a russet or neutral colour
96/18

silke russett collor *n phr as adj* of a russet or
neutral colour 142/23

silkes culler *n phr as adj* the colour of raw silk
115/9–10

singar *n* singer, especially in church 33/21;
synger 37/3, 49/38, 52/19, etc; **syngger** 12/3

skayffolde *n* scaffold (probably for spectators
at play) 38/39; **skakfoll** 38/36

skean *n* thread or yarn, of the kind made up
into skeings 34/22, 143/16; **skeane** 143/7;
skene 110/41; **skeynes** *pl* 147/10; *in phr*
skeene threedde 124/9; **skene thread** 76/22,
138/23; **skene threde** 97/1–2; **skene threed**
97/13; **skenne thread** 75/9

skine *n* (piece of) tanned or dressed skin, used
in lining garments 147/21; **skines** *pl* 118/3,
118/33, 127/13; **skins** 110/28, 111/9;
skynnes 115/14; **skynns** 95/20, 105/3,

107/9, etc; *see also* **lether skynnes, sheape skines**

skowchons *n pl* escutcheons, shields on which coats of arms were depicted 14/38; **skoutt(.)ons** 17/9

skowringe *vb n* cleaning (of cloth) 78/39

slaiters *n pl* tradesmen who laid slates on roofs 63/22

slewes *n pl* sleeves 147/21

slopes *n pl* wide, baggy breeches or hose 41/34, 45/4, 45/20, etc; **sloppes** 41/31

slopped *pp adj* (of breeches or hose) wide, baggy 25/40

slyghte *v inf* (of cloth, clothing) make smooth 147/21

spares *n pl* spars, poles, especially undressed stems of fir or similar wood of small diameter 29/26; **sparris** 14/1

stainge *pr p* restraining, steadying 55/37

staites *n pl* the government of the United Netherlands or its representatives (16th–17th century usage) 100/8, 100/12; **states** 100/34

stamell *n* a woollen cloth, or linen-wool mixture, usually dyed red 76/12, 134/5, 147/22

stamell cairsaye *n phr* a coarse ribbed cloth, dyed red (?) 76/16, **stamle carsie** 119/17–18; **stammell carsey** 119/20; **stammell kayrsaye** 138/19

stanges *n pl* poles 29/26

states *see* **staites**

stenting *n* (*sometimes attrib*) stiffening (for a doublet) 111/35; **stentinge** 105/1; **stintinge** 130/35; **stynteinge** 125/23

sterre *n* star 132/30

steward *n* governor or officer of a guild 165/25; **stewarde** 165/31; **stewardes** *pl* 22/37, 24/17, 55/30; *gen* 24/12, 26/32; **stewards** 163/16, 165/11, 165/19, etc; **stewerdes** 22/6

stoopes *n pl* drinking-vessels (or pails?) 57/23

straite *adj* tight-fitting 26/1

straken *n* a kind of coarse linen 77/28

stynte *v inf* stiffen (a doublet) with stiffening material 125/24

stynteinge *see* **stenting**

succres *n pl* 'sugars,' sweetmeats, sweet foods (?) 10/34

surgant *n* surgeon 76/40

sutes of apparell *n phr pl* suits or sets of clothes 109/14; *see also* **shiftes of apperell**

syke *see* **sik**

sylke *see* **silke**

synger, syngger *see* **singar**

sypers *n* a band or kerchief for the head or neck, or a band for a hat, originally made out of cypress (a kind of fine silk or satin) 137/9

tabroner *n* taborer, drummer 91/26

tayll *n in phr* **be tayll** by tally, by reckoning 12/16

tendering *pr p* having regard to 18/11, **tenderyng** 19/23

tentor howks *n phr pl* hooks used in stretching cloth on a frame, hence hooks used to hang cloth, etc 29/29

thauditt dyner, thauditt dynner *see* **auditt dynner**

thoyis *pron pl* those 9/8

toppes *n pl* platforms near the tops of ships' masts 10/17

toull *n* toll (precise sense uncertain) 16/22

town clerk *n* secretary of city corporation, ie, common clerk 158/31; **towne clarke** 120/41–121/1, 138/34; *see also* **clark**

tvmbleres *n pl* acrobats 73/33

tydes *n pl* loads (?) (*see endnote*) 55/15

ventyners *n pl* sellers of wine, taverners 24/1

vested *v perf 3 pl* dressed 10/37

vncostes *n pl* additional or incidental expences 14/20

vnder clarke *n* assistant to lay officer of parish church 51/35, 57/1 *see also* **clarke**

vnfre *adj* not possessed of guild membership 9/8; **wnfre** 9/10

vpper bodie *n phr* upper part of coat, etc where it fitted the body 104/41; *see also* **boddie, ouerbodies**

vsher *n* assistant master in a school 138/3

wae *error for* was (?) 24/38

waite *n* musician 48/35, 48/42, 49/33, etc;
   waitt 40/35; watt 37/40, 39/30, 43/23;
   wayt 28/3, 44/29, 47/6; waytt 30/13, 31/26,
   34/32, etc; waytte 32/22, 34/3, 36/28;
   waitees *pl* 129/35; waites 48/37, 49/12,
   49/36, etc; waittes 107/37, 111/22, 121/2,
   etc; waitts 126/37; wates 44/17, 53/16,
   112/37, etc; wattes 12/35, 13/14, 13/27,
   etc; *gen* 12/8, 43/14; wattys 31/34; waytes
   60/9, 70/15, 78/25, etc; wayts 145/18;
   wayttes 27/23, 27/25, 27/26, etc; *gen*
   30/7; weates 117/41

walkers *n pl* fullers of cloth 7/26; *gen* 7/21;
   see fullers

wardens *n pl* governors, or members of the
   governing body, of a guild 3/19, 4/14, 4/17,
   etc; wardeins 23/22; wardennes 3/20;
   wardeyns 3/17, 7/12, 7/14, etc

watyd *v perf 3 pl in phr* watyd of attended,
   went with 29/28

wayt, waytes, wayts, waytt, waytte, wayttes,
   weates *see* waite

welche fres *n phr* Welsh frieze, a kind of woollen
   cloth with a nap 42/3; *see also* ffreas

wench *n* child 105/15

whilk *pron* which 8/16

whit *adj and n* white (cloth) 52/32, 73/40,
   142/19, etc; wheete 120/11, 120/12;
   white 49/16, 49/20, 49/21, etc; whitte
   109/10; whyt 42/27, 45/3, 46/3; whyte
   138/20, 138/21; whytt 28/19, 33/39, 34/14,
   etc

windinge *n* winding sheet 141/9

wnfre *see* vnfre

wryghtes *n pl* carpenters 38/36

yatt *n* gate 10/12

yprocras *n* drink made of wine flavoured with
   spices 10/33

INDEX

Index

The index combines subject headings with places and names for ease of reference. Where the same word occurs in more than one category, the order of headings is people, places, subjects, and book or play titles (eg, Widdrington, Sir Henry precedes Widdrington, Northum).

Place names, titles, and given names appear in their modern form where this is ascertainable; surnames are normally cited in the most common form used in the text and are capitalized (I, J, U, and V therefore appear in accordance with modern usage). The headword spelling of Newcastle mayors' and sheriffs' names is based on the list in the municipal Council and Committees Diary (1961), and minor biographical information has come from C.H. Hunter Blair's annotated list in *Archaeologia AEliana*, 4th ser, 18, special volume, (1940). Both places and surnames are followed by their variant spellings in parentheses. Names of saints are indexed under St; their identification and precise dates of feast days conform to David Hugh Farmer, *The Oxford Dictionary of Saints* (Oxford, 1979). The following major sources for identification of peers and ecclesiastical officials were used: *The Dictionary of National Biography*; G[eorge] E[dward] C[okayne], *The Complete Peerage of England...*, F. Maurice Powicke and E.B. Fryde (eds), *The Handbook of British Chronology*. Where a family name is known for these dignitaries, it has been chosen as the main headword, with a cross reference from the official's title (eg, Derby, lord *see* Stanley).

The format for names and titles has been largely taken from R.F. Hunnisett, *Indexing for Editors* (Leicester, 1972). Thus family relationships, where known, have been used rather than succession numbers to distinguish members of noble families. Where no given name is known, ellipsis marks have been supplied; in cases of further doubt, a question mark follows the name. Occupations known and considered relevant are supplied (eg, Browne, John, singer). Mayors, sheriffs, and occasionally aldermen are identified as such and their dates of office supplied in parentheses from the year of election or appointment according to the municipal list; any uncertainty is indicated. The number of occurrences of a place or a name on a page in the records text is given in parentheses after the page number (eg, Chater, Christopher 58(3)).

Modern subject headings are provided with some complex groupings, such as clothing (items of) and musicians, to aid research. Individual pageants in the Newcastle cycle are listed under Corpus Christi plays (individual). Where names of monarchs fall within subject headings, they are given in chronological order; peers are listed according to their rank in the kingdom (eg, under players (travelling) the lord admiral precedes the duchess of Suffolk).

RECORDS OF EARLY ENGLISH DRAMA

York edited by Alexandra F. Johnston and Margaret Rogerson. 2 volumes. 1979.

Chester edited by Lawrence M. Clopper. 1979.

Coventry edited by R.W. Ingram. 1981.

Newcastle upon Tyne edited by J.J. Anderson. 1982.